So you really want to learn

Maths

Book 2

Serena Alexander B.A. (Hons.), P.G.C.E.

Edited by Louise Martine B.Sc. (Lon.)

Independent Schools
Examinations Board

GALORE PARK

www.galorepark.co.uk

Published by ISEB Publications, an imprint of
Galore Park Publishing Ltd,
19/21 Sayers Lane, Tenterden, Kent TN30 6BW
www.galorepark.co.uk

Text copyright © Serena Alexander
Illustrations copyright © Galore Park 2004
Cartoons by Ian Douglass
Technical drawings by Graham Edwards

Typography and layout by Typetechnique, London W1
Cover design by GKA Design, London WC2H
Printed by Replika Press, India

The publishers would like to thank Michael Ede for his extremely
valuable comments. They would also like to thank David Hanson for his
enormous dedication and help during the production of this book.

ISBN-13: 978 1 902984 31 5

First published 2004
Reprinted 2005, 2006, 2007, 2008

Details of other Galore Park publications are available at
www.galorepark.co.uk

ISEB Revision Guides, publications and examination papers may also
be obtained from Galore Park.

Author's introduction

This book is suitable for Key Stage 3 pupils in Year 7 or Year 8. It also completes the ISEB Common Entrance Mathematics syllabus at 13+ for Papers 1 and 3.

In relevant chapters the work of Book 1 is briefly revised before the topic is extended. Other topics are new and have a full introduction. There are extension exercises at the end of each chapter to extend the more enthusiastic.

In this book there is still an emphasis on sound numerical work, but, where relevant, efficient use of a calculator and sound calculator methods are also covered. In each exercise there are clear examples showing how the working should be set out, in order to develop pupils' mathematical reasoning skills.

As in Book 1 the word problems are set in relevant situations for 11 to 13 year olds: the mathematics of pocket money increases, the cost of a CD in a sale and the pricing of a school trip are all covered.

In between the chapters are activities, including puzzles and investigations. There are also some ideas for more open-ended work on statistics and practical geometry. Some of these could usefully be explored further using a suitable computer program and it is hoped that colleagues and pupils will find opportunities for further investigations.

Acknowledgements

As always my biggest thanks must go to the boys and girls of Colet Court and Newton Prep who were given the original exercises and worked through them making, as ever, frank and critical comments. I am also most grateful to my colleagues, particularly George, Sue and Matthew, for their help and support and to Michael Ede and David Hanson for the time and effort extended to the checking of this book. Finally the team at Galore Park has, as always, been wonderful in its unflagging enthusiasm.

Serena Alexander, April 2004

New 2008 Common Entrance syllabus

The requirements of the 2008 ISEB Common Entrance core syllabus for Mathematics are completely covered in both Books 1 and 2 of Galore Park's *So you really want to learn Maths* series. When first publishing the series the intention was that 11+ topics would be covered in Book 1 and all 13+ topics in Book 2. With the advent of the revised syllabus some of the 11+ topics are now only examined at 13+. These topics (see those listed below) continue to be covered comprehensively in Book 1 but will not be examined in the 11+ Common Entrance examination. They will, however, have to be covered for Common Entrance examinations at 13+.

- Negative numbers, addition and subtraction.
- Angle sum of a triangle and sum of angles at a point
- Identify all the symmetries of 2D shapes
- Recognise and use common 2D representations of 3D objects
- Know and use the properties of quadrilaterals

The topics required for Common Entrance Papers 2 and 4 are covered in Book 3.

In addition to the above there is now reference in the revised syllabus to calculating areas using algebra. Additional exercises covering this topic are now available as downloads from the Galore Park website at www.galorepark.co.uk

An appendix has been added to this edition to highlight the changes between the 2003 syllabus and the new 2008 Common Entrance syllabus (see Appendix 1 on page 393).

Contents

Chapter 1: Working with numbers

In the animal kingdom many species demonstrate the ability to recognise numbers, especially the number of their young. Many birds have a good number sense. If a nest contains four eggs, a predator could take one away without the bird abandoning the nest, but when two are removed the bird generally deserts the nest. The bird can distinguish two from three. This ability seems to be instinctive and not learned.

Very early civilisations demonstrated this same ability to recognise numbers but most did not have words for numbers larger than two. Instead they used words such as 'flocks' of sheep, 'heaps' of grain, or 'lots' of people. There was little need for a numeric system until groups of people formed clans, villages and settlements and began a system of bartering and trade that in turn created a demand for currency.

Finger numerals were used by the ancient Greeks, Romans, Europeans of the Middle Ages and, later, the Asiatics. In the days before pencil and paper hand signals were used as an official system:

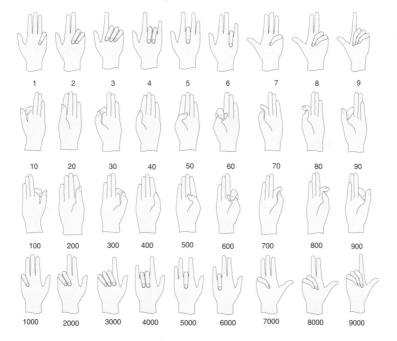

From Tobias Dantzig, 'Number: The Language of Science'. Macmillan Company, 1954, page 2.

It is believed that ordinal numbers (those used to show the place in a sequence; first, second, third etc.) and cardinal numbers (numbers used for counting one, two, three etc.) developed separately with different purposes. This is why, in many languages, we find different words for early ordinal and cardinal numbers. In some languages this extends to the third and occasionally to the fourth, but not beyond. Clearly, by the time counting got to higher numbers the link between ordinal and cardinal was established. Initially counting had 'one', 'two' and 'many'; when the need came for higher numbers the word for many was used for the first of these.

It is now generally accepted that our decimal numerals derive from a form that was developed in India and transmitted via Arab culture to Europe, undergoing a number of changes on the way. Several different ways of writing numbers evolved in India before it became possible for the existing decimal numerals to be married with the place-value principle of the Babylonians. This marriage gave birth to the number system we use today.

The four rules

You will have learnt to add, subtract, multiply and divide. Sometimes you can do this in your head and at other times you have to use a pencil and paper. As calculations become more complex, a calculator can also be used.

It would be very tempting to use a calculator for every calculation you have to do. But there may well be situations when you do not have one to hand – for example, when you're shopping or on holiday. So, it is important that you learn how to do calculations in your head and on paper.

Exercise 1.1: A challenge-Adding and subtracting

Here are 10 blocks of 10 questions in increasing difficulty. See how quickly you can complete them all in your head. Write down the answer.

1.   Copy and complete these:

   (a) 5 + 2 = _____   (f) 15 + 82 = _____

   (b) 6 + 3 = _____   (g) 36 + 43 = _____

   (c) 8 + 1 = _____   (h) 28 + 71 = _____

   (d) 4 + 3 = _____   (i) 24 + 53 = _____

   (e) 5 + 4 = _____   (j) 65 + 24 = _____

2. Copy and complete these. Remember to take care with the numbers in the tens column:

(a) 5 + 9 = _____

(b) 8 + 3 = _____

(c) 7 + 6 = _____

(d) 9 + 4 = _____

(e) 6 + 5 = _____

(f) 25 + 39 = _____

(g) 18 + 73 = _____

(h) 57 + 36 = _____

(i) 29 + 64 = _____

(j) 46 + 35 = _____

3. Ten very simple subtractions:

(a) 9 − 5 = _____

(b) 5 − 3 = _____

(c) 6 − 1 = _____

(d) 7 − 4 = _____

(e) 8 − 6 = _____

(f) 39 − 15 = _____

(g) 65 − 33 = _____

(h) 86 − 21 = _____

(i) 47 − 14 = _____

(f) 58 − 46 = _____

4. This time you have to take care with the numbers in the tens column:

(a) 12 − 4 = _____

(b) 16 − 7 = _____

(c) 11 − 2 = _____

(d) 13 − 8 = _____

(e) 15 − 7 = _____

(f) 42 − 34 = _____

(g) 56 − 27 = _____

(h) 91 − 22 = _____

(i) 33 − 28 = _____

(j) 65 − 17 = _____

5. Can you spot the trick with these?

(a) 35 + 15 = _____

(b) 45 + 14 = _____

(c) 66 + 23 = _____

(d) 47 + 13 = _____

(e) 23 + 37 = _____

(f) 65 − 36 = _____

(g) 27 − 18 = _____

(h) 63 − 24 = _____

(i) 68 − 49 = _____

(j) 44 − 35 = _____

6. There are even more nines in these:

    (a) $19 + 5$ = _____   (f) $56 - 29$ = _____

    (b) $35 + 29$ =   (g) $32 - 19$ = _____

    (c) $67 + 19$ = _____   (h) $81 - 59$ = _____

    (d) $49 + 37$ = _____   (i) $64 - 49$ = _____

    (e) $43 + 59$ = _____   (j) $77 - 69$ = _____

7. The numbers are getting larger:

    (a) $121 + 48$ = _____   (f) $165 - 23$ = _____

    (b) $325 + 124$ = _____   (g) $332 - 121$ = _____

    (c) $313 + 116$ = _____   (h) $467 - 235$ = _____

    (d) $135 + 124$ = _____   (i) $635 - 124$ = _____

    (e) $342 + 327$ = _____   (j) $757 - 131$ = _____

8. Now you have numbers to carry as well:

    (a) $147 + 45$ = _____   (f) $452 - 25$ = _____

    (b) $356 + 124$ = _____   (g) $657 - 163$ = _____

    (c) $384 + 123$ = _____   (h) $318 - 235$ = _____

    (d) $175 + 352$ = _____   (i) $452 - 361$ = _____

    (e) $616 + 347$ = _____   (j) $456 - 264$ = _____

9. These are definitely getting tougher:

    (a) $156 + 76$ = _____   (f) $164 - 85$ = _____

    (b) $485 + 173$ = _____   (g) $457 - 268$ = _____

    (c) $293 + 239$ = _____   (h) $461 - 178$ = _____

    (d) $376 + 186$ = _____   (i) $637 - 358$ = _____

    (e) $145 + 567$ = _____   (j) $378 - 289$ = _____

10. These are a real challenge:

(a) 243 + 167 = _____   (f) 402 – 123 = _____

(b) 345 + 567 = _____   (g) 607 – 288 = _____

(c) 567 + 123 = _____   (h) 308 – 159 = _____

(d) 319 + 399 = _____   (i) 402 – 361 = _____

(e) 678 + 398 = _____   (j) 706 – 358 = _____

Harder calculations

It is good to be able to calculate accurately in our heads but we also need to able to work out the answers to harder calculations on paper.

One of the reasons why mathematics exercise books have squares is to help you calculate correctly. If you think of the squares as **rows** and **columns**, then you need to make sure the numbers go into the correct **column** lining up the hundreds, tens and units.

Addition

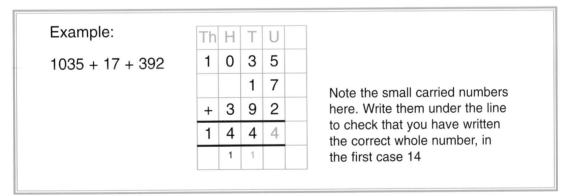

Example:

1035 + 17 + 392

Th	H	T	U
1	0	3	5
		1	7
+	3	9	2
1	4	4	4
	1	1	

Note the small carried numbers here. Write them under the line to check that you have written the correct whole number, in the first case 14

Exercise 1.2

Calculate the following by writing numbers in the correct columns. Show all your working, including the carried numbers.

1. 76 + 323
2. 245 + 460
3. 472 + 543
4. 407 + 17
5. 6 + 49 + 328

6. 6107 + 75 + 8
7. 4024 + 45 + 367
8. 48 + 147 + 39 + 1007
9. 5 + 4507 + 104 + 99
10. 9 + 909 + 99 + 9009

11. Add three thousand, four hundred and fifty-two to six hundred and forty.

12. Find the sum of four hundred and sixty-eight, seventy-five and sixteen.

13. Add one thousand and seventeen to eight hundred and eight.

14. What is fifteen plus one hundred and eight plus seven thousand and ninety-six?

15. What is eight hundred and fifteen more than six hundred and nineteen?

Subtraction

When doing mental calculations, we can see that it is simpler to do:

$$27 - 5 = 22$$
than $$27 - 9 = 18$$

This is because in the first calculation, $7 - 5 = 2$ is easy and the 20 is just left at the beginning of the calculation, minding its own business. The second calculation, $7 - 9$ is not so easy. You have to split the 20 into $10 + 10$ so that you can calculate $17 - 9 = 8$. You then have to remember the other 10 and add it back in, so $8 + 10 = 18$

When working on paper, we can make the subtraction easier by always making sure the top number is greater than the bottom number. We do this by exchanging. (Sometimes this is called borrowing but you should always pay back if you borrow anything!)

Consider 33 – 17.

We can split 33 into 30 + 3, and then into 20 + 13

This is much clearer when the numbers are in columns:

Example:

(i) 33 – 17

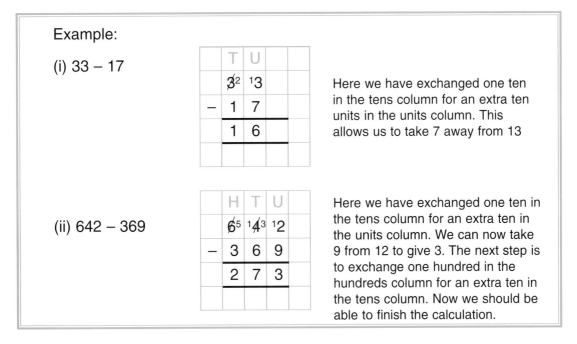

Here we have exchanged one ten in the tens column for an extra ten units in the units column. This allows us to take 7 away from 13

(ii) 642 – 369

Here we have exchanged one ten in the tens column for an extra ten in the units column. We can now take 9 from 12 to give 3. The next step is to exchange one hundred in the hundreds column for an extra ten in the tens column. Now we should be able to finish the calculation.

It is always a good idea to check your subtraction in your head by adding your answer to the number on the bottom of the calculation. This should add up to the number on the top of that calculation.

In (i) 16 + 17 = 33   In (ii) 369 + 273 = 642

When there is a zero in the top line, it is hard to see what to exchange – you cannot take 1 away from zero. In this case, what you must do is to keep going to the left until you find a whole number, then you can take 1 away from that.

Be careful to remember that the 1 could represent 'one hundred' or 'one thousand' etc., depending on which column you find this whole number in.

Here are a couple of examples to show you what we mean:

Example:

(i) 303 − 117

H	T	U
$\cancel{3}^2$	$\cancel{0}^9$	$^1 3$
− 1	1	7
1	8	6

You cannot take 1 from 0 in the tens column, so go along to 30
30 − 1 is 29

(ii) 6004 − 4139

Th	H	T	U
$\cancel{6}^5$	$\cancel{0}^9$	$\cancel{0}^9$	$^1 4$
− 4	1	3	9
1	8	6	5

You cannot take 1 away from 0 or from 00, so go along to 600

600 − 1 is 599
Now you can carry on subtracting easily.

As you did before, check your subtraction in your head by adding the answer to the number at the bottom of the calculation. This should add up to the number on the top.

In (i) 117 + 186 = 303   In (ii) 4139 + 1865 = 6004

Exercise 1.3

Calculate the following by writing numbers in the correct columns. Show all your working, including exchanged numbers:

1.   498 − 137

2.   842 − 528

3.   750 − 235

4.   637 − 374

5.   604 − 258

6.   4006 − 1238

7.   8146 − 3283

8.   9009 − 375

9.   1205 − 927

10.   5001 − 1984

11.   Subtract three hundred and ninety-eight from five hundred and forty-six.

12. Find the difference between two hundred and forty and one hundred and twenty-six.

13. Take one thousand, four hundred and five from three thousand and nine.

14. What is five hundred and sixty-one minus two hundred and twenty-eight?

15. What is two hundred and sixty-five less than six hundred and twenty-two?

Adding and multiplying

When you do calculations in your head, there may be more than one way that you could do it; people's heads work differently.

A typical example is:

2×243

You could think of this as: $243 + 243$ or 2×243

If we work them out on paper, you will see that you get the same answer:

	H	T	U			H	T	U
	2	4	3			2	4	3
+	2	4	3			×		2
	4	8	6			4	8	6

This is because multiplication is another way of thinking about repeated addition. If you know your times tables, it makes calculations even easier:

$$4 + 4 + 4 + 4 + 4 = 5 \text{ lots of } 4$$
$$= 5 \times 4$$
$$= 20$$

Exercise 1.4: Multiplication

1. Copy and complete this table square:

×	10	2	3	5	9	4	6	11	8	12	7
5											
10											
7											
9											
2											
8											
4											
11											
12											
3											
6											

Now calculate the answers to these. Show all your working clearly, including any carried numbers:

2. $7 + 7 + 7 + 7$

3. $76 + 76$

4. $125 + 125$

5. $19 + 19 + 19$

6. 2×175

7. 3×95

8. $105 + 105 + 105 + 105$

9. $217 + 217 + 217$

10. $99 + 99 + 99$

11. 9×199

Multiplication and division

When you learn your times tables you are learning four number bonds each time. Just as subtraction is the opposite of addition, division is the opposite of multiplication:

If you know that	$8 \times 9 = 72$
you also know	$9 \times 8 = 72$
and that	$72 \div 8 = 9$
and	$72 \div 9 = 8$

If you are lucky then the number divides exactly. If you're not lucky, you could have to deal with a remainder. As long as you know your times tables and can work out the remainder, then calculating the answer is easy.

Here are some examples:

$73 \div 8 = 9$ r 1 (because $8 \times 9 = 72$, $73 - 72 = 1$)

$74 \div 8 = 9$ r 2 (because $8 \times 9 = 72$, $74 - 72 = 2$)

$78 \div 8 = 9$ r 6 (because $8 \times 9 = 72$, $78 - 72 = 6$)

$73 \div 9 = 8$ r 1 (because $9 \times 8 = 72$, $73 - 72 = 1$)

$75 \div 9 = 8$ r 3 (because $9 \times 8 = 72$, $75 - 72 = 3$)

$79 \div 9 = 8$ r 7 (because $9 \times 8 = 72$, $79 - 72 = 7$)

Exercise 1.5: Division

1. Copy and complete these; they have no remainders:

   (a) $55 \div 5 =$ _____

   (b) $40 \div 5 =$ _____

   (c) $18 \div 3 =$ _____

   (d) $56 \div 8 =$ _____

   (e) $63 \div 7 =$ _____

   (f) $28 \div 4 =$ _____

   (g) $54 \div 9 =$ _____

   (h) $35 \div 5 =$ _____

   (i) $49 \div 7 =$ _____

   (j) $32 \div 8 =$ _____

2. Copy and complete these; they all have remainders:

   (a) $63 \div 6 =$ _____ r__

   (b) $13 \div 2 =$ _____ r__

   (c) $25 \div 7 =$ _____ r__

   (d) $43 \div 8 =$ _____ r__

   (e) $36 \div 5 =$ _____ r__

   (f) $29 \div 3 =$ _____ r__

   (g) $35 \div 4 =$ _____ r__

   (h) $49 \div 9 =$ _____ r__

   (i) $26 \div 6 =$ _____ r__

   (j) $59 \div 7 =$ _____ r__

3. Copy and complete these; some do have remainders and some do not:

(a) 21 ÷ 3 = _____ r__   (f) 39 ÷ 9 = _____ r__

(b) 45 : 7 = _____ r__   (g) 60 ÷ 5 = _____ r__

(c) 24 ÷ 6 = _____ r__   (h) 19 ÷ 2 = _____ r__

(d) 49 ÷ 8 = _____ r__   (i) 37 ÷ 7 = _____ r__

(e) 31 ÷ 4 = _____ r__   (j) 56 ÷ 8 = _____ r__

Harder calculations

Just as with simple addition and subtraction, it is useful to be able to calculate accurately in our heads. It is also important that we can work out the answers to harder calculations on paper.

It is easy to make a careless mistake, so it is always good practice to estimate the answer in your head first, before you do the calculation on paper.

Estimating

Consider the calculation: 419×27

Firstly estimate the answer by taking 419 to the nearest hundred: $419 \approx 400$

Then estimate 27 to the nearest ten: $27 \approx 30$

Therefore, we can say: $419 \times 27 \approx 400 \times 30$

This a much easier calculation to do: $4000 \times 3 = 12\ 000$

We can say therefore that $419 \times 27 \approx 12\ 000$

Now do the calculation properly on paper. Your answer should be 11 313 which is very close to 12 000

Here's a useful rule to know when estimating numbers: keep the estimation simple. You want each estimated value to have one digit followed by zeros.

For example, let's consider 372, 319 and 350:

For all these the first digit is a 3 in the hundreds column. All these numbers lie between 300 and 400:

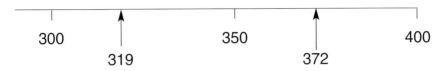

You can see that 319 is nearer 300, therefore we estimate 319 $\approx$ 300

372 is nearer to 400, and therefore 372 $\approx$ 400

But what do we do with 350 because it is exactly half way? Well, quite simply the convention is to round up, and to say 350 $\approx$ 400

Exercise 1.6: Estimation

Write each of these numbers to the nearest ten, hundred or thousand:

1. 59
2. 602
3. 1013
4. 91
5. 4567

6. 27
7. 149
8. 4500
9. 95
10. 999

When estimating calculations, remember to consider the 0s first, then worry about the numbers afterwards.

Example:

(a) 400 × 30

400 × 30 = 12 000

Here there were 3 0s behind the 3 × 4 = 12, so there will be three 0s in the answer, i.e. 12 000

(b) 400 × 500

400 × 500 = 200 000

Here there were 4 0s and because 4 × 5 = 20 there is one extra 0 in the answer, i.e. 200 000

Estimate the answers to these:

11. 32×218

12. 79×450

13. 43×623

14. 450×242

15. 1432×628

16. 125×734

17. 4200×499

18. 636×99

19. 48×863

20. 627×4761

Now do the same with division:

Example:

(a) $400 \div 20$

$400 \div 20 = 400 \div 10 \div 2$
$= 40 \div 2$
$= 20$

(b) $4000 \div 500$

$4000 \div 500 = 4000 \div 100 \div 5$
$= 40 \div 5$
$= 8$

As a general rule you could divide both the numbers in the calculation by ten. First cross off the zeros (make sure you cross off the **same** number of zeros fom each number), and then complete the resulting equation. This make things easier:

$40\emptyset \div 2\emptyset = 20$

$40\emptyset\emptyset \div 5\emptyset\emptyset = 8$

Estimate the answers to these:

21. $399 \div 24$

22. $729 \div 17$

23. $4372 \div 246$

24. $650 \div 79$

25. $8432 \div 428$

26. $1925 \div 534$

27. $4200 \div 499$

28. $3612 \div 99$

29. $587 \div 26$

30. $9999 \div 475$

31. Now take a calculator and work out the exact answers for q.11-30

Multiplication

Just like addition, it is important to put the numbers in the correct columns before you start. Then work with the units first, then the tens, and then the hundreds. Remember to put the carried numbers under the line.

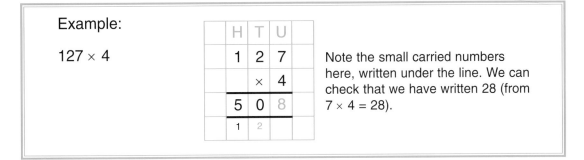

Example:

127 × 4

H	T	U	
1	2	7	
	×	4	
5	0	8	
1	2		

Note the small carried numbers here, written under the line. We can check that we have written 28 (from 7 × 4 = 28).

Exercise 1.7: Multiplication

Calculate the answers to these; show all your working, including the carried numbers:

1. 36 × 2
2. 26 × 3
3. 37 × 4
4. 43 × 5
5. 158 × 6

6. 175 × 7
7. 209 × 8
8. 326 × 9
9. 417 × 8
10. 536 × 7

In the above examples we were multiplying by a number of units. The same method can be used when we multiply by tens or by hundreds.

We know that since 8 × 7 = 56
then 8 × 70 = 560
and 8 × 700 = 5600

Here are a couple of examples. First put the 0 in the answer row as shown and then continue to multiply the other numbers:

(i)
Th	H	T	U
		3	8
	×	6	Ø
			0

(ii)
Th	H	T	U
		6	7
	×	3	Ø	Ø
			0	0

In the examples above, the frame has been set up and now all you have to do is multiply.

Example

(i) 38 × 60

Th	H	T	U
		3	8
	×	6	Ø
	2	2	8	0
2	4		

(ii) 67 × 300

TTh	Th	H	T	U
			6	7
	×	3	Ø	Ø
2	0	1	0	0
2	2			

11. 24 × 20

12. 32 × 400

13. 45 × 60

14. 39 × 300

15. 126 × 50

16. 153 × 60

17. 245 × 800

18. 316 × 90

19. 642 × 700

20. 457 × 900

Long multiplication

Consider
$$5 × 2 + 5 × 10 = 10 + 50$$
$$= 60$$
$$= 5 × 12$$

We could have written 5 × 12 as 5 × (2 + 10)

What happens when we want to multiply 52 × 23? Well, to make life easier we can split the calculation like this:

$$52 × 23 = 52 × (3 + 20)$$
$$= 52 × 3 + 52 × 20$$

It is now useful to put these numbers into frames, so that we can do various parts of the calculation.

Here are the three stages:

Stage (i) 52 × 3 Stage (ii) 52 × 20 Stage (iii) 52 × 3 + 52 × 20

Th	H	T	U		Th	H	T	U		Th	H	T	U
		5	2				5	2			1	5	6
	×		3			×	2	Ø		+ 1	0	4	0
	1	5	6		1	0	4	0		1	1	9	6

You can, though, combine all of this into one calculation:

Th	H	T	U
		5	2
	×	2	3
	1	5	6
+ 1	0	4	0
1	1	9	6

Stage (i) 52 × 3

Stage (ii) 52 × 20 – first drop the zero into the answer row and continue with the 52 × 2 calculation.

Stage (iii) finally add 156 + 1040

Exercise 1.8: Long multiplication

Do these without a calculator, showing all your working:

1. 35 × 24
2. 67 × 36
3. 45 × 27
4. 63 × 54
5. 48 × 48

6. 125 × 17
7. 244 × 26
8. 325 × 72
9. 207 × 69
10. 716 × 78

11. The school cook orders 36 boxes of crisps. There are 24 packets of crisps in a box. How many packets of crisps are there in all?

12. We have 40 new maths textbooks (*So you really want to learn Maths*, of course!). There are 326 pages in each book. How many pages are there in all?

13. 32 children are going on the skiing trip to Switzerland. The cost is £625 per child. What is the total cost?

14. How many seconds are there in 4 hours?

15. If there are 14 pounds in a stone, what is the total mass, in pounds, of a man who weighs 14 stone, 8 pounds?
(In the UK we used to weigh people in stones and pounds; in the USA they use only pounds.)

Division

The number columns are still important in division. Make sure that your answer is in the correct place. Have a look at the following example and follow it through step by step, so that you see how it is done:

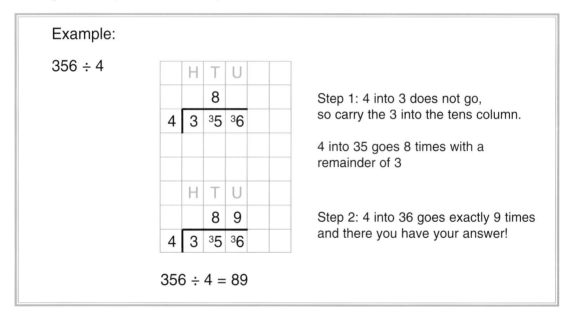

Example:

$356 \div 4$

Step 1: 4 into 3 does not go, so carry the 3 into the tens column.

4 into 35 goes 8 times with a remainder of 3

Step 2: 4 into 36 goes exactly 9 times and there you have your answer!

$356 \div 4 = 89$

Exercise 1.9: Short division

Do these without a calculator, showing all your working. Be careful! Some go exactly but others have remainders:

1. $65 \div 5$

2. $96 \div 6$

3. $79 \div 3$

4. $315 \div 5$

5. $428 \div 8$

6. $833 \div 7$

7. $428 \div 4$

8. $908 \div 8$

9. $929 \div 9$

10. $987 \div 7$

To work out the answer to these next questions, you have to think carefully about the remainders:

11. 214 children are supposed to go on a school trip in 5 buses. When the buses leave they are all full. As many children as possible have gone and there are an equal number of children on each bus. Oh no! How many children are left behind?

12. The school cook bakes 148 cakes and arranges as many of them as possible neatly on 6 plates. Each plate has the same number of cakes. The cook eats the rest. How many cakes does he eat?

13. In our school dining room there are six long tables and 250 chairs. Five of the tables have the same number of chairs and one table has a few less. How many chairs does the one table have around it?

14. There are 214 children in my school, in nine classes. There are the same number of children in most of the classes, but the top two classes have one less. How many children are in the top two classes?

Long division

Before looking at long division, remember what happens in simple division:

$$992 \div 4$$

	H	T	U	
		2	4	8
4	9	¹9	³2	

Firstly we **divide** 9 by 4

It doesn't go exactly. It goes 2 times with 1 remaining.

We get the remainder 1 because 4 **multiplied** by 2 is 8, and 9 **subtract** 8 is 1

The remainder 1 is then carried into the tens column.
You then have 19 **divided** by 4 which is 4 remainder 3 and so on.

We could in fact write this calculation out like this:

	H	T	U	
	2	4	8	
4	9	9	2	divide
	8			multiply
	1	9		subtract and pull down the next number, divide
	1	6		multiply
		3	2	subtract and pull down the next number, divide
		3	2	multiply
		–	–	subtract

We can use exactly the same principle for long division.

Example:

851 ÷ 23

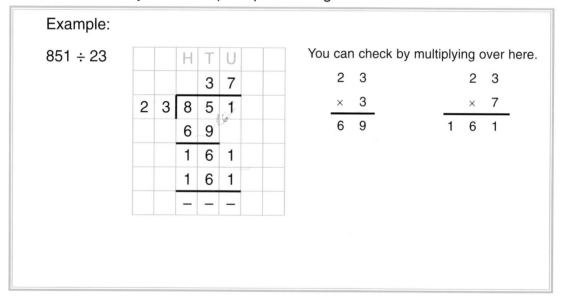

You can check by multiplying over here.

	2	3
×		3
	6	9

	2	3
×		7
1	6	1

Exercise 1.10: Long division

Do these calculations by long division. The first five have no remainders, but the last five may have:

1. 646 ÷ 17
2. 667 ÷ 23
3. 855 ÷ 19
4. 882 ÷ 42
5. 851 ÷ 37

6. 870 ÷ 24
7. 684 ÷ 36
8. 995 ÷ 31
9. 972 ÷ 27
10. 730 ÷ 39

11. Form 5X won the house point competition and now have to share a box of 323 chocolates between them. There are 19 pupils in 5X. How many chocolates does each pupil get?

12. 48 children are going on an outing to the Isle of Wight. The geography teacher has collected all the money from the children and now has £1632. How much money has each child paid?

13. The 23 children in Form 7Z have to have an eye test. It takes the same amount of time to test each child and altogether all the tests take 299 minutes. How long does each eye test take?

14. 36 cans of drink cost £27. How much does one can of drink cost?

15. A ream of paper contains 500 sheets. For our geography project our teacher shares out one ream equally between 24 of us. How many sheets do we get each and how many are left over?

Exercise 1.11: Mixed questions

Now you should be able to add, subtract, multiply and divide, both in your head and by using pencil and paper. Answer the following questions whichever way you wish, but take care to write down all your working.

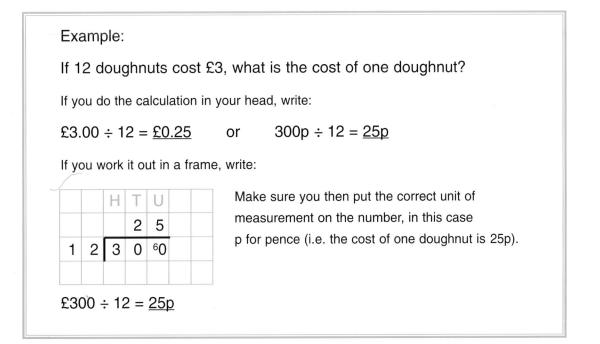

Example:

If 12 doughnuts cost £3, what is the cost of one doughnut?

If you do the calculation in your head, write:

£3.00 ÷ 12 = £0.25   or   300p ÷ 12 = 25p

If you work it out in a frame, write:

		H	T	U	
			2	5	
1	2	3	0	⁶0	

Make sure you then put the correct unit of measurement on the number, in this case p for pence (i.e. the cost of one doughnut is 25p).

£300 ÷ 12 = 25p

1. I spend 96p on eight sticks of licorice. What is the cost of one stick?

2. I spend £6 on 24 pencils. What is the cost of one pencil?

3. There are 16 ounces in a pound and 14 pounds in a stone. How many ounces are there in a stone?

4. Ash have 217 house points more than Beech. If Beech have 357, how many points do Ash have?

5. Taking part in the school Christmas production are 104 members of the choir, 9 readers and 27 musicians. How many people are there in total?

6. On a school trip 255 pupils go with 17 teachers. If each teacher has the same size group, how many children are there in each group?

7. For a science project I need six lengths of 4 m of string and eight lengths of 5 m of string. How much string is that altogether?

8. Our whole class needs to buy 1332 m of string. If string comes in balls of 24 m, how many balls do we need to buy?

9. At the school fair the cake stall sold 38 big cakes at £3 each and 75 little cakes at 24p each. How much money did the stall make in total?

10. I reckon that I spend 75 minutes, five nights a week, on homework. In a school year of 34 weeks how many minutes is that in all? How many hours is that?

11. A recipe says that I need 1500 g of flour to make 12 cakes. How many grammes do I need to make 1 cake? How many grammes do I need to make 36 cakes?

12. There is a special prize for winning 300 house points. I reckon I can get 12 house points a week. How many weeks will it take me to get 300 house points?

13. There are 1000 g in a kilogram. I use 455 g from a 2 kg bag of sugar. How much sugar is left in the bag?

14. (a) I am counting up the money from the tombola at the end of the school fair. There are 24 one pound coins, 7 two pound coins, 6 five pound notes, 14 ten pound notes, 3 twenty pound notes and 1 fifty pound note. How much money is there in total?

(b) I exchange all the money for as many twenty pound notes as possible. How many twenty pound notes do I have now?

15. The school put aside £20 000 for new computers. In the summer they bought 24 computers at £699 each. How much money did they have left?

Mixed operations

You can add, subtract, multiply and divide, but there are times when we need to do at least two of these in one calculation.

For example: $3 \times 7 + 1$

The rule is: 'do multiplication and division before addition and subtraction' and also: 'do any calculation in brackets first, followed by any index numbers'.

We use the mnemonic **BIDMAS** to remember this:

Brackets, **I**ndices, **D**ivide, **M**ultiply, **A**dd, **S**ubtract.

Remember that **indices** refers to **index numbers** or **powers**:

$$3^4 = 3 \times 3 \times 3 \times 3$$
$$= 81$$

(4 is the index number and indicates that four 3's are multiplied together)

Note that $3 \times 7 + 1 = 21 + 1$
$$= 22$$

and $\quad 1 + 3 \times 7 = 1 + 21$
$$= 22$$

Exercise 1.12: Mixed operations

Remember the BIDMAS rule when calculating the answers to these:

1. $3 + 5 \times 4$
2. $72 \div 9 - 4 \times 2$
3. $(3 + 5) \times 4$
4. $3 + 15 \div 3$
5. $3^2 + 2^3 - 2 \times 3$

6. $25 - 3 \times 7$
7. $45 \div 5 - 3 \times 2$
8. $3 \times (4 - 1)^2$
9. $(8 + 4)^2 \div (5 - 2)^2$
10. $(8 - 5)^2 \times (5 - 2)^2$

In these questions write down the calculation correctly, using brackets if necessary:

11. Take 4, add 7 and then multiply the answer by 6. What is your answer?

12. I have 9 conkers. I give 5 of them away and then I lose half of the rest. How many conkers do I have left?

13. My mother is 34. If I halve her age and then take away 5, I have my age. How old am I?

14. I am 12. If I take the square of my age and then divide it by 2, I have my grandpa's age. How old is grandpa?

Exercise 1.13: Extension questions – Babylonian numbers

It is easy to think that because we still use Roman numerals, the Romans were the earliest civilisation to use a number system, but this is not true. Many early civilisations had their own different systems. One of the most sophisticated and oldest was developed by the Babylonians about 5000 years ago. The first mathematics can be traced to the ancient country of Babylon (which lies in modern day Iraq), during the third millennium B.C.

The Babylonians recorded their mathematics on clay tablets. These were baked dry by the sun and then preserved, which is why we can study them today.

Like most early systems the numbers from one to nine were formed by a succession of simple marks, easily made with a stick in the soft clay:

1 2 3 4 5 6 7 8 9

Note the way the numbers 1, 2 and 3 were one size stroke, 4, 5, 6 a little smaller and 7, 8, 9 smaller again.

The tens were grouped with a different shape:

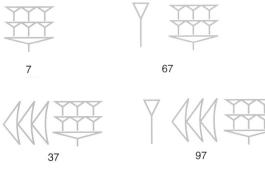

10   20   30   40   50

The Babylonians did not count in tens over 60 because their system was based on sixty. Ours, on the other hand, is based on 10

The biggest difference between the Babylonian system and those of the Greek and Roman civilisations was that it, like our own, used place value to show larger numbers.

Look at these numbers:

7   67   (the 1 on the left is in the 60 column, so you have 1 × 60 + 7 = 67)

37   97   (the 1 on the left is in the 60 column, so you have 1 × 60 + 30 + 7 = 97)

1. Copy these Babylonian numbers and write their value, in our numerals, next to them:

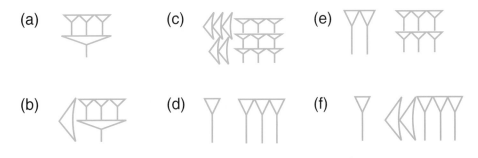

(a)   (c)   (e)

(b)   (d)   (f)

The numbers you should have written down in q.1 were (not necessarily in this order): 63, 14, 59, 83, 126, 4 If you did not get them all go and check your answers again.

2. Now get out your stick and clay tablet, and write these down in Babylonian numbers. (On second thoughts, your teacher might prefer you to use pencil and paper!):

(a) 6   (c) 56   (e) 75   (g) 127

(b) 26   (d) 64   (f) 92   (h) 142

Let's look at 142, the highest number you have looked at so far.

You should have drawn:

You have $2 \times 60 + 20 + 2 = 142$

Look at the number:

$4 \times 60 + 50 + 7 = 297$

3. Now work out these even larger numbers:

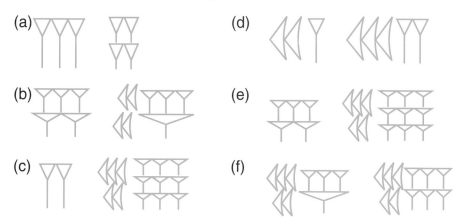

The numbers you should have written down were (not necessarily in this order): 344, 1292, 359, 184, 3296, 179

If you did not get them all, go and check your answers again.

4. Now write these down in Babylonian numbers:

(a) 306   (c) 2364   (e) 3216   (g) 1204

(b) 2472   (d) 1317   (f) 2781   (h) 3599

For your last answer you should have drawn:

$59 \times 60 + 59 = 3540 + 59 = 3599$

The next number after this would be 3600 which is 60×60 or 60^2

To write 3681 you would have to work out:

$1 \times 3600 + 1 \times 60 + 21$

and then write:

5. Now try these:

(a)

(c)

(b)

(d)

6. Now write these down in Babylonian numbers:

(a) 3666   (b) 7297   (c) 4876   (d) 5999

These numbers are written in Cuneiform script. If you had been to school 5000 years ago, this is how you would have learnt to write your numbers, using the 14 different Cuneiform numerals. (Like many early civilisations there was no symbol for 0, they just left a blank.)

7. You can see that the Babylonians were very enthusiastic about the number 60 which they also used for their system of measurement. 5000 years later which Babylonian measures do we still use?

Exercise 1.14: Summary exercise

Calculate these first ten questions either in your head or in a frame. Whichever way you use, write down the working in the way that you have been taught:

1. 173 + 312
2. 738 − 125
3. 256 + 376
4. 419 − 175
5. 65 × 3

6. 72 ÷ 8
7. 69 ÷ 8
8. 400 × 20
9. 6000 ÷ 40
10. 714 ÷ 7

Estimate the answers to these:

11. 547 × 29
12. 1635 × 541

13. 7700 ÷ 44
14. 2945 ÷ 399

Use frames to calculate carefully the answers to these questions:

15. 4878 + 567+ 17 + 517
16. 7003 − 675
17. 37 × 42

18. 649 × 27
19. 915 ÷ 8
20. 975 ÷ 28

Now solve the following problems; show your working out clearly:

21. 372 children in the school are going on a school trip. The cost of the outing is £4800. What should the school charge each pupil, approximately?

22. The school cook bakes 367 potatoes and roasts 196 potatoes. How many potatoes does he cook?

23. 48 children are going to France. They all give Mr Muddle their spending money. He collects 1680 euros in total. If all the children give him the same amount, how much money does each pupil give him?

24. I have to work out how many words I have written for my history essay. I estimate that I write 13 words on a line and that there are 48 lines on a page. If I have covered one and a half pages, roughly how many words have I written?

25. If 48 parents each pay £195 to sponsor a seat in the new theatre, how much money do they raise in total?

26. At the end of term Oak has 496 more house points than Thorn. If Oak has 724, how many points has Thorn?

27. There are 85 children in the lower school, 265 in the middle school and 267 in the upper school. How many pupils is that altogether?

End of chapter 1 activity: Dice games

For these games you will need one, two or three normal dice with six faces. Some of these games you can play by yourself and some you can play with a partner.

1. **Highest number**

    One player version

    Take one die and roll it six times. Write down the number rolled each time.

    You will then have a 6-digit number, for example: 612 322

    Using the same digits, write down the highest possible number you can from the digits you threw, i.e. 632 221

    Now that you have the idea, make six dashes in your exercise book like this:

    — — — — — —

    The aim is to make the highest number possible. Roll the die again. Write down the score on the die on one of your dashes. Do this five more times. Have you written down the highest possible number?

    If you have the highest score, then you win; otherwise you lose.

Two player version

This is exactly the same as the one player version, except that you both write down each score.

The winner is the one with the higher number.

2.   Lowest number

This is exactly the same as the highest number game, except this time the aim is to make the lowest number you can from the numbers you threw.

3.   Fraction snap
A game for two players (or you can play right hand against left hand)

Roll two dice. Place the one with the smaller score over the larger and consider the score as a fraction.

Example: $= \dfrac{2}{4} = \dfrac{1}{2}$

Now the next player rolls the dice again. If this fraction is equal to the first fraction, then the player who shouts 'SNAP' first wins a point. Keep taking it in turns to roll the dice and see who gets ten points first.

4.   Up to 20
For any number of players

Roll three dice.

Use the three scores to make as many numbers as possible (no more than 20 though!).

To make the numbers, you combine the three scores with $+ - \times$ and $\div$ and brackets.

For example: if you rolled 3, 4 and 6

$3 + 4 - 6 = 1$ $3 \times (6 - 4) = 6$
$3 \times (4 \div 6) = 2$ $4 + 6 - 3 = 7$
$3 + 6 - 4 = 5$ $4 \times (6 - 3) = 12$ and so on.

5. **Find the factors**

   For two players and two dice

   The first player calls a number between 1 and 30
   The second player rolls the two dice.
   If either score or any combination of the scores make a factor of the
   number called, then the second player wins; if not, the first player wins.
   (In this game if you throw a 1 and a 5, you can say it is 15).
   The winner is the first player in the next round.
   Once a number has been called, then it cannot be called again.
   The overall winner is the winner of the last (30th) round.

In that last game you will see there are quite a lot of strategies to help you win
the game. Some numbers are bound to have a factor and others are not. Is it
better to call these earlier or later?

6. **Battleships**

   For one player with two dice

   In your book draw a co-ordinate grid with values from 1 to 6 on both
   axes. On the grid mark out your battleship (with four xs in a straight line)
   and defend it with three mines (one x each):

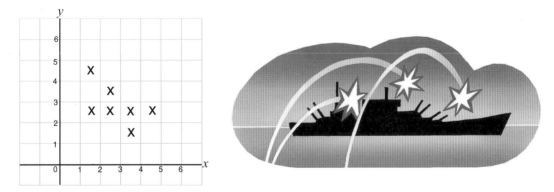

Your battleship may lie horizontally, vertically or diagonally and the mines
may touch the battleship corner to corner, but not side to side.

Now throw the dice. Use whichever die you like to be either co-ordinate.

The dice give the squares where the missiles land. If a missile lands on a
mine or a part of the battleship, then the 8 squares around it are also
exploded (making 9 squares in all).

How many throws does it take before you have sunk your battleship?

Chapter 2: Back to Babylon

How many miles to Babylon?
Three score miles and ten.
Can I get there by candlelight?
Aye, and back again.
If your feet are nimble and light,
You'll get there by candlelight.

Why would anyone want to go to Babylon? In its heyday Babylon was the centre of the civilised world, ruled over by King Nebuchadnezzar. He built the glorious "Hanging Gardens of Babylon", one of the wonders of the ancient world.

For mathematicians, Babylon is interesting because, as you found in Chapter 1, they had a numerical system like our own but based on the number 60 instead of 10.

So, why 60, you may ask. Let us remind ourselves of some of the things that we know about numbers and this will give us a clue.

Factors and multiples

Numbers that divide exactly into another number are called **factors**.

> For example: **3** and **6** are **factors** of 12

Numbers that are the result of a number (or factor) being multiplied by a whole number are called **multiples**.

> For example: **12** is a **multiple** of **6** (and also a multiple of 12, 4, 3, 2, and 1).

Without knowing it, when you learnt your times tables, you were studying factors and multiples. When whole numbers are involved, multiples give us the answer to a multiplication, and factors the answer to a division.

As	$7 \times 8 = 56$	then **56** is a multiple of **7** and of **8**
Then	$56 \div 7 = 8$	and **7** and **8** are factors of **56**

Before we move on, let us remind ourselves of the **rules of divisibility**:

- A number can be divided by **2** if it is **even**

- A number can be divided by **3** if the **sum of its digits** is a **multiple of 3**

- A number can be divided by **4** if the **last two digits** of a number **can be divided by 4**

- A number can be divided by **5** if it **ends in 5 or 0**

- A number can be divided by **6** if it is **even** and also has a **digit sum of a multiple of 3**

- A number can be divided by **9** if the **sum of its digits** is a **multiple of 9**

- A number can be divided by **10** if it **ends in 0**

There are rules of divisibility for 7, 8 and 11 but they are more complicated. It is better just to be good at these times tables and to be able to divide by 7, 8 and 11

Exercise 2.1

Now for some practice.

Example: Is 6 a factor of (i) 1341?   (ii) 2142?

(i) The digit sum of 1341 is $1 + 3 + 4 + 1 = 9$
9 is a multiple of 3
but 1341 is odd, so 6 is not a factor of 1341

(ii) The digit sum of 2142 is $2 + 1 + 4 + 2 = 9$
9 is a multiple of 3 and
2142 is even, so 6 is a factor of 2142

---

1. Write down which of these numbers has a factor of 6:
(a) 216   (b) 480   (c) 425   (d) 614   (e) 12 324

2. Are the following numbers multiples of 9?
(a) 216   (b) 891   (c) 617   (d) 6138   (e) 19 368

3. Is 7 a factor of the following?
(a) 7   (b) 27   (c) 77   (d) 717   (e) 91

4. Are the following numbers multiples of 11?
    (a) 88   (b) 121   (c) 292   (d) 374   (e) 2574

If we are asked to find **all** the factors of a number, it is a good idea to consider them in pairs. Start with 1 and go through all the ways of multiplying, to get your number, until you start repeating yourself.

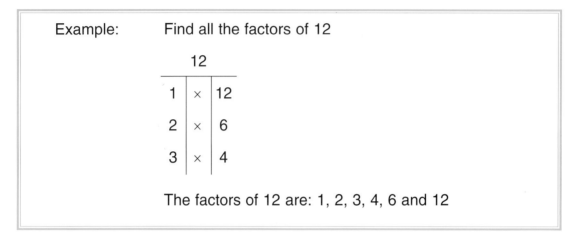

Example: Find all the factors of 12

12

1 × 12

2 × 6

3 × 4

The factors of 12 are: 1, 2, 3, 4, 6 and 12

5. List all the factors of:
    (a) 3   (b) 37   (c) 71   (d) 83   (e) 101

6. List all the factors of:
    (a) 1   (b) 25   (c) 64   (d) 9   (e) 144

7. List all the factors of:
    (a) 10   (b) 16   (c) 24   (d) 60   (e) 100

8. What is special about 60?

You should have noticed something special about the numbers in q.5 and q.6.

The numbers in q.5 had very few factors; in fact they had only two: themselves and 1; these are called **prime numbers**. Remember the number 1 itself is NOT a prime number because it does not have TWO factors.

Prime numbers and prime factors

A prime number has two factors, itself and 1

Exercise 2.2

1.   List all the prime numbers from 1 to 50

2.   Are the following prime numbers?
     (a) 87   (b) 91   (c) 107   (d) 207   (e) 231

3.   If $12 = 3 \times 4$ and $4 = 2 \times 2$, then $12 = 2 \times 2 \times 3$ is a product of its prime factors.
     In the same way write these numbers as products of their prime factors:
     (a) 16   (b) 40   (c) 120   (d) 28   (e) 100

Another thing to remember:
If you get bored with writing: $3 \times 3 \times 3 \times 3 \times 3$
You could write it as an **index number**: $\mathbf{3 \times 3 \times 3 \times 3 \times 3 = 3^5}$

The little 5 is called an **index number** and it **indicates how many** 3s are **multiplied** together.

So, we could have written 12 as $12 = 2^2 \times 3$

4.   Write the answers to q.3 again, using index numbers.

5.   These are numbers written as a product of prime factors in index form.
     What are the numbers?
     (a) 2×3^2 (b) $2^2 \times 3^2$ (c) $2^3 \times 3^2 \times 5$ (d) $2^2 \times 3^2 \times 5^2$ (e) $2^3 \times 5^2 \times 11$

The method we used in q.3 is fine for finding the prime factors of smaller numbers. But for larger numbers it is better to use successive division by prime numbers. Life is made easier if you start with the smallest.

Example: Find the prime factors of (i) 1287   (ii) 786

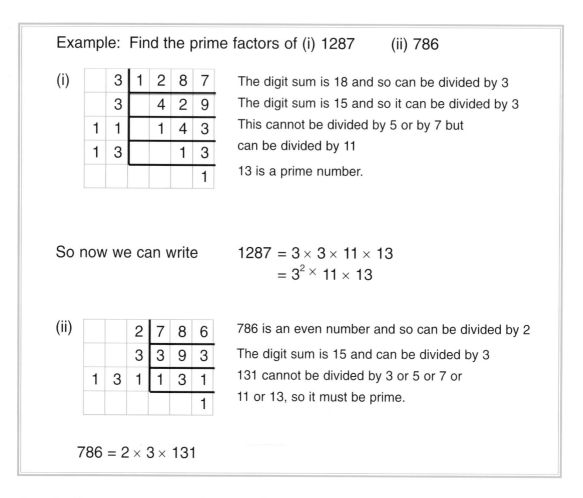

(i)

3	1	2	8	7
3		4	2	9
1 1		1	4	3
1 3			1	3
				1

The digit sum is 18 and so can be divided by 3

The digit sum is 15 and so it can be divided by 3

This cannot be divided by 5 or by 7 but

can be divided by 11

13 is a prime number.

So now we can write
$$1287 = 3 \times 3 \times 11 \times 13$$
$$= 3^2 \times 11 \times 13$$

(ii)

	2	7	8	6
	3	3	9	3
1 3 1	1	3	1
			1

786 is an even number and so can be divided by 2

The digit sum is 15 and can be divided by 3

131 cannot be divided by 3 or 5 or 7 or

11 or 13, so it must be prime.

$$786 = 2 \times 3 \times 131$$

6. In the same way as shown in the example above, write these numbers as a product of their prime factors:
(a) 252   (b) 1155   (c) 798   (d) 11 475   (e) 6215

7. Write down the **largest** number that is a factor of:
(a) both 24 and 45   (b) both 40 and 56   (c) both 100 and 120

8. Write down the **smallest** number that is a multiple of:
(a) both 8 and 10   (b) both 16 and 20   (c) both 20 and 25

The numbers in q.7 are called **highest common factors** or **H.C.F.**, and the answers in q.8 are called **lowest common multiples** or **L.C.M.**

You can deduce them quite simply for smaller numbers, but for larger numbers it helps to look at the **prime factors**.

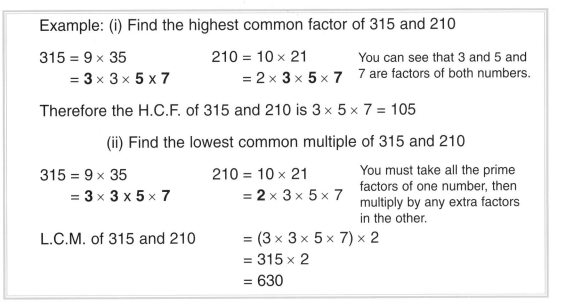

Example: (i) Find the highest common factor of 315 and 210

315 = 9 × 35   210 = 10 × 21   You can see that 3 and 5 and
   = **3** × **3** × **5** x **7**   = 2 × **3** × **5** × **7**   7 are factors of both numbers.

Therefore the H.C.F. of 315 and 210 is 3 × 5 × 7 = 105

(ii) Find the lowest common multiple of 315 and 210

315 = 9 × 35   210 = 10 × 21   You must take all the prime
   = **3** × **3** x **5** × **7**   = **2** × 3 × 5 × 7   factors of one number, then
                                            multiply by any extra factors
                                            in the other.

L.C.M. of 315 and 210   = (3 × 3 × 5 × 7) × 2
                               = 315 × 2
                               = 630

Another way of looking at H.C.F.s and L.C.M.s is to put all the factors of the numbers into a Venn diagram:

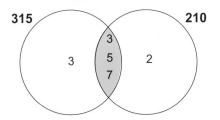

The H.C.F. is the product of the factors in the dark overlapping area: 3 × 5 × 7
The L.C.M. is the product of all the factors: 2 × 3 × 3 × 5 × 7

Exercise 2.3

1. What is the **highest common factor** of?
    (a) 24 and 144   (c) 144 and 180   (e) 400 and 640
    (b) 132 and 198   (d) 224 and 504   (f) 630 and 882

2. What is the **lowest common multiple** of?
    (a) 12 and 45   (c) 60 and 72   (e) 400 and 640
    (b) 60 and 144   (d) 224 and 504   (f) 630 and 882

3.   Consider the numbers from 1 to 100:
     (a) Which is the largest number that is a multiple of both 3 and 7?
     (b) What is the smallest number that is a multiple of both 8 and 6?
     (c) What is the largest number that has 3 as a factor?
     (d) What is the largest number that has 6 as a factor?
     (e) What is the largest number that has both the numbers 3 and 5 as factors?
     (f) Which numbers have only two factors?
     (g) Which numbers have an odd number of factors?
     (h) Which is the largest number that is a factor of 360?
     (i) How many numbers contain the digit 7?
     (j) How many numbers contain the digit 0?

Squares and their roots

We reminded ourselves about index numbers in the last exercise and saw that:

$3 \times 3 = 3^2$

If we think of this as a dot drawing, it becomes:

• • •

• • •

• • •

A 3×3 pattern makes a square.

When we use the index number ^{2}, we call it 'squared'. 3^2 is **three squared** because it can make a dot square with three dots on each side.

Exercise 2.4

1.   Draw dot patterns to show:
     (a) $4^2 = 16$ (b) $2^2 = 4$ (c) $6^2 = 36$

2.   Without drawing dot patterns, work out the value of:
     (a) 7^2 (b) 9^2 (c) 11^2

The answers to these questions are 'square numbers' which as you now know means the numbers can make a square pattern of dots.

3. List all the square numbers from 1 to 100, in order.

4. Look at this sequence of numbers:
0, 3, 8, 15, 24, 35, ...
(a) Continue the pattern for three more terms.
(b) Compare with your sequence of square numbers. What do you notice?

5. Look at this sequence of numbers:
3, 6, 11, 18, 27, 38, ...
(a) Continue the pattern for three more terms.
(b) Compare with your sequence of square numbers. What do you notice?

6. Generate a number sequence by this rule:
Start with 0
Add 1 and write down your answer.
Add 3 to that number. Write down that answer.
Continue until you have 10 numbers.
Describe these numbers.

We will look at this pattern later on when we have learnt a bit more about algebra.

7. Imagine a square of 49 dots. How many dots are on one side of the square?

This number is the square root of 49

If $3^2 = 3 \times 3 = 9$
Then the square root of 9 = 3

The special sign for square root is rather like a tick: $\sqrt{9} = 3$

8. Find the square root of the following numbers:
(a) 16   (b) 4   (c) 36

9. Evaluate ('find the value of'):
(a) $\sqrt{100}$ (b) $\sqrt{81}$ (c) $\sqrt{1}$ (d) $\sqrt{25}$ (e) $\sqrt{64}$ (f) $\sqrt{144}$

10. The Babylonians studied square numbers and used them in their mathematics. In particular they noticed special groups of three squares, where two of the squares added up to the third. Can you find two such groups of three in your list of square numbers?

11. Now you have your groups of three squares, write down the 3 square roots associated with each. Draw two triangles whose sides are the same lengths, in cm, as the square roots. Measure the largest angle in each. What do you notice?

This phenomenon has long been attributed to the Greek mathematician Pythagoras because he brought the knowledge to Europe. However, it is interesting to see that in fact the Babylonians got there first!

Cubes and their roots

Just as $3 \times 3 = 3^2$ and is called 3 squared, there is a special name for 3^3

We could draw a cube with sides of 3 units:

$3 \times 3 \times 3$ makes a cube

When we use the index number ^{3}, we call it 'cubed'. 3^3 is **three cubed** because it can make a cube of side three.

Exercise 2.5

1. Evaluate:

   (a) 2^3 (b) 3^3 (c) 4^3

2. Copy and complete this table, with values of n from 1 to 12:

n	n^3
1	1
2	8
...	
12	

If $3^3 = 3 \times 3 \times 3 = 27$

then 3 is called the cube root of 27

this has a special tick sign: $\sqrt[3]{27} = 3$

3.   Find the cube roots of the following numbers:
     (a) 8   (b) 125   (c) 1000

4.   Evaluate:

     (a) $\sqrt[3]{64}$ (b) $\sqrt[3]{729}$ (c) $\sqrt[3]{216}$ (d) $\sqrt[3]{343}$ (e) $\sqrt[3]{512}$

5.   Write down two numbers that are both a square number and a cube number.

6.   When we looked at the squares, we found a group of three where two of them added up to the third. Can you do that with cubes?

Perhaps that is something you might leave for a rainy day. If you do find two different cubes that add up to a third cube, then you will make mathematical history! This is the starting point for a more general theorem now known as **Fermat's Last Theorem**.

Triangle numbers

Earlier we arranged dots into a square pattern.

We can also arrange dots into triangles, either like this:

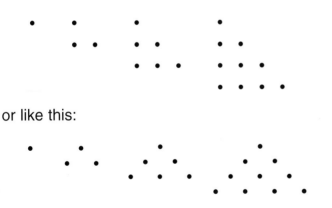

or like this:

Whichever way you arrange the dots, they make the same number sequence:

1 = 1
1 + 2 = 3
1 + 2 + 3 = 6

Exercice 2.6

1. Copy the sequence above and continue it until you have calculated the first ten triangle numbers.

2. Write your ten triangle numbers out in a row and beneath it write the sum of each pair, like this:

    1 3 6 10 ...

      4 9 ...   and so on

    What do you notice about your pairs?

    You could show the above using a picture. Look at this one:

    The black dots are the 4th triangle number, 10
    The white dots are the 3rd triangle number, 6
    See how one fits neatly with the other to make a
    square and see how $10 + 6 = 16$ which is 4^2

3. Draw some more pairs of triangle numbers that fit together to make squares.

To explore the interesting properties of triangle numbers further, it helps to have a neat way of writing them down. We can do this by calling them T numbers, short for triangle, and writing them down like this:

$T_1 = 1$
$T_2 = 1 + 2 = 3$
$T_3 = 1 + 2 + 3 = 6$
$T_4 = 1 + 2 + 3 + 4 = 10$

We could have summarised q.3 like this:
The sum of two consecutive triangle numbers is always a square:

$T_1 + T_2 = 1 + 3 = 4 = 2^2$
$T_2 + T_3 = 3 + 6 = 9 = 3^2$

4. Multiply each triangle number by 9 and add 1

    $9 \times T_1 + 1 = 9 \times 1 + 1 = 10 = T_4$
    $9 \times T_2 + 1 =$

    What do you notice?

5. Continue your list of triangle numbers until T_{15}
    Now make a list of the digits in the unit column.
    What do you notice?

When we looked at the rules of divisibility, we saw that the digit sum of multiples of 3 was a multiple of 3

6. Find the digit sum of each triangle number and from this the 'digital root'. (If the digit sum is 9, then the digital root is 9 but if the digital sum is 18 the digital root is $1 + 8 = 9$)
    What do you notice?

7. Multiply each triangle number by 8 and add 1:

    $8 \times T_1 + 1 = 8 \times 1 + 1 = 9$
    $8 \times T_2 + 1 =$
    What do you notice?

You can see how interesting triangle numbers are, but what we have not yet looked at is how you can find the 100th triangle number without having to do lots of adding up. Once you have looked at the next paragraph and answered q.8 and q.9, you should be able to find the 100th triangle number easily.

Try fitting together two triangle numbers, but this time the same size:

You see we have 2 × the 4th triangle number:
$2 \times 10 = 20$

Look closely at the rectangle we have made. It has sides of 4 and 5 and
$4 \times 5 = 20$

8. Draw some more consecutive triangle numbers fitted together in pairs to make rectangles. What do you notice?

9. Multiply together the lengths of the sides, then divide your answer by 2
    What do you notice?

10. Without drawing, use this fact to calculate the value of:
    (a) T_{10} (b) T_{20} (c) T_{100}

More clues

If you look at the worksheet for the next exercise you will find a table square and a 1 to 100 square. This time we are going to look at the last digit of each multiple.

Exercise 2.7

You will need a calculator for this exercise. Using the worksheet, complete the table square and then take ten different colours:

1. Colour each number that ends in 2 in one colour. Make a list of the possible multiples:
    $2 \times 6 = 12$, $3 \times 4 = 12$, $2 \times 11 = 22$ etc.

2. Colour each number that ends in 3 with another colour. Make a list of the multiples.

3. Continue with numbers that end with 4 through to 9, then do 0 and 1

    Look at your lists of multiples. Those that end in 2 have a very long list; those that end in 7 have a very short list.

4. (a) The column that is the 11 times table has the same pattern as which other column?
    (b) The column that is the 12 times table has the same pattern as which other column?
    (c) Colour the numbers in the 1 to 100 square as instructed. What is the name given to the numbers in the 1 to 100 square that are not coloured?

You can see that if you multiply the last two digits of any two numbers together, then the last digit of THAT product is the same as the last digit of the product of the two WHOLE numbers.

So 12×72 will have $2 \times 2 = 4$ as the last digit. Check this using your calculator.

5. Give the last digit only of these products:
    (a) 23×45 (c) 21×65 (e) 47×22
    (b) 34×98 (d) 36×27 (f) 99×38

In the last chapter we looked at estimating answers:
$31 \times 92 \approx 30 \times 90$ and $30 \times 90 = 2700$

6. Using estimating and the rule about the last digit, find which of these calculations must be wrong, and state the reason why:
   (a) 31 × 99 =   (i) 3069   (ii) 2699   (iii) 2708
   (b) 29 × 42 =   (i) 818   (ii) 1029   (iii) 1218
   (c) 31 × 58 =   (i) 1058   (ii) 1798   (iii) 1218
   (d) 78 × 52 =   (i) 4056   (ii) 456   (iii) 35 016
   (e) 72 × 51 =   (i) 3616   (ii) 3492   (iii) 3672
   (f) 99 × 39 =   (i) 2718   (ii) 3861   (iii) 4081

7. Use your calculator to check the answer to the six multiplications above.

8. The class teacher has some number tiles which she has stuck up to show the answers to some multiplications but the number tiles have fallen off the wall. Use estimating and the last digit rule to make the calculations work:
   (a) 37 × 25 =   (Tiles are 2, 5, 9)
   (b) 29 × 78 =   (Tiles are 2, 2, 2,6)
   (c) 45 × 87 =   (Tiles are 1, 3, 5, 9)
   (d) 32 × 49 =   (Tiles are 1, 5, 6, 8)
   (e) 29 × 58 =   (Tiles are 1, 2, 6, 8)
   (f) 81 × 61 =   (Tiles are 1, 4, 4, 9)

Inspired guesswork

Sometimes we have a problem that we cannot solve with a straightforward +, −, x, ÷ solution. In this situation we have to do some guesswork. If we think about what we are doing, we can often find a solution very quickly.

Example: My classroom is 4 m longer than it is wide and its perimeter is 36 m. What is its length?

Width	Length	Perimeter	Note
2 m	6 m	16 m	Too small
3 m	7 m	20 m	Too small
4 m	8 m	24 m	Too small
(After 4 m you might notice that the pattern of numbers for the perimeter goes up in fours and thus be able to work out the answer.)			
7 m	11 m	36 m	Exactly

The length is therefore 11 m.

Exercise 2.8

1. My brother is three years older than I am. The product of our ages is 54 How old am I?

2. My mother is three times as old as I am. The sum of our ages is 52 How old am I?

3. Last year I was three times as old as my brother. In two years time I will be twice as old. How old is my brother now?

4. I have twice as much pocket money as my brother but £1 less than my sister. Altogether we get £6. How much pocket money does my sister get?

5. I give one half of my sweets to Ollie and one third of them to Millie. I have 6 left. How many sweets did I start with?

6. Japhet had several camels. On a long walk across the desert one third of his camels got sore feet and had to be left behind. One quarter of his camels were sold to a dealer on the way. He arrived at the other end with 10 camels. How many camels did he start with?

7. On a sponsored swim I swam three times as far as Rose. Rose was sponsored for twice as much per length. We raised £72 between us. How much money did I raise?

8. I looked at my father's calendar. If you did not count the 52 weekends at all and took off the eight bank holidays, then he is at work 10 times as many days as he is on holiday. How many days is he on holiday (it is not a leap year)?

9. I have £10 more saved up than my brother and £4 less than my sister. Altogether we have £30. How much money has my brother?

10. I have a collection of micro-machines. I can put them in an odd number of rows (but greater than 1) with the same prime number of cars in each row. If I have more than 100 and less than 110 micro-machines, how many do I have exactly?

Exercise 2.9: Pythagoras' perfect numbers

Perfect numbers are numbers whose factors add up to the number itself (the factors obviously cannot include the actual number).

Let us see what we can find:

1: factors are {1}   factor sum is 1 - imperfect
10: factors are {1, 2, 5}   factor sum is 8 - imperfect
12: factors are {1, 2, 3, 4, 6}   factor sum is 16 - imperfect

1.   Try to find the first two perfect numbers.

The Babylonians knew about perfect numbers, so did the Hittites and the Hebrews. St Augustine is reputed to have said, "God created the world in six days because that number is perfect."

2.   Why do you think there are 28 days in February?

From the number series you have been looking at, consider the numbers that occur in ancient and modern history. See if you can say if they are perfect, triangular, prime, square or special in any other way:

3.   (a) There are 10 laws of Moses.
(b) 7 is lucky.
(c) You come of age at 21
(d) The French refer to a fortnight as 'quinze jours' (15 days).
(e) The Romans had 10 months of 36 days (at one point!).

Can you think of any other 'special' numbers?

Exercise 2.10: Extension questions – Using factors to multiply

In the example of 125 × 23 we used long multiplication to solve the problem. However, most of us are better at some multiplication calculations than others. For example, you may not know your 24 times table but you should know your 8 and 3 times tables. You can, therefore, see that 8 × 3 = 24, and that 24 − 1 = 23

We can use this information to work out the answer:

Look at the sum like this: $125 \times 23 = 125 \times (24 - 1)$
$$= 125 \times (8 \times 3 - 1)$$
$$= 125 \times 8 \times 3 - 125 \times 1$$
$$= 1000 \times 3 - 125$$
$$= 3000 - 125$$
$$= 2875$$

This might look like a lot of work, but some of the stages can be done in your head and then you only need to write down the complicated bits.

Notice that $125 \times 8 = 1000$

The numbers ending in 25 or 75 are interesting in that some are factors of 100, or 1000

1. Complete these multiplication tables up to 10:
   $1 \times 25 = 25$ $1 \times 125 = 125$ $1 \times 225 = 225$
   $2 \times 25 = 50$ $2 \times 125 = 250$ $2 \times 225 = 450$
   $3 \times 25 = $ ____ $3 \times 125 = $ ____ $3 \times 225 = $ ____ etc.

2. Copy and complete this multiplication:
   $24 \times 19 = 24 \times (20 - 1)$
   $$= 24 \times 20 - 24 \times 1$$
   $$= \underline{\quad} - \underline{\quad}$$
   $$= \underline{\quad}$$

3. Do these multiplication calculations in the same way:
   (a) 25×19 (c) 43×29 (e) 39×45
   (b) 32×19 (d) 29×25 (f) 63×39

4. Work out the answer to these multiplication calculations:
   (a) 25×21 (c) 225×31 (e) 51×225
   (b) 125×31 (d) 41×25 (f) 125×62

5. Now try these, by dividing the second number into two factors:

> Example: 75×24
>
> $$75 \times 24 = 75 \times 8 \times 3$$
> $$= 600 \times 3$$
> $$= 1800$$

(a) 25×24 (c) 55×27 (e) 215×18
(b) 35×48 (d) 105×64 (f) 65×28

Using factors to find square roots

The square numbers 1, 4, 9, 16 ... can be written as 1^2, 2^2, 3^2, 4^2,...
This is because they are 1×1, 2×2, 3×3, 4×4, ...

Thus 4 is the square root of 16 (which is 4×4)
    3 is the square root of 9 (3×3)
    2 is the square root of 4 (2×2) etc.

If we break down **perfect** squares into their prime factors, we can find their square roots.

$36 = 2 \times 2 \times 3 \times 3 = (2 \times 3) \times (2 \times 3)$ thus square root of 36 is $2 \times 3 = 6$

or

$$\sqrt{36} = \sqrt{2 \times 2} \times \sqrt{3 \times 3}$$
$$= 2 \times 3$$
$$= 6$$

6. Break the following numbers into their prime factors and then find the square roots:

(a) 144   (c) 1296   (e) 1225
(b) 2025   (d) 900   (f) 1764

If you are given the number 28 it can be written:

$$28 = 2 \times 2 \times 7$$

You **cannot** find its square root from the prime factors.

However, if you are given the product 28×7

$$28 \times 7 = 2 \times 2 \times 7 \times 7$$

$$\text{Therefore } \sqrt{28 \times 7} = 2 \times 7$$
$$= 14$$

7. Break the following products into their prime factors and then find the square root of each product:
    (a) 28×28 (c) 12×27 (e) 525×189
    (b) 56×14 (d) 72×50 (f) 220×55

8. Can you find the cube roots of the following products in the same way?
    (a) 18×12 (c) 98×28 (e) $147 \times 42 \times 12$
    (b) 56×49 (d) $21 \times 12 \times 28$ (f) $56 \times 63 \times 231$

Exercise 2.11: Summary exercise

1. Write down which of these numbers are multiples of 6:
    (a) 226   (c) 1434   (e) 231
    (b) 234   (d) 132   (f) 9000

2. Write down which of the above numbers can be divided by:
    (a) 5   (b) 9   (c) 7

3. List all the factors of:
    (a) 64   (b) 24   (c) 300

4. Consider the following numbers:
    7   10   4   32   25

    From the numbers above write down one that is:
    (a) a prime.   (d) a square number.
    (b) a factor of 16   (e) the cube root of 64
    (c) a multiple of 8   (f) a triangle number

5. Write the following numbers as products of their prime factors:
    (a) 48   (b) 196   (c) 315

6. Evaluate:
    (a) $2^2 \times 3^3$ (b) $2^3 \times 5^2$ (c) $2^2 \times 3 \times 5^2$

7. Find the highest number that is a factor of both 144 and 196

8. Find the lowest number that is a multiple of both 24 and 56

9. Draw the first four triangle numbers and calculate the value of the 7th.

10. By a logical method of trial and improvement solve these problems:
    (a) My grandfather left me some money in his will. He left my brother half as much as me, and my sister the same as my brother and me together. If my grandfather left us £750, how much did we each get?
    (b) We have a rectangular garden. Its length is 5 m longer than its width and its area is 204 m^2. How long is the garden?

End of chapter 2 activity: The number game

Having been through this chapter, you should now know lots of things about numbers. Before you move onto the next topic here are some puzzle games for you to play. Warm up by trying to answer the following questions. All the answers are numbers less than 100:

1. I am thinking of a number. It is a prime number and it is even. What is my number?

2. I am thinking of a number. It is a multiple of three and a factor of 12, but is not 12 or 3; what is my number?

3. I am thinking of a number. It is a square number that is less than 50 and the sum of its digits is 13; what is my number?

4. I am thinking of a number greater than 50 and it is a prime number. Its last digit is 3, and the sum of the digits is 10; what is my number?

5. My number is a factor of 455 and 693, but is not 1; what is my number?

6. My number is the highest multiple of 3 and 4 that is less than 100; what is my number?

7. My number is a triangle number that is divisible by 11; what is my number?

8. My number is a factor of 60, but is not a multiple of 5, or a square number, or a prime number. What is my number? (There are two possible answers.)

9. My number is a prime number between 25 and 75, and the sum of its digits is a square number. What is my number?

10. My number is a square number and a triangle number. What is my number?

Now that you have warmed up, it is time to play the game.

On the worksheet you will see several 1 to 100 squares. You and your opponent both need a worksheet. Here's how to play:

1. Think of a number. Write it over your first square. Your opponent will do the same.

2. The youngest player asks the first question in the first game. After that take it in turns.

3. Now ask a question. As in the warm up questions you should ask a question that will give you some information about your opponent's number. The answer can only be 'yes' or 'no'. Whatever the answer to your question, you should be able to eliminate many of the numbers on your square.

    Possible questions could be:

Is your number even?	(If the answer is 'yes', cross out all odd numbers.)
Is it a multiple of 3?	(If 'yes', cross out all non multiples of 3)
Is it prime?	(If 'no', cross out all primes.)
Does it contain the digit 7?	(If 'yes', cross out all numbers not containing the digit 7)

4. You keep asking questions until you get the answer 'no'. Then it is your opponent's turn.

5. He or she can ask you questions until your answer is 'no', then it is your turn again.

6. As you eliminate numbers, you should end up with a very small selection remaining that have not been crossed out. When you reach this stage, your final question(s) might be something like:

    Is your number 37?

7. The winner is the player who works out his / her opponent's number first.

Chapter 3: Fractions

We have seen how some early number systems were not based on 10 but on 60. This is because 60 was a useful base because it has so many factors.

Divisions under early number systems were a real problem. It was difficult to divide using their symbols. Consider how a Roman child might see 36 ÷ 9:

XXXVI ÷ IX

To get around this problem, division would often be done by consulting tables. You can see now why 60 was a good number. It has so many factors that it can be divided exactly by many numbers.

We see this particularly with the Ancient Egyptians. The Egyptians were great traders and this meant that they needed to use fractions, particularly for the division of food supplies. For example, a division of 2 loaves among 5 men would require the fraction: $\frac{2}{5}$

As new situations arose the Egyptians developed special techniques for dealing with the notations they already had. Compound fractions (i.e. where the numerator is greater than one) were normally expressed as a sum of the unit fraction.

For example: $\frac{3}{8} = \frac{1}{4} + \frac{1}{8}$

Fractions were so important to the Egyptians that of the 87 problems in the Rhind Mathematical Papyrus only 6 did not involve fractions. Because the Egyptians performed their multiplications and divisions by doubling and halving, scribes would create tables with calculations of fractions along with integers. These tables would be used as references, so that temple personnel could carry out the fractional divisions on the food and supplies.

You may not be quite as used to calculating with fractions as the Ancient Egyptians, but by now you should be familiar with equivalent fractions, mixed numbers, simplifying, addition and subtraction. We will just remind you of some of these and then you can try the first three exercises.

Equivalent fractions

Equivalent fractions are fractions that have the same value.

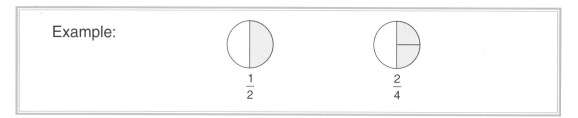

Example:

$$\frac{1}{2} \qquad\qquad \frac{2}{4}$$

We can draw diagrams to show equivalent fractions, or we can work them out numerically by multiplying or dividing the top and bottom by the same number:

$$\frac{3}{8} = \frac{3}{8} \times \frac{3}{3} \quad \text{or} \quad \frac{18}{24} = \frac{18}{24} \div \frac{6}{6}$$

$$= \frac{9}{24} \qquad\qquad = \frac{3}{4}$$

When we are simplifying a fraction, we should finish with the smallest possible numbers.

For example: $\frac{18}{24} = \frac{9}{12} = \frac{6}{8} = \frac{3}{4}$

All four fractions are of equal value, but $\frac{3}{4}$ is the fraction **in its simplest form (lowest terms).**

Note that the bottom number is called the **denominator** and the top number the **numerator**. For some of the questions that follow you need to find the **lowest common denominator**, just like you had to find lowest common multiples in the last chapter.

Exercise 3.1

1. Replace the stars to make these fractions equivalent (note that the star represents a different number in each case):

    (a) $\frac{3}{4} = \frac{*}{12}$ (b) $\frac{2}{7} = \frac{*}{14}$ (c) $\frac{4}{9} = \frac{*}{27}$ (d) $\frac{5}{6} = \frac{15}{*}$

2. Write these fractions in their lowest terms:

    (a) $\frac{10}{12}$ (b) $\frac{15}{18}$ (c) $\frac{8}{48}$ (d) $\frac{14}{56}$ (e) $\frac{60}{100}$

3. Draw a 5 cm by 6 cm rectangle in your book four times. Divide each rectangle up to illustrate these fractions:

   (a) $\frac{7}{30}$　　　(b) $\frac{4}{15}$　　　(c) $\frac{5}{6}$　　　(d) $\frac{1}{10}$

Example:　　　Write 25p as a fraction of £2

£2 = 200p

Fraction $= \frac{25}{200}$

$= \frac{1}{8}$

---

4. Write the first quantity as a fraction of the second, giving your answer in its simplest form:

   (a) 50p as a fraction of a £1
   (b) 24 as a fraction of 60
   (c) 48 as a fraction of 360
   (d) 350 g as a fraction of a kilogramme
   (e) 35p as a fraction of £5
   (f) 36 cm as a fraction of a metre
   (g) 125 cm as a fraction of 4 m
   (h) 750 ml as a fraction of 2 litres

5. Copy and complete: $\frac{3}{8} = \frac{}{40}$ and $\frac{2}{5} = \frac{}{40}$　Which is larger, $\frac{3}{8}$ or $\frac{2}{5}$?

6. In the same way write down the larger of these pairs of fractions:

   (a) $\frac{3}{5}$ or $\frac{5}{8}$　　　(c) $\frac{5}{6}$ or $\frac{7}{8}$　　　(e) $\frac{4}{9}$ or $\frac{3}{7}$

   (b) $\frac{3}{4}$ or $\frac{2}{3}$　　　(d) $\frac{3}{7}$ or $\frac{5}{12}$　　　(f) $\frac{3}{5}$ or $\frac{5}{9}$

7. I poured myself a drink from a two litre bottle of cola. My glass holds 125 ml. What fraction of the whole bottle is in 1 glass?

8. I have saved up £15 towards a jacket costing £75. What fraction of the £75 have I saved?

9. I cut off 12 m from a ball of string 45 m long. What fraction of the string have I cut off?

10. We have driven 350 km. Our total journey is 480 km. What fraction of our journey have we left to go?

11. In our year there are 45 children, only 24 of whom are going on the ski trip. What fraction of the children are not?

12. I pick 36 conkers and give 8 to my sister, 6 to my brother and put 4 in my pocket. I then give half of the rest to my best friend. What fraction of the original total have I kept for myself?

Equivalent fractions, decimals and percentages

We have seen how different civilisations developed different number systems. In Ancient Egypt, for example, fractions were used as a form of division; in our decimal number system we use decimal fractions, or decimals.

Compare these two number lines:

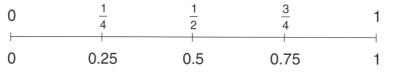

Let us remind ourselves why the fraction $\frac{1}{4} = 0.25$, $\frac{1}{2} = 0.5$ and $\frac{3}{4} = 0.75$

The numerical system we use is called the decimal system because it is based on powers of ten. (Ten in Latin is *decem*). Earlier we looked at writing and calculating with numbers greater than one. These numbers are given their value by the relative position of the digits. If we extend the number line to the right of the units column, we can look at numbers less than one.

Thousands Hundreds Tens Units ▪ Tenths Hundredths Thousandths.

The important **POINT** is between units and tenths. This is the decimal point and it separates numbers less than 1 from those greater than 1.

As with numbers greater than one, the value of a digit is given by its position in the above columns. As before we fill up spaces with 0s:

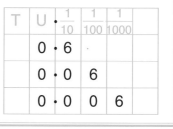

	If we place a 6 in the tenths column, it is 6 tenths	$0 \cdot 6$
If we place a 6 in the hundredths column, it is 6 hundredths	$0 \cdot 0\ 6$
If we place a 6 in the thousandths column, it is 6 thousandths	$0 \cdot 0\ 0\ 6$

Therefore, if we write 0.5, we are saying $\frac{5}{10}$ which is equivalent to $\frac{1}{2}$

If we write 0.25, we are saying $\frac{25}{100}$ which is equivalent to $\frac{1}{4}$

If we write 0.75, we are saying $\frac{75}{100}$ which is equivalent to $\frac{3}{4}$

Another way of looking at numbers is as percentages. The word 'percentage' means 'out of a hundred'. Therefore, any fraction written out of 100 can also be written as a percentage.

So, if we write 0.5, we are saying $\frac{5}{10}$ which is equivalent to $\frac{50}{100}$ or 50%

If we write 0.25, we are saying $\frac{25}{100}$ which is equivalent to 25%

If we write 0.75, we are saying $\frac{75}{100}$ which is equivalent to 75%

Exercise 3.2

1. Write these fractions as decimals:

    (a) $\frac{1}{10}$ (b) $\frac{3}{10}$ (c) $\frac{7}{10}$ (d) $\frac{9}{10}$

2. Write these fractions as percentages:

    (a) $\frac{1}{100}$ (b) $\frac{43}{100}$ (c) $\frac{7}{10}$ (d) $\frac{9}{10}$

3. Write these percentages as (i) decimals and then (ii) fractions in their lowest terms:

    (a) 20%   (b) 40%   (c) 60%   (d) 80%

4. Write these decimals as (i) percentages and then (ii) fractions in their lowest terms:

    (a) 0.25   (b) 0.45   (c) 0.65   (d) 0.95

Here is one that is worth learning because it keeps cropping up:

12.5% = 0.125 = $\frac{125}{1000}$ = $\frac{1}{8}$

Once you know the equivalent value of $\frac{1}{8}$, you can work out $\frac{3}{8}$ etc. by multiplying.

---

5. Write these fractions as (i) decimals and then (ii) percentages:

    (a) $\frac{3}{8}$ (b) $\frac{5}{8}$ (c) $\frac{7}{8}$

6.   The other way of thinking about fractions and percentages is to understand that:

$$\frac{1}{4} = 1 \div 4 = 0.25$$

Use a calculator to check all your fraction-to-decimal answers above.

Here is another that is worth learning because it does not go exactly:

$$\frac{1}{3} = 1 \div 3 = 0.3333\ldots$$

We call this 0.3 recurring and we write it like this: $0.\dot{3}$

---

7.   Use a calculator to work out the decimal equivalent of:

(a) $\frac{1}{6}$ (b) $\frac{2}{3}$ (c) $\frac{5}{6}$ (d) $\frac{1}{9}$

Now make sure that you know perfectly all the fraction, decimal and percentage equivalents we have worked out in this exercise.

Mixed numbers and improper fractions

All the fractions we have looked at so far have been smaller than 1 (proper fractions), but we often talk of fractions with whole numbers attached:

I am twelve and a half.
It is quarter past two.

We call these numbers **mixed numbers** because they are a mixture of a whole number and a fraction. If we need to turn mixed numbers into fractions, we end up with **improper fractions**. They are called improper fractions because the **numerator** (that's the number on top) is bigger than the **denominator** (that's the number on the bottom) and the fraction is top heavy.

Exercise 3.3

> Example: (i) Write $\frac{25}{6}$ as a mixed number.
>
> $$\frac{25}{6} = 4\frac{1}{6} \qquad (25 \div 6 = 4 \text{ remainder } 1)$$
>
> (ii) Write $2\frac{1}{4}$ as an improper fraction.
>
> $$2\frac{1}{4} = \frac{9}{4} \qquad (4 \times 2 + 1 = 9)$$

1. Write these mixed numbers as improper fractions:

(a) $1\frac{3}{4}$ (c) $2\frac{1}{7}$ (e) $10\frac{3}{10}$ (g) $7\frac{3}{7}$ (i) $4\frac{7}{12}$ (k) $9\frac{1}{9}$

(b) $3\frac{2}{5}$ (d) $6\frac{4}{5}$ (f) $8\frac{4}{9}$ (h) $12\frac{2}{5}$ (j) $15\frac{3}{4}$ (l) $5\frac{5}{12}$

2. Write these improper fractions as mixed numbers:

(a) $\frac{13}{4}$ (c) $\frac{19}{9}$ (e) $\frac{93}{12}$ (g) $\frac{23}{8}$ (i) $\frac{27}{2}$ (k) $\frac{101}{5}$

(b) $\frac{21}{6}$ (d) $\frac{42}{7}$ (f) $\frac{84}{11}$ (h) $\frac{29}{10}$ (j) $\frac{19}{4}$ (l) $\frac{65}{13}$

Adding fractions

We can only add fractions when they have the same denominator.

If we are asked $\frac{1}{10} + \frac{3}{10}$, we can see the $3 + 1 = 4$, because the denominator (10) is the same in both fractions. The answer is therefore $\frac{4}{10}$

However, if we are asked $\frac{3}{10} + \frac{7}{12}$, we cannot directly add tenths to twelfths.

We have to write both fractions as **equivalent fractions**, with a **lowest common denominator.**

In this example the lowest common multiple of 10 and 12 is 60, so we multiply the top and the bottom of each fraction with a multiple that will make 10 up to 60 i.e. 6, and 12 up to 60 i.e. 5:

$$\frac{3}{10} = \frac{3 \times 6}{10 \times 6} = \frac{18}{60} \quad \text{and} \quad \frac{5}{12} = \frac{5 \times 5}{12 \times 5} = \frac{25}{60}$$

We can then write the fraction addition like this:

Example:

$$\frac{3}{10} + \frac{5}{12} = \frac{18}{60} + \frac{25}{60}$$

$$= \frac{18 + 25}{60}$$

$$= \frac{43}{60}$$

Exercise 3.4

Add these fractions, remembering to put the answer in its simplest form. If the answer is an improper fraction, e.g. $\frac{13}{12}$, write it as a mixed number: $1\frac{1}{12}$

1. $\frac{2}{5} + \frac{1}{4}$

2. $\frac{1}{7} + \frac{3}{5}$

3. $\frac{2}{3} + \frac{1}{5}$

4. $\frac{5}{6} + \frac{3}{5}$

5. $\frac{2}{15} + \frac{4}{9}$

6. $\frac{3}{10} + \frac{3}{8}$

7. $\frac{5}{6} + \frac{3}{4}$

8. $\frac{5}{6} + \frac{3}{10}$

9. $\frac{5}{12} + \frac{3}{8}$

Addition with mixed numbers

When you add mixed numbers you have an extra stage in the calculation. The first step is to add the whole numbers and then to do the fraction bit as we saw above.

Example:

$$3\frac{1}{8} + 2\frac{11}{12} = 5\frac{3 + 22}{24}$$ In this case we have an extra stage.

$$= 5\frac{25}{24}$$ First deal with the whole numbers 3 + 2 = 5 then do the fraction addition as we did

$$= 6\frac{1}{24}$$ before.

10. $1\frac{1}{5} + 3\frac{2}{3}$ **14.** $5\frac{3}{8} + 3\frac{1}{16}$ **18.** $1\frac{1}{6} + 3\frac{3}{10}$

11. $2\frac{1}{7} + 3\frac{3}{5}$ **15.** $2\frac{4}{5} + 2\frac{2}{15}$ **19.** $4\frac{5}{6} + 2\frac{3}{4}$

12. $1\frac{2}{5} + 4\frac{1}{8}$ **16.** $6\frac{5}{12} + 3\frac{5}{8}$ **20.** $5\frac{1}{12} + 3\frac{2}{3}$

13. $7\frac{2}{9} + 2\frac{2}{15}$ **17.** $3\frac{5}{8} + 3\frac{3}{10}$ **21.** $3\frac{3}{4} + 3\frac{2}{3}$

Subtraction

Subtraction of fractions follows the same first steps as addition. First find the lowest common denominator, then work out the equivalent fractions and finally do the subtraction:

Exercise 3.5

Example: $$\frac{3}{5} - \frac{1}{3} = \frac{9}{15} - \frac{5}{15}$$
$$= \frac{9 - 5}{15}$$
$$= \frac{4}{15}$$

1. $\frac{4}{5} - \frac{2}{3}$ **4.** $\frac{7}{8} - \frac{5}{6}$ **7.** $\frac{5}{8} - \frac{2}{5}$

2. $\frac{2}{3} - \frac{1}{4}$ **5.** $\frac{5}{12} - \frac{1}{4}$ **8.** $\frac{6}{7} - \frac{3}{4}$

3. $\frac{5}{7} - \frac{1}{6}$ **6.** $\frac{7}{12} - \frac{1}{5}$ **9.** $\frac{7}{8} - \frac{5}{6}$

Subtracting with mixed numbers

Example: $$3\frac{3}{7} - 1\frac{1}{4} = 2\frac{12 - 7}{28}$$
$$= 2\frac{5}{28}$$

First subtract the whole numbers.

Then do the fraction subtraction as we did before.

10. $3\frac{4}{7} - 1\frac{2}{5}$ 13. $6\frac{2}{5} - 3\frac{2}{9}$ 16. $6\frac{2}{3} - 2\frac{2}{9}$

11. $5\frac{2}{3} - 2\frac{2}{7}$ 14. $5\frac{4}{9} - 1\frac{1}{3}$ 17. $4\frac{3}{4} - 1\frac{2}{3}$

12. $4\frac{4}{5} - 1\frac{1}{3}$ 15. $4\frac{4}{7} - 3\frac{1}{4}$ 18. $7\frac{5}{6} - 3\frac{5}{8}$

As in any other subtraction there will be times when the first subtraction is not possible (5 – 9); as usual you must then **borrow** from the next number on the left. Remember that you are not borrowing ten units – you will be borrowing 8 eighths, 12 twelfths, 16 sixteenths or whatever:

Example: $3\frac{1}{3} - 1\frac{3}{4}$ $= 2\frac{4-9}{12}$ 4 – 9 cannot be done, so we borrow 12 twelfths.

$= 1\frac{16-9}{12}$ 12 + 4 = 16
The calculation is now 16 – 9

$= 1\frac{7}{12}$

19. $2\frac{2}{5} - 1\frac{2}{3}$ 23. $5\frac{3}{7} - 2\frac{4}{5}$ 27. $2\frac{1}{4} - 1\frac{5}{6}$

20. $4\frac{3}{8} - 1\frac{2}{5}$ 24. $2\frac{3}{5} - 1\frac{9}{10}$ 28. $4\frac{1}{9} - 2\frac{5}{6}$

21. $1\frac{1}{5} - \frac{2}{3}$ 25. $1\frac{1}{3} - \frac{7}{8}$ 29. $1\frac{2}{7} - \frac{3}{4}$

22. $3\frac{3}{4} - 1\frac{7}{8}$ 26. $2\frac{2}{7} - \frac{2}{3}$ 30. $5\frac{1}{6} - 1\frac{5}{8}$

Exercise 3.6

To answer each of these questions, write out the fraction calculation:

1. I bought a packet of 'Ringos'. Five sixths of them were stuck together; what fraction were not stuck together?

2. I drink $\frac{7}{12}$ of a large bottle of cola and my friend drinks $\frac{2}{3}$ of a bottle of the same size. Who drinks the most cola?

3. When I measure myself I find that I am 1.4 metres tall, and that my head is 20 cm. What fraction of my total height is my head?

4. I have a ball of string eight and a half metres long. I use five and five sixths of a metre on my technology project. How much string is left?

5. In a bag of 'Gummos' one quarter of the sweets are red, two fifths are green, and the rest are orange. What fraction of the sweets are orange?

6. Prince Absolute has to make a journey of 8 leagues. $2\frac{3}{8}$ leagues of the journey are through forest and $1\frac{1}{5}$ leagues are through desert. The rest is of the journey is across plains. How many leagues are across plains?

7. What is greater, the sum of a half plus three fifths or the difference between one and a half and two fifths?

8. A triathlete runs for one and a quarter hours, swims for 45 minutes and cycles for two and two fifths of an hour. How long does he take in all?

A fraction of an amount

Here are some everyday examples of where we consider fractions of an amount.

'Half an hour' is 30 minutes. We divide 60 minutes by 2

'Half a metre' is 50 cm. We divide 100 cm by 2

'Three quarters of an hour' is 45 minutes because 60 minutes is divided by 4, and then multiplied by 3

Exercise 3.7

> Example: (i) Find $\frac{1}{5}$ of 25
>
> $\frac{1}{5}$ of 25 = 25 ÷ 5
>
> = 5
>
> (ii) Find $\frac{3}{4}$ of 1 m. Give the answer in cm.
>
> $\frac{3}{4}$ of 1m = 100 ÷ 4 × 3
>
> = 25 × 3
>
> = 75 cm

1. Find $\frac{1}{4}$ of 16

2. Find $\frac{1}{7}$ of 35

3. Find $\frac{1}{8}$ of 104

4. Find $\frac{1}{9}$ of 126

5. Find $\frac{1}{4}$ of 81

6. Find $\frac{1}{8}$ of 74

7. Find $\frac{3}{4}$ of 48

8. Find $\frac{2}{3}$ of 72

9. Find $\frac{3}{5}$ of 1 m. Give the answer in cm.

10. Find $\frac{2}{3}$ of 1 hour. Give the answer in minutes.

11. Find $\frac{3}{4}$ of 1 kg. Give the answer in grams.

12. Find $\frac{5}{8}$ of 3 km. Give the answer in km and m.

For more complicated fractions of an amount we may need to write down the calculation.

Remember that 'of' can be written as × (multiply).

Example: What is $\frac{2}{5}$ of 240?

$$\frac{2}{5} \text{ of } 240 = \frac{2}{5} \times 240$$

These calculations are simplest if both terms are fractions, and so we can write the 240 as $\frac{240}{1}$

The calculation becomes $\frac{2}{5} \times \frac{240}{1}$

We can simplify this in the same way that we simplify equivalent fractions, by dividing top and bottom by the same common factor:

$$\frac{2}{{}_1\cancel{5}} \times \frac{\cancel{240}^{48}}{1} = \frac{96}{1} = 96$$

Example: Find $\frac{7}{9}$ of 135

$$\frac{7}{9} \text{ of } 135$$

$$= \frac{7}{{}_1\cancel{9}} \times \frac{\cancel{135}^{15}}{1}$$

$$= 7 \times 15$$

$$= 105$$

13. Find $\frac{3}{7}$ of 420

20. Find $\frac{5}{9}$ of 423

14. Find $\frac{5}{16}$ of 240

21. Find $\frac{9}{40}$ of 520

15. Find $\frac{3}{26}$ of 130

22. Find $\frac{7}{18}$ of 126

16. Find $\frac{4}{25}$ of 125

23. Find $\frac{5}{24}$ of 312

17. Find $\frac{11}{36}$ of 612

24. Find $\frac{7}{18}$ of 216

18. Find $\frac{5}{14}$ of 364

25. Find $\frac{7}{26}$ of 208

19. Find $\frac{9}{16}$ of 712

26. Find $\frac{5}{34}$ of 306

Multiplying fractions

In the above examples we multiplied a whole number by a fraction. We use the same principle when we have to multiply a fraction by a fraction:

$$\frac{2}{7} \times \frac{21}{26} = \frac{\cancel{42}^{3}}{\cancel{182}_{13}}$$

$$= \frac{3}{13}$$

In this example there was quite a complicated multiplication: 7×26

There is no reason why we cannot divide by the factors **before** the multiplication. This then allows us to do easier calculations:

Example: $\frac{2}{7} \times \frac{21}{26} = \frac{\cancel{2}^{1}}{\cancel{7}_{1}} \times \frac{\cancel{21}^{3}}{\cancel{26}_{13}}$
$= \frac{3}{13}$

2 divides into 2 and into 26
7 divides into 7 and into 21
We end up with 1×3 as the numerator
and 1×13 as the denominator.

Exercise 3.8

1. $\frac{2}{3} \times \frac{9}{10}$

2. $\frac{4}{5} \times \frac{15}{16}$

3. $\frac{9}{14} \times \frac{7}{12}$

4. $\frac{6}{7} \times \frac{2}{9}$

5. $\frac{20}{21} \times \frac{14}{15}$

6. $\frac{4}{9} \times \frac{3}{4}$

7. $\frac{8}{9} \times \frac{3}{10}$

8. $\frac{5}{8} \times \frac{16}{25}$

9. $\frac{2}{3} \times \frac{4}{5}$

10. $\frac{12}{25} \times \frac{10}{21}$

11. $\frac{6}{7} \times \frac{4}{9}$

12. $\frac{2}{9} \times \frac{3}{8}$

13. $\frac{7}{10} \times \frac{5}{14}$

14. $\frac{20}{21} \times \frac{8}{9}$

15. $\frac{24}{25} \times \frac{9}{16}$

We can use the same principle with three or more fractions multiplied together:

Example: $\dfrac{4}{5} \times \dfrac{10}{21} \times \dfrac{7}{8} = \dfrac{\overset{1}{\cancel{4}}}{\cancel{5}} \times \dfrac{\overset{2}{\cancel{10}}}{\cancel{21}_3} \times \dfrac{\overset{1}{\cancel{7}}}{\cancel{8}_2}$

$= \dfrac{1 \times \overset{1}{\cancel{2}} \times 1}{1 \times 3 \times \cancel{2}_1}$

$= \dfrac{1}{3}$

Here are a few quite challenging questions:

16. $\dfrac{2}{3} \times \dfrac{6}{7} \times \dfrac{14}{15}$ **19.** $\dfrac{5}{6} \times \dfrac{4}{7} \times \dfrac{14}{15}$ **22.** $\dfrac{5}{7} \times \dfrac{11}{15} \times \dfrac{14}{33}$

17. $\dfrac{4}{5} \times \dfrac{15}{16} \times \dfrac{2}{3}$ **20.** $\dfrac{7}{9} \times \dfrac{6}{15} \times \dfrac{3}{14}$ **23.** $\dfrac{7}{9} \times \dfrac{4}{7} \times \dfrac{12}{13}$

18. $\dfrac{8}{9} \times \dfrac{6}{7} \times \dfrac{21}{22}$ **21.** $\dfrac{2}{9} \times \dfrac{6}{11} \times \dfrac{4}{5}$ **24.** $\dfrac{3}{4} \times \dfrac{7}{15} \times \dfrac{10}{21}$

25. $\dfrac{2}{7} \times \dfrac{5}{6} \times \dfrac{7}{8} \times \dfrac{4}{5}$ **27.** $\dfrac{3}{14} \times \dfrac{4}{5} \times \dfrac{7}{18} \times \dfrac{10}{13}$

26. $\dfrac{10}{11} \times \dfrac{2}{5} \times \dfrac{22}{25} \times \dfrac{5}{8}$ **28.** $\dfrac{1}{2} \times \dfrac{3}{4} \times \dfrac{5}{6} \times \dfrac{7}{8} \times \dfrac{9}{10} \times \dfrac{11}{12}$

Dividing with fractions

When we write $4 \times \dfrac{1}{2}$ we get the answer 2 because four halves are 2.

This calculation could also be $4 \div 2 = 2$

or $\dfrac{4}{2} = 2$

or $\dfrac{1}{2}$ of 4 is 2

or we could use decimals: $4 \times 0.5 = 2$

or even: 50% of 4 is 2

All the above calculations mean the same. They are just several different ways of saying the same thing.

Exercise 3.9

Write these in as many different ways as you can:

1. $\frac{1}{4}$ of 8

2. $6 \div 2$

3. $10 \times \frac{3}{5}$

4. $9 \div 4$

5. $6 \times \frac{2}{3}$

6. $10 \div 3$

7. $\frac{1}{8}$ of 16

8. 25 % of 12

9. 0.3×3

We can see that $\div 2$ is the same as $\times \frac{1}{2}$; similarly $\div \frac{1}{2}$ is the same as $\times 2$; in other words the $\div$ sign changes to $\times$ and the fraction turns upside down.

This works for all fractions, so $\div \frac{3}{4}$ is the same as $\times \frac{4}{3}$

$$\text{Examples: (i) } 4 \div \frac{4}{5} = \frac{4}{1} \times \frac{5}{4}$$
$$= \frac{{}^1 \cancel{4}}{1} \times \frac{5}{\cancel{4}_1}$$
$$= 5$$

$$\text{(ii) } \frac{2}{3} \div \frac{4}{5} = \frac{2}{3} \times \frac{5}{4}$$
$$= \frac{{}^1 \cancel{2}}{3} \times \frac{5}{\cancel{4}_2}$$
$$= \frac{5}{6}$$

Exercise 3.10

Do these divisions. If your answer is an improper fraction, you should turn it into a mixed number:

1. $\frac{3}{5} \div \frac{6}{7}$

2. $\frac{3}{4} \div \frac{7}{8}$

3. $\frac{2}{3} \div \frac{8}{9}$

4. $\frac{8}{9} \div \frac{2}{3}$

5. $\frac{7}{12} \div \frac{5}{9}$

6. $\frac{9}{10} \div \frac{3}{5}$

7. $\frac{11}{12} \div \frac{9}{10}$

8. $\frac{5}{9} \div \frac{10}{21}$

9. $\frac{4}{5} \div \frac{8}{9}$

10. $\frac{5}{6} \div \frac{5}{9}$

11. $\frac{2}{3} \div \frac{4}{9}$

12. $\frac{4}{5} \div \frac{7}{10}$

13. $\frac{4}{5} \div \frac{15}{16}$ **17.** $\frac{11}{24} \div \frac{33}{36}$ **21.** $\frac{24}{25} \div \frac{8}{15}$

14. $\frac{4}{5} \div \frac{16}{25}$ **18.** $\frac{9}{10} \div \frac{3}{5}$ **22.** $\frac{25}{36} \div \frac{5}{9}$

15. $\frac{1}{3} \div \frac{2}{9}$ **19.** $\frac{7}{12} \div \frac{14}{72}$ **23.** $\frac{4}{39} \div \frac{8}{13}$

16. $\frac{7}{15} \div \frac{2}{3}$ **20.** $\frac{15}{49} \div \frac{5}{7}$ **24.** $\frac{24}{35} \div \frac{3}{10}$

Exercise 3.11: Mixed operations

Remember BIDMAS (see page 23 if you cannot remember the rule from Book 1) to calculate the answers to these:

1. $\frac{3}{8} + \frac{2}{5} \times \frac{5}{6}$ **6.** $\frac{3}{4} + \frac{2}{3} \times \frac{3}{8}$

2. $\left(\frac{1}{2}\right)^2 + \frac{1}{3}$ **7.** $\left(\frac{1}{4} + \frac{2}{3}\right) \times \frac{3}{11}$

3. $\frac{3}{8} + \frac{5}{6} \div \frac{2}{3}$ **8.** $\frac{2}{3} + \frac{3}{5} \div \frac{7}{10}$

4. $\left(\frac{1}{8} + \frac{2}{5}\right) \times \frac{5}{6}$ **9.** $\left(\frac{2}{3} + \frac{3}{5}\right) \div \frac{7}{10}$

5. $\left(\frac{1}{3}\right)^2 - \left(\frac{1}{6}\right)^2$ **10.** $\frac{3}{8} + \left(\frac{1}{4}\right)^2$

Problems with fractions

Example: I travel at 45 mph for 40 minutes. How far do I go?

$40 \text{ mins} = \frac{2}{3} \text{ hour}$

$\text{distance} = 45 \times \frac{2}{3}$

$= \frac{\overset{15}{\cancel{45}}}{1} \times \frac{2}{\cancel{3}_1}$

$= 30 \text{ miles}$

Exercise 3.12

1. I travel at 60 mph for 45 minutes. How far do I go?

2. A space rocket travels at 3000 km per hour for 5 minutes. How far does it go?

3. I buy $\frac{3}{4}$ kg of tomatoes at £1.20 a kg and a cabbage weighing $\frac{3}{8}$ kg at 80p a kg. How much money do I spend?

4. I have a ball of string $4\frac{1}{2}$ m long and I use $\frac{1}{2}$ of it. How many metres are left?

5. I have a ball of string $8\frac{1}{2}$ m long and I use $3\frac{3}{8}$ m of it. How many metres are left?

6. In my lunch break of three quarters of an hour, I spend a third of it playing conkers. What fraction of an hour is that?

7. In my morning break of a third of an hour, I spend half of it playing football. How many minutes is that?

8. One third of our class are girls and one half of them have music lessons. If all the girls that have music lessons have to go to a meeting, what fraction of the class is left behind?

9. One sixth of a class of 24 are in detention. Three quarters of these are boys. How many boys are in detention?

10. One third of my class have packed lunches. A quarter of these are boys. All the girls that have a packed lunch sit together. What fraction of my class is this?

Extension Exercise 3.13

Use the four rules for addition, subtraction, multiplication and division of fractions, and remember BIDMAS to do these questions:

1. $2\frac{5}{6} - \frac{8}{15}$

2. $\dfrac{\frac{2}{3} - \frac{4}{7}}{\frac{2}{15}}$

3. $3\frac{3}{4} - \frac{13}{18}$

4. $\dfrac{\frac{3}{4} + \frac{3}{7}}{\frac{5}{18}}$

5. $\dfrac{2\frac{1}{3} - 1\frac{4}{9}}{\frac{8}{9}}$

6. $\dfrac{1\frac{1}{7} - \frac{7}{10}}{\frac{3}{14}}$

7. $\dfrac{\frac{2}{9} + \frac{1}{6}}{\frac{2}{9}}$

8. $\dfrac{\frac{4}{5}}{\frac{2}{7}} - \dfrac{\frac{1}{4}}{\frac{1}{5}}$

9. $\dfrac{\frac{7}{15} - \frac{5}{12}}{\frac{7}{8} - \frac{5}{6}}$

10. $\dfrac{\frac{3}{5} + \frac{2}{7}}{\frac{4}{7} - \frac{3}{10}}$

11. $1 - \frac{1}{4}\left(1 - \frac{1}{4}\left(1 - \frac{1}{4}\right)\right)$

12. $1 - \frac{1}{4}\left(1 - \frac{1}{3}\left(1 - \frac{1}{5}\right)\right)$

13. $1 - \frac{1}{4}\left(1 + \frac{1}{2}\left(1 - \frac{3}{4}\right)\right)$

14. $1 - \frac{1}{8}\left(1 + \frac{1}{4}\left(1 - \frac{2}{5}\right)\right)$

15. (a) The teacher asked the class to work out the sum of the series:

$\frac{1}{1} + \frac{1}{2} + \frac{1}{3} + \frac{1}{4} + \frac{1}{5} \ldots$

stopping when the sum exceeded $2\frac{1}{2}$
What would the final answer be?

(b) Molesworth was not paying attention, as usual, and the series he was summing was:

$\frac{1}{1} + \frac{1}{2} + \frac{1}{4} + \frac{1}{8} + \ldots$ What was Molesworth's final answer?

16. (a) $\frac{1}{2} \times \frac{2}{3} \times \frac{3}{4} \times \frac{4}{5}$

(b) $\left(1 - \frac{1}{2}\right)\left(1 - \frac{1}{3}\right)\left(1 - \frac{1}{4}\right)\left(1 - \frac{1}{5}\right)\ldots\left(1 - \frac{1}{20}\right)$

(c) $\left(1 + \frac{1}{2}\right)\left(1 + \frac{1}{3}\right)\left(1 + \frac{1}{4}\right)\left(1 + \frac{1}{5}\right)\ldots\left(1 + \frac{1}{20}\right)$

(d) $\left(1 - \frac{1}{4}\right)\left(1 - \frac{1}{9}\right)\left(1 - \frac{1}{16}\right)\left(1 - \frac{1}{25}\right)\ldots\left(1 - \frac{1}{400}\right)$

Summary Exercise 3.14

1. What fraction of each rectangles is shaded?

(a) 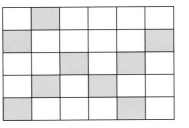   (b)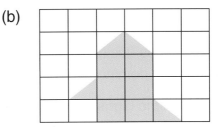

2. Complete this table of equivalent fractions, decimals and percentages:

Fraction	Decimal	Percentage
$\frac{3}{4}$		
	0.65	
$\frac{4}{5}$		
		12.5%

3. (a) $\frac{3}{4} + \frac{5}{6}$ (b) $2\frac{3}{5} + 3\frac{5}{7}$ **4.** (a) $\frac{5}{8} - \frac{2}{5}$ (b) $4\frac{2}{3} - 2\frac{5}{8}$

5. Find $\frac{1}{7}$ of 350

6. Find $\frac{3}{8}$ of 3 kg. Give your answer in grams.

7. (a) $\frac{2}{5} \times \frac{15}{16}$ (b) $\frac{15}{16} \times \frac{7}{20}$ **8.** (a) $\frac{2}{15} \div \frac{4}{5}$ (b) $\frac{15}{16} \div \frac{9}{32}$

9. Which of these is the odd one out:

    (a) $\frac{1}{4}$ of 25   (b) $25 \div 4$ (c) $\frac{25}{4}$ (d) $4 \div 25$ (e) $6\frac{1}{4}$

10. I cut three quarters of a metre of ribbon from a piece two and a third metres long. What fraction of the ribbon was left?

11. One sixth of my class chose to play football and one quarter chose netball. What fraction chose neither?

12. $\dfrac{\frac{3}{4} + \frac{5}{6}}{\frac{2}{3} - \frac{3}{5}}$ **13.** $1 - \frac{1}{4}\left(1 + \frac{1}{4}\left(1 - \frac{1}{4}\right)\right)$

End of Chapter 3 activity: 'Equivalent fraction' dominoes

On the worksheet you will find a set of dominoes. Cut these out and play dominoes.

The traditional game (For up to 4 players)

Turn all the pieces upside down and shuffle them around the table. Each player takes one domino in turn until all players have seven.

The player with the highest double starts (i.e. the piece showing a double half). If no one has the double half, then find it from the remaining pieces and place it on the table. The player who picks up the last piece then starts.

The player places the double on the table (unless it's already there) and the other players have to add a matching (i.e. an equivalent fraction) domino to the first. For example:

$$\boxed{\dfrac{3}{4}\ \Big|\ \dfrac{1}{2}}\quad\boxed{\dfrac{18}{36}\ \Big|\ \dfrac{4}{36}}$$

The next player then has to match one of his or her dominoes up to one of the ends of the chain. For example:

$$\boxed{\dfrac{3}{4}\ \Big|\ \dfrac{1}{2}}\quad\boxed{\dfrac{18}{36}\ \Big|\ \dfrac{4}{36}}\quad\boxed{\dfrac{1}{9}\ \Big|\ \dfrac{3}{9}}$$

The next player then adds on to the end of the chain and so on. If the chain is getting too long then it can bend like this:

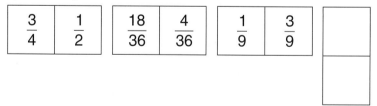

If a player cannot go, he passes and forfeits his turn. The winner is the first player to put down all his pieces, and the score is the sum of all the numbers on the remaining players' dominoes.

The puzzle

The dominoes on the worksheet can be placed in a continuous rectangle with no pieces left out. All touching squares must be equal in value. Can you make this rectangle?

Chapter 4: Probability

The probability scale

We know that some things will definitely happen and others will definitely not, but there are other things that **could** happen. It is useful to know how likely it is that these events could happen. After all, if there is an 80% chance of rain tomorrow, you may decide not to go to the park.

When you play certain games, you often come across probability, or chance. For example:

> It is **impossible** that I will roll a total of 1 with two normal dice.
> It is **certain** that I will roll a total of more than 1 with two normal dice.
> If I toss a coin there is an **even chance** that I will see heads or tails.

If an event is impossible, we say that there is a probability of 0
If an event is certain, it has a probability of 1

If an event has an even chance, then it has a probability of 1 in 2 or $\frac{1}{2}$
Probabilities can be written as fractions, or as decimals: 0.5, or as percentages: 50%

These can be entered on a probability scale:

impossible	possible	even chance	probable	certain
0	$\frac{1}{4}$	$\frac{1}{2}$	$\frac{3}{4}$	1

or:

impossible	possible	even chance	probable	certain
0	0.25	0.5	0.75	1
0	25%	50%	75%	100%

Exercise 4.1

1. Write down:
    (a) an event that is impossible
    (b) an event that is possible
    (c) an event that has an even chance of happening
    (d) an event that is probable
    (e) an event that is certain

2. The weather forecast says that there is a 75% chance of a shower tomorrow.
    (a) What would you **NOT** plan to do?
    (b) What is the probability that there will not be a shower?

3. The weather forecast says that there is a 0.1 chance of a shower tomorrow.
    (a) What would you plan to do?
    (b) What is the probability that there will not be a shower?

4. The forecast says that on Tuesday there is a 1 in 2 chance of rain, on Wednesday there is a 0.25 chance of rain but on Thursday they are 99% certain that it will be a glorious day.
    (a) Which would be the best day to spend outside?
    (b) What is the chance of no rain on Tuesday: possible, even chance or probable?
    (c) What is the chance of no rain on Wednesday: possible, even chance or probable?

5. Make a copy of the probability scale and mark on it the probability of the following events; the first one is done for you:

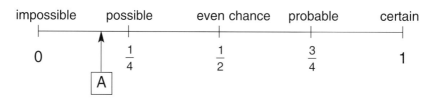

    A: I will throw a 1 with a normal die.
    B: I will toss a coin and get 'heads'.
    C: I will watch television tonight.
    D: There will be salad for lunch.
    E: Man will land on Mars in the next decade.
    F: It will rain tomorrow.

6. I throw a normal die 5 times. List these possibilities in the order they are most likely to happen, least likely first:

    A: I throw an odd number.
    B: I throw a 3
    C: I throw a square number.
    D: I throw at least 2
    E: I throw less than 5

The probability of an event

In q.5 there were three types of events:
Events that you have control over (I will watch television).
Events about which you can have a sensible guess (Men will land on Mars).
Events where you can calculate the theoretical probability (I will toss 'heads').

In q.6 you could see which event was the most likely by using the following rule:

$$\frac{\text{Number of favourable outcomes}}{\text{Total number of possibilities}}$$

This works if all outcomes are equally likely.

So, if we were throwing a die, we could write:

Probability of throwing a three = $P(3) = \frac{1}{6}$

We can always write a probability as a fraction but, as we said at the beginning of this chapter, it can also be written as a decimal or as a percentage:

Probability of throwing an odd number (there are 3 possibilities : 1, 3, 5)
the probability is: $P(\text{odd number}) = \frac{3}{6} = 0.5 = 50\%$

Remember if in doubt, use fractions.

Games of chance

Because so many games are based on **chance** as well as **skill**, questions about probability often use examples involving cards and dice. So, here are some basic facts you should learn about dice and cards:

A **normal die** has six faces and these are numbered from 1 to 6 with dots. Other types of **dice** could be numbered in different ways and have more faces, so watch out!

A pack of cards has 4 suits (clubs, diamonds, hearts, and spades) and each suit has 13 cards. In each suit there is an Ace, the numbers 2 to 10, a Jack (or Knave) a Queen and King. The Knave, Queen and King are called 'royal cards'. Diamonds and hearts are red, spades and clubs are black. It's worth getting hold of a pack of cards and having a look, if you haven't already done so.

Exercise 4.2

1. When you throw a normal die, write down the probability of throwing:
    (a) an odd number   (d) at least 2
    (b) a 3   (e) less than 5
    (c) a square number

2. When one card is chosen at random from a normal pack of cards, give the probability of choosing:
    (a) a club
    (b) a King
    (c) a royal card
    (d) a red Ace
    (e) a black card

3. When a letter is chosen at random from the letters of the word 'MATHEMATICS', what is the probability of choosing a vowel?

4. I have a die with 8 faces numbered from 1 to 8
    Write down the probability of throwing:
    (a) a 6
    (b) an even number
    (c) a prime number
    (d) a square number
    (e) a multiple of 3

5. Look at this 5-sided spinner:
    Give the probability of spinning:
    (a) 1
    (b) 2
    (c) an odd number
    (d) an even number

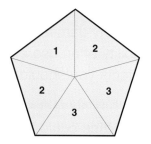

6. Look at this 5-sided spinner.
This time some numbers are coloured:

Write down the probability of spinning:
(a) a green 2
(b) a green number
(c) a green odd number

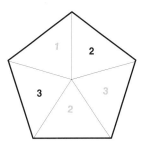

Finding the probability of an event NOT happening

From the spinners you saw above, the probability of spinning an even number is $\frac{2}{5}$ and the probability of spinning an odd number is $\frac{3}{5}$

In this case a number will either be odd or even. You will notice that:
$\frac{2}{5} + \frac{3}{5} = 1$, and 1 is therefore the probability that an event must happen.

This is because an event must either happen or not happen, so we can say:

$$P \text{ (event)} + P \text{ (not that event)} = 1$$

This is another way of writing:

Probability of an event not happening = (1 − probability of that event happening)

Exercise 4.3

Example:

If a number is chosen at random from the first 10 positive integers, what is the probability of that number **not** being square?

First 10 positive integers are 1, 2, 3, 4, 5, 6, 7, 8, 9, 10

The square numbers are 1, 4, 9

So we can write: $\qquad$ $P \text{ (square)} \quad = \frac{3}{10}$

And therefore: $\qquad$ $P \text{ (not square)} = 1 - \frac{3}{10}$

$$= \frac{7}{10}$$

1. If a number is chosen at random from the first 20 positive integers, give the probability of that number:
   (a) being odd
   (b) being prime
   (c) not being prime
   (d) not being a multiple of 3
   (e) not being a cube
   (f) not being a factor of 360
   (g) not being a triangle number

2. If a card is chosen at random from a standard pack of 52 cards, write down the probability of that card's being:
   (a) a Queen
   (b) not more than 8
   (c) not an Ace
   (d) not a royal card

3. An 8-sided spinner is numbered from 1 to 8
   Give the probability of spinning:
   (a) a prime number
   (b) not a prime number
   (c) not less than 6
   (d) not more than 4
   (e) at least 7
   (f) less than 9

4. I have a bag of 20 coloured sweets. Four of them are red, three green, seven orange and the rest yellow. If I take one out of the bag at random, give the probability of picking:
   (a) a red sweet
   (b) a yellow sweet
   (c) not a red sweet
   (d) not orange or yellow
   (e) not a colour of the rainbow

Sometimes one action can change the situation

For example, if I eat the sweet that I choose at random from a bag, there are fewer sweets in the bag (by one) and fewer of the colour that I took (also by one).

In the bag described in q.4 above, imagine that I took an orange sweet and then ate it. That would leave 19 sweets in the bag and only 6 of these would be orange.

The probability that the next sweet I take is orange is 6 out of 19 or $\frac{6}{19}$

From looking at this sort of example you can see why we usually use fractions to describe probability!

Exercise 4.4

1. I have a bag of 20 coloured sweets. 4 of them are red, 3 are green, 7 are orange and the rest are yellow. I eat a yellow one. If I take another sweet out of the bag at random, give the probability of my picking:
    (a) a yellow sweet
    (b) a green sweet

2. I have a drawer full of 26 socks. 9 of them are grey, 11 of them are black and the rest are white. If I take 1 sock out of the drawer at random, give the probability that it is:
    (a) white
    (b) black
    (c) grey

    In fact the first sock that I take out is white. I do not replace the sock. Write down the probability that the next sock is:
    (d) white
    (e) black

3. For the school tombola we are told that the winning tickets will be those that end with a 0 or 5. There are 500 tickets and 100 prizes.
    (a) If I buy a ticket, what is the probability that I will win a prize?
    (b) After 1 hour, 350 people have bought tickets and 40 prizes have been won. What is the probability of winning a prize now?

4. I am playing a game of cards. I have been dealt an Ace, a King and a Queen and my friend has been dealt an Ace, a Knave and a 10
(a) What is the probability that the next card I am dealt is a Knave?
(b) I am dealt a 10
What is the probability that the next card my friend is dealt is also a 10?

5. We are playing a game in our maths lesson with a die. The teacher rolls the die and it is a 5
She rolls the die a second time. Write down the probability that it:
(a) is a 4
(b) is a 5
(c) makes more than 5
(d) makes a total of 8 with the first die
(e) Which of the answers above would be different if the teacher had rolled a 3 the first time? Suppose she had rolled a 1?

Probability with two events

Tossing a coin gives you either heads or tails, but if you toss 2 coins the first coin could be heads or tails and the second coin could be heads or tails. This means that you could end up with 1 of 4 possible combinations:

(head, head) (head, tail) (tail, head) (tail, tail)
i.e. 4 possibilities

It can be easier to see all the possibilities if we put the events in a table called a **possibility space**:

		First Coin	
		H	T
Second coin	H	(H, H)	(T, H)
	T	(H, T)	(T, T)

From the table we can easily see that:

$P(H,H) = \frac{1}{4}$

Exercise 4.5

1. Copy and complete this possibility space to show the possible outcomes when throwing 2 dice:

		First die					
		1	2	3	4	5	6
Second die	1	(1,1)	(2,1)	(3,1)	(4,1)	(5,1)	(6,1)
	2	(1,2)	(2,2)	(3,2)	(4,2)	( )	( )
	3	( )	( )	( )	( )	( )	( )
	4	( )	( )	( )	( )	( )	( )
	5	( )	( )	( )	( )	( )	( )
	6	( )	( )	( )	( )	( )	( )

When throwing 2 dice give the probability of throwing:

(a) a double 6   (d) a total of 4   (f) at least 5
(b) any double   (e) more than 6   (g) a 4 on either die
(c) a total of 7

2. The game 'catch the mouse' has 2 dice. One is a normal die with numbers from 1 to 6 and the other has coloured spots on the 6 faces: three blue spots, two red spots and one yellow spot. Complete this possibility space to show the possible outcomes when you throw the two dice together:

		Coloured die					
		B	B	B	R	R	Y
Numbered die	1	(B,1)	(B,1)	(B,1)	(R,1)	(R,1)	(Y,1)
	2	(B,2)	(B,2)	(B,2)	(R,2)	( )	( )
	3	( )	( )	( )	( )	( )	( )
	4	( )	( )	( )	( )	( )	( )
	5	( )	( )	( )	( )	( )	( )
	6	( )	( )	( )	( )	( )	( )

Give the probability of throwing:
(a) a blue spot and a 3   (c) a red spot
(b) a yellow spot and a 3   (d) a 6

3. The game 'tell me' has a 5-sided spinner with letters on and a 4-sided spinner with colours:

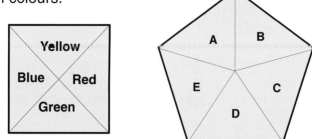

Draw a possibility space showing all the possible outcomes when both spinners are spun. Write down the probability of spinning:
(a) a red
(b) a blue and a D

4. (a) Draw a possibility space showing all the possible outcomes when you throw one normal die and another die that is numbered 1, 1, 2, 2, 3, 4.

(b) Use your possibility space to find the probability that you will throw:
(i) a double 2	(iv) a total of 6
(ii) any double	(v) at least 8
(iii) a double 6	(vi) over 8

Exercise 4.6: Extension questions

In all the probabilities that we have looked at so far, the events have all had an equal chance of happening.

Look at this spinning wheel:

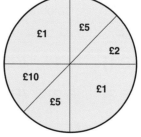

Although the wheel is divided into six sections, these sections are **not equal**. This means that there is **not an equal chance** of picking each section.

2 out of 6 sections might win £1, but the probability of winning £1 is higher than $\frac{2}{6}$ (or $\frac{1}{3}$). If you imagine that in fact the spinner is divided into 8 equal sections and that 2 sections are joined together, where the £1s are, you can easily see that the probability of winning £1 is $\frac{4}{8} = \frac{1}{2}$

1. In the circular spinner on page 82 the wheel is divided into 8 equal sections, but then 2 sections are joined together:

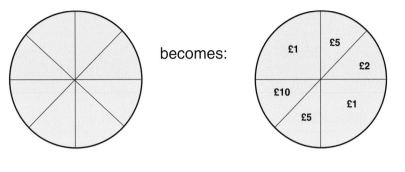

becomes:

(a) Give the probability of winning: (i) £10   (ii) £5   (iii) £1

(b) If it costs £1 to have a spin of the wheel, what is the probability of your winning more than you pay?

2. Look at these spinners:

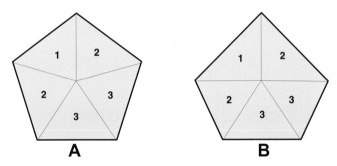

(a) With spinner A, give the probability of spinning:
   (i) 1
   (ii) 2
   (iii) an odd number

(b) With spinner B, give the probability of spinning:
   (i) 1
   (ii) 2
   (iii) an odd number

(c) I have to spin a total of 4 to win a game. Would I be better off spinning A twice, spinning B twice or spinning A and B together? Explain your answer.

3. In a game called 'Old Macdonald' I have to throw a plastic pig. The way the pig lands decides what move I can make next. I throw the pig 100 times and get the following results:

Position	Move	Tally	Frequency
On four legs	Stay still	̶H̶H̶ ̶H̶H̶ ̶H̶H̶ III	18
On right side	Move right	HH HH HH HH HH HH I	31
On left side	Move left	HH HH HH HH HH HH HH III	38
Nose down	Move forward	HH III	8
Tail down	Move back	HH	5
Total			100

(a) If I were to throw the pig once more, write down the probability, based on the results above, that it lands:
 (i) on four legs
 (ii) on its left or right side
 (iii) not on a side
 (iv) either tail down or nose down

(b) If I were to throw the pig another 100 times, would I get the same results? Explain your answer.

(c) At the same time as throwing the pig, I throw a normal die. The die tells me how many squares I move. Draw up a possibility space showing all the possible combinations of throwing the pig and the die together.

(d) My friend Jake says that the probability of moving forward three squares is $\frac{1}{30}$; is he right? Explain your answer. If he is wrong, what do you think the correct probability is?

Exercise 4.7: Summary exercise

1. Draw a probability scale. Show the probability of these events on the scale:
    (a) There will be a moon in the sky tonight.
    (b) It will rain tomorrow.
    (c) England will win the next football World Cup.
    (d) Next year is a leap year.
    (e) I will brush my hair before I go to bed.

2. If a letter is chosen from the word PROBABILITY, write down the probability that it is:
    (a) a vowel   (c) the letter P
    (b) a consonant   (d) a letter with rotational symmetry

3. If a card is chosen at random from a normal pack of cards give the probability that it will be:
    (a) a Knave   (d) a black King or a red 9
    (b) more than 8   (e) a heart
    (c) a red 'royal' card   (f) a Knave or a heart

4. If a normal die is rolled, give the probability that it will be:
    (a) 5
    (b) at least 4
    (c) a factor of 36

5. I throw a coin and roll a die at the same time. Copy and complete this possibility space to show the possible combinations:

		Die					
		1	2	3	4	5	6
Coin	H	(1,H)	(2,H)	(3,H)	(4,H)	(......)	(......)
	T	(1,T)	(2,T)	(......)	(......)	(......)	(......)

Give the probability of throwing:
(a) a head and an odd number
(b) a tail and a number greater than 4
(c) a prime number and either a head or tail
(d) a tail and a number greater than 6

6. I roll 2 dice; both are cubes but their numbering is rather different. Here are the nets of the cubes, showing the number of dots on each:

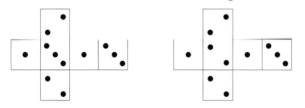

Complete this possibility space, showing the possible outcomes when both dice are rolled:

		First die					
		1	1	2	2	3	3
Second die	1	(1,1)	(1,1)	(,)	(,1)	(,1)	(,)
	1	(1,1)	(1,1)	(,1)	(,1)	( )	( )
	2	( )	( )	( )	( )	( )	( )
	2	( )	( )	( )	( )	( )	( )
	2	( )	( )	( )	( )	( )	( )
	3	( )	( )	( )	( )	( )	( )

(a) What is the probability of rolling a double 3?
(b) What is the probability of rolling a double?
(c) What is the probability of rolling a total of 4?
(d) What is the probability of getting at least 5?
(e) What possible totals could you throw?
(f) Which is the most likely?

7. I bought a bag of mixed mini candy bars; there were four nutty bars, three plain chocolate bars, five crispy bars and two coconut bars. If I took one bar at random, give the probability that it was:
(a) coconut
(b) nutty

My little sister ate one coconut bar and one plain chocolate bar. Now when I take one bar at random, give the probability that I choose:
(c) coconut
(d) nutty

End of chapter 4 activity: Designing a board game

In this chapter there was a question about a game called 'Old Macdonald' (Exercise 4.6 q.3). In this you had to move around a board and the direction in which you moved depended on the position where a pig landed.

You could easily design your own board game. Here are some ideas. Before you start, you might want to do some research into games. Perhaps everyone in the class could bring in an unusual game for you all to talk about.

1. What makes a good game? List all the games you enjoy. Note whether they are games of chance or games of skill, or a mixture of both.

2. For games that involve chance, write down these elements of chance. There may be more than one. For some games the element of chance depends on what your opponent does.

3. Decide what you think works best. Now create a game where you could use two or more elements of chance. It might be throwing one or two dice to allow you to move, and picking up some cards from time to time. You will need to put your game into a context. Here are a few ideas:
    – purely mathematical on a grid of squares or hexagons
    – a general knowledge game, where the question you get depends on where you land
    – a race game like ludo or snakes and ladders
    – a game based on a popular book or film
    – a game with letters

4. When you have planned your game, draw the game board accurately.

5. Write down the rules.

6. This is the clever bit – assuming your game involves chance, what advice can you give someone about how to win the game? Does it matter who goes first? What choices could you make? Could you change the rules a little so that there is some skill as well as chance?

7. When you are happy with your game, then play it! If you enjoy it, then you could try to market it – now there is some exciting mathematics!

Chapter 5: Handling data

Mean and range

Pupills in my class have been growing bean plants. We all used a different amount of fertiliser because we wanted to see which plants grew the best. Last week we measured them to see how tall they were. My plant was 68 cm high. Although I am very pleased with its growth, it doesn't mean it has grown as well as it could have done. To make this judgement, I have to compare it with the height of everyone else's plant.

These are the heights in centimetres of the class's plants:

72	56	42	68	55
63	45	71	43	62
59	56	54	70	67
64	52	61	48	62

Seeing this information like this doesn't really tell us anything. What we need to do is analyse it.

Firstly it would be interesting to see the difference between the highest and the lowest value. This is called the **range**.

Range = 72 − 42
          = 30

Now I can see that my plant, measuring 68 cm, was not the tallest and was not the shortest. I might now like to know whether it was above average.

What is the **average**? The average is a way of expressing the value of the mid point of a set of numbers. There are different ways of finding the average, the most common of which is calculating the **mean** of a set of numbers.

The **mean** is the **total** of the numbers divided by **the number** of numbers. This is also called the **arithmetic average**.

$$\text{mean} = \frac{\text{total of numbers}}{\text{number of items}}$$

> Example: mean height $= \dfrac{\text{total height of all plants}}{20}$
>
> $\qquad\qquad\qquad = \dfrac{1170}{20}$
>
> $\qquad\qquad\qquad = 58.5$

I can now see that my plant at 68 cm is well above the mean height of 58.5 cm and in fact very close to the tallest.

Exercise 5.1

1. Find the mean and range of these numbers:
   (a) 1, 2, 2, 3, 4, 4, 5
   (b) 21, 45, 67, 72, 95
   (c) 1.4, 6.2, 3.4, 5.1, 7.8, 3.2, 6.7, 4.8, 8.1, 2.6
   (d) 1234, 1345, 1672, 1593

2. These are my exam marks:
   English: 64%   Maths: 71%   French: 62%
   Science: 75%   History: 58%   Geography: 75%

   What was my mean mark?

3. Every week we have a mental maths test. These are my marks so far this term:

         14   18   15   17   16   18   14

   These are my friend Sam's marks. He was away 1 week so he has 1 less mark than I:

         12   18   19   14   18   15

   Who has the higher average?

4. Our football team has played 10 games this season. Here are the scores for each (the first number shows our goal scores, the second our opponents):

   2 – 2   0 – 4   1 – 3   2 – 0   1 – 1
   0 – 3   3 – 1   2 – 1   2 – 0   1 – 2

   (a) What was the mean and range of our goal scores?
   (b) What was the mean and range of our opponents' goal scores?

5. Here are the ages of 6 children:
    10y 10m, 11y 5m, 10y 7m, 10y 8m, 11y 1m, 10y 5m

    What is the mean age of the children?

Sometimes we are given the average figure and a number of items, and are asked to calculate the total. If this is the case, all we need to do is rearrange the equation used for calculating the mean.

$$\text{mean} = \frac{\text{total}}{\text{number of items}}$$

To calculate the total, the rearranged calculation becomes:

mean × number of items = total

Here are some questions for you to practise this:

6. My exam average was 63%. If I sat six exams, what was the total of all my marks?

7. In science I weigh measures of five compounds. The mean mass of these is 253 g. What do they weigh altogether?

8. Our netball team of seven players has a mean average mass of 43 kg.
    (a) What is the total mass of the team?
    (b) Our substitute weighs 39 kg. What is the total mass of the team including the substitute?
    (c) What is the mean mass of the team if we include the substitute?

9. There are 18 people in my class. Our mean mark in the French exam was 68%.
    (a) What was the total of all our marks?
    (b) Mademoiselle has marked my paper incorrectly. She has given me 68% instead of 86%. When she corrects her mistake, what does the mean mark for the class become?

10. The mean age of a class of 15 children is 12 years and 3 months.
    (a) What is the sum of all our ages?
    (b) A new boy joins the class. The mean is recalculated to include him and now becomes 12 years 2.5 months. What is the new boy's age?

Looking at data: The median

Look again at the heights of the class's bean plants (page 88):

72	56	42	68	55
63	45	71	43	62
59	56	54	70	67
64	52	61	48	62

We have already learned how to find the mean height, but a different way of looking at the average of the heights is to look at the **median** or the 'middle' height.

First we must put the heights in order:
42, 43, 45, 48, 52, 54, 55, 56, 56, 59, 61, 62, 62, 63, 64, 67, 68, 70, 71, 72

Because there are 20 heights, the middle height will be the average of the tenth and eleventh.

$$\frac{59+61}{2} = 60$$

We can now say that the **median** is 60

To find the median of 3, 9, 8, 5, 1, 5, 7, 6:

1. Put them in order : 1, 3, 5, 5, 6, 7, 8, 9   8 numbers

2. The median is the mean of fourth and fifth = $\frac{5+6}{2}$ = 5.5

To find the median of 3, 7, 2, 5, 7, 9, 4, 6, 8, 3, 7:

1. Put them in order : 2, 3, 3, 4, 5, 6, 7, 7, 7, 8, 9   11 numbers

2. The median will be the sixth number (the middle) = 6

The mode

The **mode** is yet another way of looking at the average of a sample of the data. It refers to the value that occurs most frequently or most often. If each value occurs only once, there is no mode. The group of items with value equal to the mode is called the **modal group.** The number of times each value appears is called the **frequency.** In the 2 examples above the mode would have been 5 in the first and 7 in the second.

The mode is particularly useful when analysing measurements such as shoe size, when there is no half-way value between one size and the next (i.e. there is no size 36.25).

Exercise 5.2

1. Find the median and mode of these sets of numbers:
   (a) 3, 4, 4, 5, 6, 6, 6, 7, 8
   (b) 1, 2, 2, 3, 3, 3
   (c) 17, 19, 20, 20, 24, 25, 29

2. Find the median and mode of these sets of numbers:
   (a) 7, 5, 1, 5, 4, 3, 5, 7, 9
   (b) 16, 18, 13, 15, 13, 18, 19
   (c) 0.02, 0.2, 2, 0.22, 0.202, 0.2, 0.202, 2.2

3. Find the range, the mean, the median and the mode of these sets of numbers:
   (a) 98, 46, 65, 42, 38, 46
   (b) 4.2, 5.2, 4.6, 5.0, 4.4, 4.9, 4.2, 4.6, 5.0, 4.2
   (c) 100, 112, 104, 106, 108, 111, 104, 111

4. Find the range and the mean, mode and median for these sets of numbers:

   (a) $\frac{1}{2}$, $\frac{3}{4}$, $\frac{1}{4}$, $\frac{1}{8}$, $\frac{3}{8}$, $\frac{1}{2}$, $\frac{1}{8}$, $\frac{5}{8}$

   (b) $2\frac{1}{4}$, $2\frac{1}{4}$, $2\frac{3}{4}$, $1\frac{3}{4}$, $2\frac{1}{4}$, $2\frac{1}{4}$

   (c) $7\frac{1}{5}$, $6\frac{1}{4}$, $5\frac{2}{5}$, $7\frac{1}{5}$, $6\frac{3}{4}$

5. Find the mean and median of any set of consecutive numbers. What do you notice?

6. I have 10 numbers. Their range is 3. Their mode is 4, their mean is 5.5 and the median is 6. What are the numbers?

Displaying data: Frequency tables and frequency diagrams

A picture is often easier to read than a table of numbers. In mathematics the pictures we use to display data are known as tables, diagrams and charts. The simplest picture to use is a bar chart. The height of each bar tells you the relevant frequency of each piece of data and usually the width of the bar represents a number or an object. It can also represent a range of numbers. Before we can draw the chart, we need to sort the data out into useful groups. We can do this by using tallies in a **frequency table**.

Exercise 5.3

1. These are marks for a recent French vocabulary test.

16	20	19	23	18	24	18	17	*(The marks are out of 25.)*

20	21	18	16	22	24	19	16

22	19	17	17	20	25	21	16

(a) Copy and complete this frequency table to show the distribution of the marks:

Mark	Tally	Frequency
16		
17		
18		
19		
20		
21		
22		
23		
24		
25		
Total		

(b) What is the range of marks?

(c) What are the mean, the mode and the median?

(d) What does this tell you about the marks, if anything?

2. We have been growing bean plants from seed. These are the heights in centimetres of the plants:

14	15	12	13	16	15

17	17	13	16	15	14

15	15	14	15	16	18

(a) Copy and complete this tally table to show the information above:

Heights	Tally	Frequency
12		
13		
14		
15		
16		
17		
18		
Total		

(b) What is the mean height of the plants?

(c) What is the range of heights?

In the first 2 questions we had the original data, but sometimes we are only given the frequency table. Here are some examples:

3. This frequency table shows the distribution of marks for a French vocabulary test:

Mark	Frequency
12	1
13	2
14	4
15	2
16	7
17	3
18	1
Total	20

(a) What was the range of marks?

(b) What was the mode?

(c) (i) How many children are in the class?

(ii) If the marks are put in order, which two would give you the median?

(iii) What is the median? (Not 15!)

(d) To find the mean you need to find the total of all 20 marks. What is the total? (Not 95!)

(e) Calculate the mean.

4. (a) Calculate the range, mode, median and mean of this set of data:

Score	Frequency
17	2
18	0
19	1
20	2
21	5
22	6
23	3
24	0
25	1
Total	20

(b) Draw a frequency diagram to show this information.

(c) Could you find the range, mode, median and mean from the frequency diagram only? Explain your answer.

5. Look at this frequency diagram showing the distribution of marks out of 10 for our Latin test (my class is not very good at Latin!):

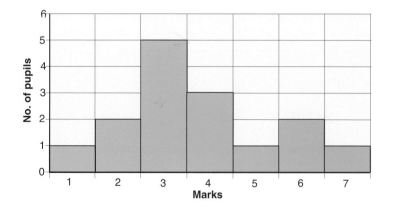

(a) What was the range of marks?
(b) What was the mode?
(c) What was the median?
(d) Calculate the mean.

6. We did a traffic survey for prep. I stood outside my house for 20 minutes and filled in a tally table to show how many vehicles passed me. Here is the result:

Type of vehicle	Tally	Frequency
Car	ⅢⅠ ⅢⅠ ⅢⅠ ⅢⅠ III	
Van	ⅢⅠ II	
Lorry	I	
Motorbike	III	
Bicycle	IIII	
Total		

(a) Complete the frequency column and calculate the total. What was the modal group?

(b) Why can you not work out a median and a mean?

Displaying data: Pie charts

Another way to look at information is in a **pie chart**. Like a pie, these diagrams are circular and divided into slices. A pie chart is used to show the proportion of various amounts that add up to a whole. For example, your parents may have had a breakdown of their local tax into money spent on education, housing, and services such as transport and waste disposal.

Here is an example from North Lanarkshire:

Council Budget 2003/2004 (Net)

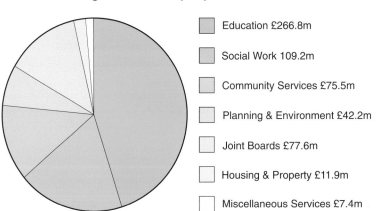

Education £266.8m

Social Work 109.2m

Community Services £75.5m

Planning & Environment £42.2m

Joint Boards £77.6m

Housing & Property £11.9m

Miscellaneous Services £7.4m

Here is the breakdown of another council's expenditure:

Education	£400 million
Social Work	£80 million
Community Services	£120 million
Planning and Environment	£70 million
Other	£50 million
Total	£720 million

This can be shown on a pie chart. When you are drawing a pie chart, it helps to look at the fraction of the whole pie that every slice represents and then work out the angle.

Start by noting that the total is £720 million (remember there are 360° in a full circle). £1 million will therefore be represented by $\frac{360°}{720} = \frac{1}{2}°$

The next step is to work out the angles that will represent all the other measures. You may need to use a calculator to work out the angles, but do write down the calculations you perform. The easiest thing to do is to make a table like the one below to show your calculations.

Expenditure	Amount in £m	Calculation	Angle
Education	400	$\frac{360°}{720} \times 400$	200°
Social Work	80	$\frac{360°}{720} \times 80$	40°
Community S	120	$\frac{360°}{720} \times 120$	60°
Pl and Env.	70	$\frac{360°}{720} \times 70$	35°
Other	50	$\frac{360°}{720} \times 50$	25°
Total	720		360°

Do always check that the total of the angles comes to 360° before you draw your pie chart. Use your protractor to draw the pie chart. If you have drawn it correctly, the pie will be full; there should be no empty spaces and no overlap.

Although the amount of expenditure between the two councils is very different, the pie chart makes it very easy to see that the second council spent a higher proportion on education.

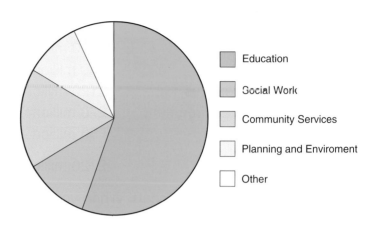

- Education
- Social Work
- Community Services
- Planning and Enviroment
- Other

Exercise 5.4

1. A year group of 36 pupils carried out a survey to look at the number of brothers and sisters that they all had. Draw a pie chart to show the results of their survey:

No. of brothers and sisters: No. of pupils:

No. of brothers and sisters:	No. of pupils:
0	9
1	12
2	9
3	5
4	1

(a) Copy and complete this table to work out the angles:

No. of brothers and sisters	Frequency	Calculation	Angle
0	9	$\frac{360^{\circ}}{36} \times 9$	
1	12		
2	9		
3	5		
4	1		10°
Total	36		360°

(b) Draw a pie chart to show this information.

2. I conducted a survey of my class of 30 pupils to find out approximately how many hours of television they watched each week. These were my results:

0 – 2 hours   1 pupil
2 – 4 hours   3 pupils
4 – 6 hours   5 pupils
6 – 8 hours   12 pupils
8 – 10 hours   6 pupils
More than 10 hours   3 pupils

    (a) Write out a frequency table like the one in q.1 to display this information.
    (b) Complete the table by calculating the angles.
    (c) Display this information on a pie chart.

3. We have 240 pupils at our school. When we looked at how they come to school, we discovered the following:
60 pupils walk to school.
48 come to school on the school bus service.
96 come to school by car.
36 come to school on public transport.

    (a) Write out a frequency table like the one in q.1 to display this information.
    (b) Complete the table by calculating the angles.
    (c) Show this information on a pie chart.
    (d) If a child at the school is selected at random, what is the probability that he or she walks to school?

4. 72 pupils went on a school trip. They all brought a packed lunch. Each packed lunch contained a sandwich, a drink and one other item. The other items were as follows:
10 had a yoghurt
18 had an apple
8 had a banana
12 had a chocolate bar
the rest each had a bag of crisps.

    (a) Write out a frequency table like the one in q.1 to display this information.
    (b) Complete the table by calculating the angles.
    (c) Display this information on a pie chart.
    (d) Mr Munch wanted a crisp. If he selected a child at random, what would the probability be that he picked one with a bag of crisps?

Interpreting pie charts

Consider these two pie charts. They compare the things that the children in Year 8 and Year 4 like doing after school:

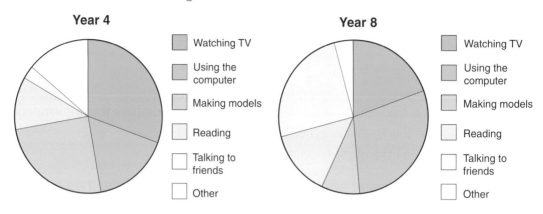

The charts show that the older children prefer using the computer and talking to friends more than the younger children do. Although we do not have exact figures, we can see that about a quarter of the Year 4 children like making models, but only about a tenth of the Year 8 children do.

Exercise 5.6: Extension questions

1. We asked the people in my class what they were doing at 7 p.m. last night. This chart shows the answers:

    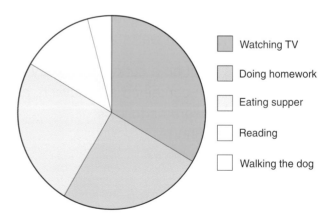

    (a) What fraction of the children were watching TV?
    (b) What fraction of the children were doing their homework?
    (c) If I picked a child at random, what would be the probability that he was eating supper at 7 p.m.?
    (d) If 6 children were reading, how many children were in the class?
    (e) How many were walking the dog?

2. The parents conducted a survey of how children come to school in the morning. This pie chart shows the results:

    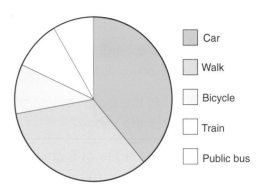

    (a) Roughly what fraction come to school by car?
    (b) If 40 come by bicycle, how many children took part in the survey?

    The school introduced a school minibus service and now one half of those who used to come by car use the school minibus.

    (c) Sketch another pie chart showing the new breakdown of morning transport.

3. This pie chart shows where the pupils in the school went on holiday last year:

    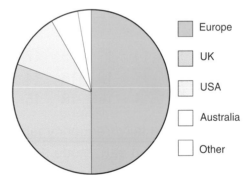

    (a) What was the most popular destination?
    (b) If three tenths of the school stayed in the UK, what fraction spent their holiday in the USA?
    (c) In fact a quarter of those going to Europe went to France. What fraction of the whole school went to France?
    (d) 60 children stayed in the UK. How many went to Europe?

4. In geography I did a survey in the local park to find out what people did there. This pie chart shows the various activities:

    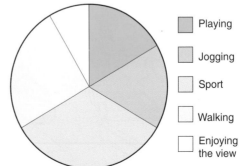

    Write a report of these results. Write as much detail as you can. Think what time of day I might have asked the questions. Would I have had the same results at a different time?

Exercise 5.7: Summary exercise

1. Here are the heights in metres of 6 children:
    1.42   1.35   1.41   1.50   1.38   1.46

    (a) What is the mean height of the children?
    (b) What is the range?

2. Here are the ages of 5 children in years and months:
    11y 6m, 10y 4m, 10y 6m, 11y 4m, 10y 11m

    (a) What is the mean age of the children?
    (b) A sixth child joins the group and the mean age of the 6 children
        becomes 11 years and 1 month. What is the age of the sixth child?

3. What is the mean, median and mode of these sets of numbers:
    (a)   3   4   4   4   5   6   7   7   8
    (b)   2.1   1.8   1.6   2.3   1.8   2.1   1.4   2.1   1.9
    (c)   14.1   12.4   13.2   14.1   12.8   13.8

4. Here are the marks for the recent mental arithmetic test. The marks are
    out of 20:
    15   16   14   13   15   17
    11   15   17   12   16   14
    13   19   14   16   18   15

    (a) Draw a tally/frequency table to show the results.
    (b) Find the mean, mode and median of the marks.
    (c) Show the results on a pie chart.

5. Look at this frequency diagram showing how many people are in each car that comes to school in the morning:

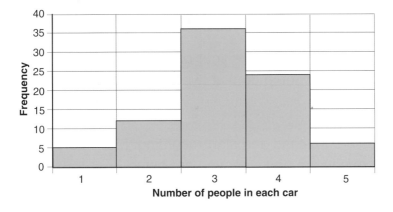

(a) How many cars had 3 people in them?
(b) How many more cars had 4 people in them than 2?
(c) How many cars were there in all?
(d) How many people were there in all the cars?
(e) What was the mode?
(f) What was the mean number of people in each car?

End of chapter 5 activity: A traffic survey

In this chapter you may have noticed that several questions were about traffic and travelling. Here are some ideas for conducting your own surveys. You will be able to practise the things you have learnt in this chapter and have some fun at the same time.

1. Traffic

There are many questions that you might like to ask about the traffic that runs past your school:

What type of vehicle?
What colour of vehicle?
How many buses?
When is the traffic at its busiest?

Before you start you must firstly:

1.   Decide what it is that you want to know about the traffic.

2.   Make up a recording sheet so that you can record your observations.

3.   Decide when you are going to make your observations and for how long. For example, you might want to do it at two different times of day.

When you are fully prepared:

4.   Find somewhere safe to stand and start recording. Make sure that an adult knows where you are and what you are doing.

5.   When you have your results, you can make your report. Use any of the charts and tables that you have studied in this chapter to make your report more interesting.

2. Travelling to or from school

Several other questions you will have come across looked at how pupils travelled to and from school, and how many people were in a car.

Here's how you could conduct your own survey:

1.   Ask your class how they came to school in the morning.

2.   Ask anyone who travelled by car how many people were in it (do not forget to ask your teacher too!).

3.   Ask people where they came from. You might find a pattern.

4.   Put together a questionnaire for other classes. When you are happy with it, ask your teacher to give it out.

5.   When you have your results, think about what sort of things you want to find out. It might be the sort of information we have already mentioned, or it might be that you want to see if there is a difference as pupils get older, or you might want to compare travel to different destinations.

6.   Write a report about the results of your survey. Try to use many of the things you have learnt from this chapter to make your report interesting.

Chapter 6: Working with decimals

Ancient Babylonia

We saw in Chapter 3 how decimal fractions are equivalent to fractions. Many early civilisations used fractions. However, it was only those with a place value system, such as the Babylonians, who could work with the equivalent of decimals.

The number above was found on an old Babylonian tablet. It is an approximation for the square root of two. The symbols, as you hopefully remember from Chapter 2, are 1, 24, 51 and 10. Because the Babylonians used a base 60, or sexagesimal system, this number is actually read as:

$1 \times 1 + 24 \times 1/60 + 51 \times 1/3600 + 10 \times 1/216000$, or about 1.414212

It is interesting that they did not use anything to separate the units column from the first place of sexagesimals. The decimal point was in fact introduced much later. Francesco Pellos, or Pellizzati, a native of Nice, published a 'commercial arithmetic' at Turin in 1492. It was in this paper that the first use of a decimal point was made. However, the idea did not catch on at the time. In fact, the use of the decimal point in the form we now use is generally attributed to John Napier. He used it in his work *Descriptio*, in 1616.

Decimal arithmetic: Adding and subtracting

Just as with normal adding and subtracting, it is important that the rows are lined up so that numbers are in the correct column. As you once wrote H T U above any calculation, and carefully put the digits in the correct column, so once again you must carefully put the digits in the correct column. You must also carefully put the decimal points underneath one another.

In the following 2 examples you have to add extra zeros to make the rows have the same number of digits after the decimal point:

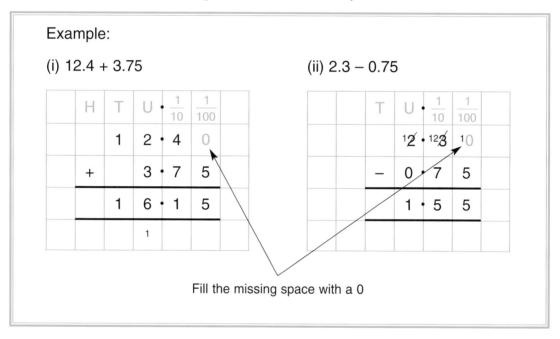

Example:

(i) 12.4 + 3.75

(ii) 2.3 − 0.75

Fill the missing space with a 0

Exercise 6.1

Calculate the answers to these; show all your working, including any carried or exchanged numbers:

1. 7.6 + 9.9
2. 3.5 − 2.7
3. 4.72 + 5.43
4. 4.07 − 1.15
5. 16.324 + 4.806

6. 14.125 − 3.091
7. 3.024 + 14.5 + 0.67
8. 4.8 − 2.19
9. 14 + 4.175 − 9.364
10. 9.91 + 0.09 − 3.127

11. 17.6 + 8.124

12. 130.5 − 2.745

13. 404.72 + 5.637 + 28

14. 5 − 1.432

15. 6 + 2.7 + 7.64

16. 20 − 0.673

17. 2.03 − 1.999

18. 4.567 − 2.7

19. 104 + 0.64 − 11.674

20. 11.9 − 1.636 + 6.737

Multiplying decimals

If 6 × 4 is 24, what is 0.6 × 4?

It's not that difficult. Remember that we can think of multiplying as successive adding.

So: 0.6 × 4 = 0.6 + 0.6 + 0.6 + 0.6
           = 2.4

Calculations that we cannot do in our head can be put into a frame. As in previous calculations, it is important to keep the decimal points beneath each other.

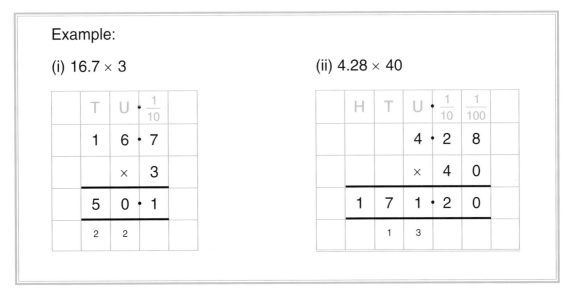

Example:

(i) 16.7 × 3

(ii) 4.28 × 40

Remember, when multiplying by multiples of 10, to pull the zero down into the answer line before you start multiplying.

Exercise 6.2

Calculate the answers to these; show all your working, including any carried numbers:

1.	1.7×3	**6.**	11.07×6
2.	0.45×4	**7.**	20.8×9
3.	3.25×7	**8.**	6.7×7
4.	16.09×5	**9.**	20.06×8
5.	4.26×8	**10.**	21.09×6
11.	3.72×20	**16.**	67.05×300
12.	16.8×40	**17.**	49.86×4000
13.	3.708×50	**18.**	5.68×50
14.	16.09×70	**19.**	72.96×500
15.	32.87×80	**20.**	6.405×6000

Multiplying decimals by a decimal

Consider this question: find the area of a rectangle 50 cm by 30 cm.

The answer is 1500 cm² (because $50 \times 30 = 1500$). However, suppose the question had asked for the answer to be given in square metres. All you would need to do is to remember that there are 10 000 square centimetres in a square metre. The calculation would become: $1500 \div 10\ 000 = 0.15$ m².

We could do this calculation slightly differently by converting the centimetres in the question into metres before we do the calculation. The calculation would then become:

Area $= 0.3$ m $\times 0.5$ m
$= 0.15$ m²

The answer is interesting because it is smaller than the numbers we multiplied together. This makes more sense if we look at the problem in two dimensions:

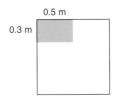

0.5 m

0.3 m

The area is 0.15 square metres, or 15 hundredths of the whole square metres

If we multiply a positive number by a number less than one, we get a smaller answer.

- If we multiply tenths by tenths, we get hundredths.
- If we multiply tenths by hundredths, we get thousandths etc.

Example:

(i) $0.3 \times 5 = 1.5$ Tenths x whole gives tenths.

(ii) $2.5 \times 0.3 = 0.75$ Tenths x tenths gives hundredths.

(iii) $1.2 \times 0.06 = 0.072$ Tenths x hundredths gives thousandths.

Exercise 6.3

Calculate the answers to these:

1. 0.4×0.7 6. 0.12×0.6

2. 0.4×0.07 7. 0.004×0.8

3. 0.04×0.007 8. 0.204×3

4. 0.07×4 9. 0.101×0.05

5. 0.8×0.5 10. 1.2×0.05

You may have had difficulty deciding where the decimal point should go. If you did, another way of thinking about this is to look at the numbers after the decimal point. In our example we had:

Area = 0.3 m × 0.5 m   Here there are 2 numbers after the decimal point, so
     = 0.15 m²   there are 2 numbers after the decimal point in the
                              answer.

Look at this example:

1.24×0.06 In this example there are 4 numbers after the decimal

$124 \times 6 = 744$ point, which means there will be 4 numbers after the

$1.24 \times 0.06 = 0.0744$ decimal point in the answer.

Check your answers to the first 10 questions and then do q.11-20 in the same way as the example above. Use a multiplying frame if you cannot do the multiplication in your head.

11. 1.55×1.2

12. 3.96×0.4

13. 4.8×1.2

14. 0.87×0.4

15. 1.35×0.06

16. 6.7×0.08

17. 4.5×0.12

18. 5.09×0.07

19. 0.056×0.05

20. 9.105×0.6

For these you will need to do long multiplication first and then work out the answer with the decimal point in the correct place:

21. 3.6×5.2

22. 4.8×0.75

23. 6.5×0.084

24. 12.2×3.4

25. 45.2×4.2

26. 2.14×0.52

27. 3.12×0.14

28. 2.08×0.35

29. 1.07×0.036

30. 5.6×1.08

When you were doing the above calculations, you should have been thinking:

	3.6×4.5		There is a total of 2 numbers after the decimal point.
so if	36×45	$= 1620$	
then	3.6×4.5	$= 16.20$	There should be 2 numbers after the decimal point in the answer.

Once you have done the multiplication, you can work out the answer to other related questions:

if	36×45	$= 1620$	
then	3.6×0.45	$= 1.620$	Here there are 3 numbers after the decimal point in the answer.
and	0.36×450	$= 162$	Divide by 100 then multiply by 10 is equivalent to divide by 10.
and	3.6×4500	$= 16200$	Divide by 10 then multiply by 100 is equivalent to multiply by 10.

Exercise 6.4

Write down the answers to these:

1. If $47 \times 83 = 3901$, give the answer to:
   (a) 4.7×8.3 (b) 470×0.83 (c) 8300×0.47

2. If $68 \times 29 = 1972$, give the answer to:
   (a) 6.8×2.9 (b) 680×0.29 (c) 6800×0.29

3. If $45 \times 63 = 2835$, give the answer to:
   (a) 4.5×6.3 (b) 4500×0.63 (c) 6300×0.045

4. If $645 \times 24 = 15\ 480$, give the answer to:
   (a) 64.5×2.4 (b) 6450×0.24 (c) 2400×6.45

5. If $928 \times 815 = 756\ 320$, give the answer to:
   (a) 9.28×8.15 (b) 9280×0.815 (c) 81500×0.928

Dividing decimals

When we divide a decimal, we follow the same principles used in normal division:

Here's a straightforward division $14 \div 2 = 7$

And here's one with a decimal $1.4 \div 2 = 0.7$

For more complicated problems we may need to write the calculation out. It is important that the decimal points stay above each other in the division.

Unlike normal division, the first one or more zeros can be important, since they tell us where the decimal point is:

Example: (i) $1.95 \div 5$

```
          0 · 3  9
      5 | 1 · 9  ⁴5
```

(ii) $1.068 \div 12$

```
            0 · 0  8  9
     1  2 | 1 · 0  6  ⁷8
```

Exercise 6.5

Do these in your head if you can. If not, write out the division calculation:

1. $1.8 \div 3$
2. $0.45 \div 9$
3. $0.025 \div 5$
4. $1.2 \div 6$
5. $1.32 \div 12$

6. $0.042 \div 6$
7. $7.2 \div 8$
8. $5.4 \div 9$
9. $0.84 \div 12$
10. $0.0121 \div 11$

11. $2.1 \div 7$
12. $4.2 \div 6$
13. $0.014 \div 2$
14. $1.44 \div 12$
15. $0.108 \div 9$

In the next exercise you will need to do long division with decimals. Write the calculations out as shown in the example below:

Example: $13.68 \div 19$

Exercise 6.6

1. $87.4 \div 19$
2. $12.48 \div 26$
3. $1.587 \div 23$
4. $15.75 \div 35$
5. $26.68 \div 46$

6. $51.30 \div 54$
7. $0.952 \div 17$
8. $243.6 \div 29$
9. $2.592 \div 72$
10. $0.1404 \div 26$

Sometimes extra zeros have to be added, so that we can keep dividing until we have a final answer.

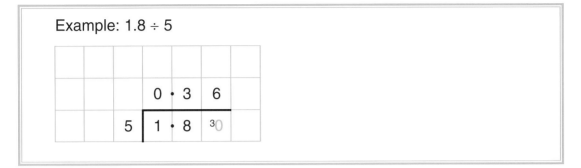

Example: 1.8 ÷ 5

Exercise 6.7

Remember to add extra zeros. There should not be any remainders in these questions:

1. 2.5 ÷ 2   **6.** 4.05 ÷ 12   **11.** 1.06 ÷ 8

2. 0.9 ÷ 4   **7.** 0.27 ÷ 6   **12.** 12.1 ÷ 4

3. 0.03 ÷ 6   **8.** 3.12 ÷ 12   **13.** 10 ÷ 8

4. 0.06 ÷ 12   **9.** 0.77 ÷ 5   **14.** 0.405 ÷ 6

5. 1.03 ÷ 4   **10.** 0.027 ÷ 12   **15.** 3.1 ÷ 4

Division by decimals

How many halves are there in 4?

We can write this as   4 ÷ 0.5

The answer is 8. We can work this out simply if we know that 40 ÷ 5 is 8

When the question is more complicated (for example 40 ÷ 0.005), it is very difficult to work out exactly where the decimal point goes in the answer. Is it 0.08, 0.8, 8, 80, 800, 8000 or 80 000?

It is particularly important in division to check your answer:

40 ÷ 0.005 gives 80	Check: 80 × 0.005 = 0.4	Wrong
40 ÷ 0.005 gives 8000	Check: 8000 × 0.005 = 40	Right

Because dividing by a decimal is difficult, it is better if we try to make it simpler by first eliminating the decimal point. Here is an example to show you what we mean:

Firstly let's write $40 \div 0.005$ as $\frac{40}{0.005}$

Now we want to eliminate the decimal point. We can do this by multiplying 0.005 by 1000 to make 5

But remember that whatever you do to the bottom of the calculation, you must do to the top. So now multiply the 40 by 1000 as well, so our calculation becomes:

Example: $40 \div 0.005 = \frac{40}{0.005} \times \frac{1000}{1000}$

$$= \frac{40000}{5}$$

$$= 8000$$

That's much easier!

Exercise 6.8

Do the first 12 in your head but check by multiplication that your decimal point is in the right place:

Example: $4 \div 0.2 = 20$ Check: $0.2 \times 20 = 4$

1.	$8 \div 0.2$	**6.**	$3.2 \div 0.8$
2.	$0.16 \div 0.4$	**7.**	$24 \div 0.3$
3.	$1.2 \div 0.3$	**8.**	$0.0014 \div 0.07$
4.	$36 \div 0.12$	**9.**	$210 \div 0.3$
5.	$0.024 \div 0.06$	**10.**	$180 \div 0.006$

You may need to write the working out in full for the following, as we did in the example just before Exercise 6.8

11. $1.05 \div 0.6$
12. $0.000\,24 \div 0.03$
13. $3.2 \div 0.8$
14. $0.64 \div 0.008$
15. $2.8 \div 0.007$
16. $0.063 \div 0.09$
17. $4.5 \div 0.005$
18. $0.0036 \div 0.9$
19. $480 \div 0.6$
20. $0.000\,12 \div 0.6$

If you know the answer to a multiplication, you can work out the answer to other related questions. For example:

If $\quad 36 \times 45 = 1620$
then $\quad 1620 \div 45 = 36$
and $\quad 16.2 \div 45 = 0.36$ (divide by 100 because it's 16.2 not 1620)
and $\quad 16.2 \div 3.6 = 4.5$ (check by multiplying $3.6 \times 4.5 = 16.20$)

Exercise 6.9

Write down the answers to these:

1. If $58 \times 16 = 928$, give the answer to:
   (a) $928 \div 1.6$ (b) $928 \div 0.58$ (c) $92.8 \div 0.016$

2. If $36 \times 85 = 3060$, give the answer to:
   (a) $3060 \div 8.5$ (b) $306 \div 0.36$ (c) $3.06 \div 0.085$

3. If $56 \times 29 = 1624$, give the answer to:
   (a) $162.4 \div 2.9$ (b) $16.24 \div 0.56$ (c) $1.624 \div 0.29$

4. If $248 \times 79 = 19\,592$, give the answer to:
   (a) $19.592 \div 24.8$ (b) $195.92 \div 0.79$ (c) $195\,920 \div 2.48$

5. If $245 \times 124 = 30\,380$, give the answer to:
   (a) $3038 \div 12.4$ (b) $3.038 \div 2.45$ (c) $30.38 \div 0.124$

Measurement and the metric system

You may have noticed that in Britain we use a metric system for most units of measurements, but we still measure long distances in miles, which is the older imperial unit of measurement. It probably never occurs to many of us that the measures we use today were the result of heated political debate in the nineteenth century. In 1874, William Rankine, a British Engineer, wrote this poem, 'The Three Foot Rule':

> *Some talk of millimetres, and some of kilograms,*
> *And some of decilitres, to measure beer and drams;*
> *But I'm a British Workman, too old to go to school,*
> *So by pounds I'll eat, and by quarts I'll drink, and I'll work by my*
> *three foot rule.*

> *A party of astronomers went measuring the Earth,*
> *And forty million metres they took to be its girth;*
> *Five hundred million inches, though, go through from Pole to Pole;*
> *So let's stick to inches, feet and yards, and the good old three foot rule.*

The traditional measures used in Britain have evolved over centuries. Britain as a nation was involved heavily in trade and so the measures it used became standard and, by the end of the eighteenth century, were used by both Britain and America.

In France, on the other hand, there was no standardization. It has been estimated that France had about 800 different names for measures at this time and, taking into account different values used in different towns, around 250 000 differently-sized units.

In 1790 France was in the middle of a revolution but their National Assembly was determined to make improvements. It was agreed that a new measurement system based on a length from nature should be adopted. The system should have decimal subdivisions, and all measures of area, volume, weight etc. should be linked to the fundamental unit of length.

The chairman of the Commission of Weights and Measures proposed the length of $\frac{1}{10\,000\,000}$ of the distance from the pole to the equator of the Earth. They might have got international agreement on this had they not declared that this distance would be determined by an accurate survey of the distance between Dunkerque and Barcelona. The Royal Society in London declared that this was based on a measurement of France and the Americans were not prepared to accept the word of the French mathematicians for its length.

Over the next century the European countries, and their colonies, adopted the new units, but Britain and America resisted.

Metric units

We measure length in **metres (m)**

10 mm	= 1 centimetre (cm)
100 cm	= 1 metre (m)
1000 millimetres (mm)	= 1 metre (m)
1000 metres	= 1 kilometre (km)

We measure mass in **grams g**

1000 milligrams (mg)	= 1 gram (g)
1000 grams	= 1 kilogram (kg)
1000 kg	= 1 tonne (t)

We measure volume in **litres l**

1000 cubic centimetres (cm³)	= 1 litre (l)
1000 millilitres (ml)	= 1 litre (l)
100 centilitres (cl)	= 1 litre (l)

Exercise 6.10

Write these quantities in terms of the new unit given. It helps if you always start by writing down the basic conversion fact before you start. Make sure you read the units in the question carefully; this will help you to avoid making silly mistakes:

> Example:
>
> (i) Write 54 cm in metres.
> $$100 \text{ cm} = 1 \text{ m}$$
> Therefore 54 cm = 0.54 m
>
> (ii) Write 35 kg in grams.
> $$1 \text{ kg} = 1000 \text{ g}$$
> Therefore 35 kg = 35 000 g

1. Write in metres:
   (a) 25 cm   (b) 480 mm   (c) 5.3 km   (d) 258 cm

2. Write in grams:
   (a) 25 kg   (b) 3750 mg   (c) 0.625 kg   (d) 3.6 t

3. Write in litres:
   (a) 220 ml   (b) 3634 ml   (c) 2.8 cl   (d) 5 ml

4. Write in cm:
   (a) 24 mm   (b) 2.7 km   (c) 35 m   (d) 0.07 m

5. Write in kg:
   (a) 350 g   (b) 4.5 t   (c) 25 mg   (d) 7.5 g

6. Write in ml:
   (a) 1.4 l   (b) 0.35 l   (c) 45 cl   (d) 0.7 cl

7. Write in mm:
   (a) 3.2 cm   (b) 4.5 m   (c) 0.7 m   (d) 0.4 km

8. Write in mg:
   (a) 3.2 g   (b) 5.5 g   (c) 165 g   (d) 0.06 kg

9. Write in km:
   (a) 3.5 m   (b) 4050 m   (c) 320 000 cm

Calculating with quantities

If we need to calculate with quantities, we must make sure that they are all in the same units before we start. This means that some units may have to be changed.

Exercise 6.11

Add the following, giving your answer in the units indicated:

Example:

1.2 m + 23 cm + 15 mm (give units in cm).

First remember it helps to note down the basic conversions facts:
1 m = 100 cm and 10 mm = 1 cm

So we can now write:
1.2 m + 23 cm + 15 mm = 120 cm + 23 cm + 1.5cm
= 144.5 cm

---

1. 5 m + 672 cm + 65 mm (give units in cm)

2. 3500 g + 1.7 kg + 375 mg (give units in g)

3. 0.678 km − 4525 cm (give units in m)

4. 375 ml × 8 (give units in l)

5. 2 km ÷ 8 (give units in m)

6. 5.7 t ÷ 12 (give units in g)

7. I need 12 lengths of rope. Each length must be 75 cm long. How many metres of rope should I buy?

8. Our class is making chocolate crispies for the summer fair. I don't have any cocoa, so I have to go and buy some. 12 crispies need 45 g of cocoa. How much cocoa should I buy to make 240 crispies?

9. I need to buy 2.4 kg of raisins, but raisins come in bags of 150 g. How many bags do I need to buy?

10. I have a plank that is 2.2 m long. I cut it into five equal pieces with four cuts, but I lose 1.5 mm of wood with each cut. How long are my four pieces of plank, in centimetres?

11. I am making cement in my science lesson. I mix 4 kg of sand with 1.2 kg of cement and 600 g of water. I pour the cement into 4 equal-sized moulds. What is the mass of cement in each mould?

12. I add 4 cupfuls of raspberry flavouring and 2 cupfuls of banana flavouring to a 4 litre carton of milk. I pour the resulting milkshake into 10 glasses. If each glass contains 475 ml, how much is in one cupful?

Exercise 6.12: Extension questions

For more complicated calculations it is important that the parts of the calculation are done in the correct order, especially if you are using a calculator:

For example: $\dfrac{42.84}{19.61 - 13.49}$

First of all it is useful to estimate the answer:

$$\frac{42.84}{19.61 - 13.49} \approx \frac{42}{6} \approx 7$$

Method 1: Using the memory button on your calculator

Enter 19.61 − 13.49 and the = button. You should get 6.12

Enter 6.12 into the memory, (usually there is a Min or M+ button). Then clear the screen.

Now enter 42.84 and ÷ then MR and = to get the answer: 7
(Refer to your calculator instruction manual if this does not work!)

Method 2: Using brackets

Think of the calculation as being 42.84 ÷ (19.61 − 13.49)

Enter the keys in that order, using your bracket keys, and you should get the answer 7
This is usually the better method to use.
(Refer to your calculator instruction manual if this does not work!)

1. $\dfrac{119.5}{18.86 - 5.61}$

5. $\dfrac{38.48 + 232.23}{40.41 - 16.87}$

2. $\dfrac{74.49}{8.22 - 2.49}$

6. $\dfrac{745.29 + 196.69}{28.75 + 7.48}$

3. $\dfrac{130.55}{50.27 - 31.62}$

7. $\dfrac{887.49 - 584.65}{17.25 - 14.57}$

4. $\dfrac{82.9}{18.87 - 2.29}$

8. $\dfrac{375.92 - 112.58}{49.39 - 36.85}$

Exercise 6.13: Summary exercise

Do **not** use a calculator for this exercise.

1. (a) 5.6 + 14 + 0.056   (b) 3.4 − 0.675

2. (a) 5 × 0.04   (b) 0.4 × 0.06   (c) 0.5 × 0.08

3. (a) 0.8 ÷ 4   (b) 36 ÷ 0.6   (c) 3.2 ÷ 0.008

4. (a) 2.5 × 0.38   (b) 0.63 × 9.5

5. 1.568 ÷ 49

6. If 56 × 84 ÷ 4704, give the answer to:
   (a) 0.56 × 8.4   (c) 47.04 ÷ 56
   (b) 560 × 0.84   (d) 4.704 ÷ 0.084

7. Copy and complete these:
   (a) 1.3 g = _____ mg   (c) 7.2 km = _____ m
   (b) 53 mm = _____ m   (d) 0.072 ml = _____ l

8. (a) 4.5 m + 450 cm + 36 mm = _____ (cm)
   (b) 4.2 t + 56 kg + 765 g = _____ (kg)
   (c) 5 l ÷ 8 = _____ (ml)
   (d) 240 mg × 5 = _____ kg

9. I am the dining room monitor. I fill up all the cups on my table from a 2 litre jug of water. If I can fill up 8 cups from one jug, how much water goes in each?

10. I make a cake with 1.2 kg of flour, 450 g of sugar and 450 g of butter and 45 mg of cocoa. What is the total mass of these ingredients?

11. In order to raise money for charity, I run 2.2 km every day for 5 days. Harry runs the same total distance as I do, but in four days. How many metres more does Harry run each day than I do?

End of chapter 6 activity: Imperial units

How did it all begin?

It was the Greeks who developed the 'foot' as their fundamental unit of length. Legend has it that this Greek unit was based on an actual measurement of Hercules' foot.

People measured a yard of cloth by the distance between the end of the outstretched arm and their chin.

The Romans measured their pace steps at about 2.5 feet. 1000 double paces formed a mile.

You may have noticed that, although we measure small distances in metres, we still measure long ones in miles. Our system of metric units has been in place for a very short time compared to the old imperial units, and it is a good idea to be familiar with both.

1. Find a tape measure that is marked in inches (in). Measure your height, your girth (the distance around your stomach), the height of a door. Now measure these in metric units.

2. Find some weighing scales that are marked in pounds (lb) and stones. Weigh yourself. Now weigh yourself in kg. Weigh some other things too.

3. Find a pint glass and a litre container. Fill the pint glass and pour the contents into the litre container.

4. From your experiments work out some rough equivalent comparisons of metric and imperial units (for example 1 foot ≈ 30 cm).

Now see how your comparisons compare to the ones we use:

1 metre ≈ 39 inches (or 3 feet and 3 inches)	(multiply by $3\frac{1}{4}$)
1 kilometre = $\frac{5}{8}$mile	(multiply by 5 divide by 8)
1 kilogram = 2.2 pounds	(add $\frac{1}{10}$ and multiply by 2)
1 litre = 1.75 pints	(multiply by 7 and divide by 4)
1 foot = 0.3 metres	(multiply by 3 and divide by 10)
1 mile = $1\frac{3}{5}$ kilometres	(multiply by 8 and divide by 5)
1 pound = 0.45 kilograms	(divide by 2 and subtract $\frac{1}{10}$)
1pint = 0.6 litres	(multiply by 3 and divide by 5)

Time for some history

The worksheet can be used for the next 3 questions:

5. The following is a story in which imperial units are used. Rewrite it using metric units. You need to know that there are 16 ounces (oz) in one pound (lb) of weight.

    (a) Connie was going shopping for her mother. She walked **two miles** into the village. Connie bought **2 lb** of potatoes and **8 oz** of mushrooms.

    (b) Connie walked **100 yards** down the road to the Haberdashers shop. Connie then bought **3 yards** of blue ribbon and **5 feet** of knicker elastic.

    (c) Connie was tired and the shopping was heavy and so she stopped at the sweet shop and bought **4 ounces** of wine gums.

6. Here is a story in metric units. Rewrite it in imperial units.

    (a) Digby bicycled **4 km** to the shops where he bought a **2 kg** weight and 6 weights of **300 g**.

    (b) Digby also bought **200 m** of fishing twine and **50 cm** of string.

    (c) Digby was thirsty and so he also bought a **500 ml** bottle of water.

7. Write some stories of your own and give them to a friend to rewrite.

Chapter 7: Algebra 1 – Expressions and formulae

When we looked at averages in Chapter 5, we wrote down a rule for calculating the mean:

$$\text{Mean} = \frac{\text{total}}{\text{number of items}}$$

We often meet rules in mathematics. Sometimes we write them in words, like the one above, and at other times we decide that words take far too long to write down and we use simple letters instead.

Here is a rule that you probably know:

$$A = bh$$

It is a shorthand way of writing:

Area of a rectangle = base times height

When we write rules like this, we are writing a **formula** using **algebra**.

Algebra was brought from ancient Babylon, Egypt and India to Europe via Italy by the Arabs. The first treatise on algebra was written by Diophantus of Alexandria in the 3rd century AD. The word **algebra** derives from the Arabic **al-jabr** or literally 'the reunion of broken parts'. It gained widespread use through the title of a book '*ilm al-jabr wa'l-mukabala*' – the science of restoring what is missing and equating like with like – written by the mathematician Abu Ja'far Muhammad (c.800-847). He has subsequently become known as *al-Khwarazmi, the man of Kwarazm* (now Khiva in Uzbekistan). He introduced the writing down of calculations in place of using an abacus.

In *So you really want to learn Maths* Book 1 we learnt some simple rules of algebra and used them to solve equations.

The rules of algebra

- When using algebra, we use symbols or letters to represent numbers.

- We can add and subtract the same letters, or numbers, but cannot add unlike letters or letters to numbers.
  $a + a + a = 3a$ but $a + b = a + b$

- We do not use multiplication signs, or division signs:
  $3 \times x = 3x$ $x \div 3 = \frac{x}{3}$

- $3 \times x$ may equal $3x$ but $1 \times x = x$. We never write $1x$ or $0x$

- The x in algebra is written as a curly x, not the x that means multiply.

- An **expression** is just a string of terms: $3x + 4y$
  You cannot solve an expression, but you may be able to **simplify** it.

- An **equation** contains an equals sign: $2 + x = 6$
  You can **solve** equations.

- Equals signs should **always** go neatly **underneath** each other.

Exercise 7.1

Use the rules above to simplify these expressions:

Example:

(i) $a + a + a + a = 4a$
(ii) $3 \times b = 3b$
(iii) $6d \div 2 = 3d$

---

1. $a + a + a$

2. $5 \times x$

3. $m + m + m - m$

4. $p + p + q + q$

5. $4 \times y + 3 \times y$

6. $s + s - t - s - t$

7. $4d \div 2$

8. $\dfrac{10x}{5}$

9. $a + 5 + a + 5$

10. $c - c - c - c$

Remember that we can collect identical letters together when we are adding or subtracting and we can write any expression without the × or ÷ sign.

Example:

(i) $3a + 4b - 2a + 3b = a + 7b$

(ii) $3a \times 4b = 12ab$

(iii) $12x \div 2y = \dfrac{12x}{2y}$

$$= \dfrac{6x}{y}$$

---

11. $2a \times 3b$

12. $2p + 3q - 4p + q$

13. $m + 2n - 3n + m$

14. $4x \times 5y$

15. $8x \div 2y$

16. $4a + 3b + 2a - b$

17. $5m - 5 - 7m + 4$

18. $15m \div 5n$

19. $2p \times 5q$

20. $8a + 2b - 2a - 2b$

Multiples of x and powers of x

Consider the areas of these squares:

The area of the first square: $1 \times 1 = 1^2 = 1$

The area of the second square: $2 \times 2 = 2^2 = 4$

The area of the third square: $3 \times 3 = 3^2 = 9$

The area of the other square: $x \times x = x^2$

We cannot simplify x^2 any further.

Just as any number times itself can be written with an index number, so too can:

$$x \times x \times x = x^3 \qquad x \times x \times x \times x \times x = x^4$$

It is very important not to confuse this with $3 \times x = 3x$ or $x + x + x = 3x$

Make sure you understand why before you move on. If you are a little unsure, then imagine the calculation where $x = 2$

$$x \times x \times x = x^3 \qquad\qquad 2 \times 2 \times 2 = 2^3 = 8$$

$$3 \times x = 3x \qquad\qquad 3 \times 2 = 2 + 2 + 2 = 6$$

Do you see how important it is to understand this correctly?

Exercise 7.2

Here are some examples to test you. Simplify these:

1. (a) $x \times x$ (b) $x + x$ (c) $2 \times x$ d) $2 \times 2 \times x$

2. (a) $x + x + x$ (b) $3 \times x$ (c) $x \times x \times x$ (d) $3 \times x \times 3$

3. (a) $4 \times x$ (b) $x \times x \times x \times x$ (c) $2 \times x \times 2 \times x$

4. (a) $a \times x$ (b) $a \times x \times x$ (c) $a \times a \times x$ (d) $a \times x \times a \times x$

5. (a) $b \times b$ (b) $2 \times b \times b$ (c) $2 \times a \times b$ (d) $a \times b \times a \times b$

6. (a) $x \times y + x$ (b) $x \times y + x \times x$ (c) $x \times y + x \times y$ (d) $x \times x + 2 \times x \times x$

Remember to gather together terms that are like each other.

Example:

$$2 \times x \times x \times y + x \times x \times y = 2x^2y + x^2y$$
$$= 3x^2y$$

---

7. (a) $2 \times a \times b + a \times a$ (b) $2 \times a \times a + a \times a$

8. (a) $2 \times a \times b + a \times b \times b$ (b) $2 \times a \times b + 3 \times a \times b$

9. (a) $s \times t \times u + s \times t \times t$ (b) $2 \times s \times t \times t - s \times t \times t$

10. (a) $3 \times x \times y \times x - x \times x \times y$ (b) $3 \times x \times y \times x - x \times y \times y$

More about algebra and index numbers

We may need to combine expressions in algebra, for example:

$$2x^2 \times 3x^3 = 2 \times x \times x \times 3 \times x \times x \times x$$
$$= 6x^5$$

It is important not to confuse adding and multiplying:

$$a^2b + a^2b + a^2b = 3a^2b \qquad a^2b \times a^2b \times a^2b = a^6b^3$$

Exercise 7.3

Simplify these expressions, if possible:

1. $a \times a^2 \times a^3$

2. $3a \times 2a^2 \times a^3$

3. $3b + b^2 + 2b^3$

4. $2b^2 + b^2 + 3b^2$

5. $2ab \times a^2b \times 3ab^2$

6. $4x^2y + x^2y + 3x^2y$

7. $4xy + x^2y - xy$

8. $4xy + x^2y - xy^2$

9. $3ac \times a^2b \times 4bc$

10. $2bc + a^2b + 4ac$

Combining multiplication and division

A fraction in algebra may be cancelled down in the same way as a numerical fraction. Algebraic fractions may have common factors in the same way as ordinary fractions and can be cancelled by dividing top and bottom by the same number or letter:

$$3xy^2 \div 6xy = \frac{3xy^2}{6xy}$$
$$= \frac{{}^{1}\cancel{3} \times \cancel{x} \times \cancel{y} \times y}{{}_{2}6 \times \cancel{x} \times \cancel{y}}$$
$$= \frac{y}{2}$$

Exercise 7.4

Simplify these fractions. Check that your answer is in the simplest form possible:

1. $\dfrac{6ab}{2}$

2. $\dfrac{6ab}{3}$

3. $\dfrac{6ab}{12}$

4. $\dfrac{6ab}{a}$

5. $\dfrac{6ab}{b}$

6. $\dfrac{6ab}{12a}$

7. $\dfrac{6ab}{3b}$

8. $\dfrac{6ab}{ab}$

9. $\dfrac{6ab}{6ab}$

10. $\dfrac{6ab}{15ab}$

11. $\dfrac{3xy}{6}$

12. $\dfrac{12p^2}{6p}$

13. $\dfrac{4n^2}{6n}$

14. $\dfrac{3ab}{6b}$

15. $\dfrac{4mn}{6n}$

16. $\dfrac{20xy}{4y}$

17. $\dfrac{24ab}{12b}$

18. $\dfrac{3x^2}{x}$

19. $\dfrac{3x^2}{x^2}$

20. $\dfrac{8ab}{2b^2}$

Which number is indexed?

Sometimes it hard to see exactly what the index number is referring to. If this is the case, you must look carefully to see if there are any brackets:

Consider the difference between:

$2a^2$ and $(2a)^2$

$2a^2 = 2 \times a \times a$ and $(2a)^2 = (2a) \times (2a)$

$$= 2 \times a \times 2 \times a$$

$$= 4 \times a \times a \quad \text{or} \quad 4a^2$$

On other occasions, the index number is also indexed.

If you are confused, you must remember that the index number represents a multiplication:

$$(3^2)^2 = (3^2) \times (3^2) \quad \text{and} \quad (b^2)^2 = (b^2) \times (b^2)$$
$$= 3 \times 3 \times 3 \times 3 \qquad\qquad = b \times b \times b \times b$$
$$= 3^4 \qquad\qquad\qquad\qquad = b^4$$

Exercise 7.5

Simplify these, if possible, and check that your answer is in its simplest form:

1. 3^2

2. 3×2^2

3. $(3 \times 2)^2$

4. $(3b)^2$

5. $3 \times a^2$

6. $(4x)^2$

7. $(x^2)^2$

8. $3 \times 2b^3$

9. $3(2b)^3$

10. $2(3b)^3$

Now that you can simplify an expression by adding, subtracting, multiplying and dividing, try this mixed exercise:

Exercise 7.6

1. $2x + 5x$

2. $a \times a \times a$

3. $3ax - ax$

4. $\dfrac{6xy}{3}$

5. $(2b)^2$

6. $c^2x + 2c^2x - 3c^2x$

7. $a^2 \times 3a$

8. $3y \times 2y$

9. $\dfrac{ab}{a}$

10. $\dfrac{b^2}{b}$

11. $\dfrac{(2b)^2}{b}$

12. $\dfrac{3a + 3a}{6a}$

13. $\dfrac{3a \times 3a}{6a}$

14. $\dfrac{3ab + ab - 2ab}{6b}$

15. $3 \times (3b)^2$

16. $3x + 2y - 5x - y$

17. $7 - 3x + 4 - 6x$

18. $\dfrac{3b^2}{3b - b}$

19. $3a \times 2b \times 3bc$

20. $\dfrac{3a \times 2b \times c}{2ab}$

More about algebra

Now that we know the shorthand way to write expressions in algebra, we can start to look at expressions and formulae.

When we know the value of x, we can **substitute** the x to find the value of the **expression.**

There is no reason why x cannot be negative. But before we look further at substitution, we need to be sure of using arithmetic with negative numbers.

Negative numbers

In *So you really want to learn Maths* Book 1 we learnt the following rules about negative numbers:

$3 - 5 = -2$	$3 + 5 = 8$	$3 - (-5) = 3 + 5$ $= 8$	$3 + (-5) = 3 - 5$ $= -2$
$-3 - 5 = -8$	$-3 + 5 = 2$	$-3 - (-5) = -3 + 5$ $= 2$	$-3 + (-5) = -3 - 5$ $= -8$

Exercise 7.7

Calculate the answers to these, using the rules above:

1. $-6 - 4$

2. $6 - 9$

3. $-8 - (+6)$

4. $-5 + (-3)$

5. $-9 - (-4)$

6. $6 + (-2)$

7. $-3 - (+5)$

8. $6 + (-6)$

9. $-7 - (-3)$

10. $8 - 5$

11. −9 − 6

12. 8 − 12

13. −13 + (−5)

14. −7 + (−14)

15. 13 − (−9)

16. −2 + (−7)

17. −7 − (+8)

18. −7 + 9

19. −3 − 8

20. − (−3) − (+8)

Multiplying with negative numbers

If 2 + 2 + 2 + 2 is the same as 4 × 2 = 8

then (−2) + (−2) + (−2) + (−2) = 4 × (−2) = −8

What about (−4) × (−2)?

We cannot really draw −4 lots of −2, but we could say that as −4 is the same as −(+4), then:

$$(-4) \times (-2) = - (+4) \times (-2)$$
$$= - (-8)$$
$$= +8 \text{ or } 8$$

From this we can see that multiplying by a negative changes the sign:

$$4 \times -2 = -8 \qquad -4 \times 2 = -8 \qquad -4 \times -2 = +8$$

Using negative numbers with a calculator

On your calculator you should find a button like this +/- or (−) . The 'change sign' button +/- changes the sign of a number just entered. The 'negative' button (−) is pressed before a number is entered, to make it negative. These must not be confused with the − button which is used **only** for the subtraction operation.

To check the calculations below, you need to follow one of these four key sequences, depending on the type of calculator you have:

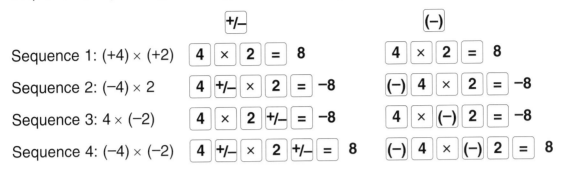

Exercise 7.8

Calculate these and then check your answers with a calculator.

1. 4×3
2. $(-4) \times 5$
3. $(-4) \times (-8)$
4. $5 \times (-6)$
5. $(-3) \times (-5)$

6. $(-2) \times (-9)$
7. 3×8
8. $(-4) \times (+8)$
9. $(+4) \times (-5)$
10. $(-2) \times (-6)$

11. $(-6) \times (-9)$
12. $(-4) \times (+4)$
13. $6 \times (+4)$
14. $(+6) \times (-6)$
15. $(-4) \times (+9)$

16. $5 \times (-5)$
17. $(-7) \times 3$
18. $(-8) \times 2$
19. $(+5) \times (-8)$
20. $(-7) \times (-8)$

Dividing with negative numbers

When you learnt your multiplication tables, you should also have learned to use them to divide:

If $2 \times 4 = 8$
then $8 \div 4 = 2$ and $8 \div 2 = 4$

On the last page we saw that $4 \times (-2) = -8$
And so from this $4 = -8 \div (-2)$ and $-2 = -8 \div 4$

Here's a useful rule to remember:

A negative number divided by another negative number gives a positive result (number).

A negative number divided by a positive number or a positive number divided by a negative number gives a negative result (number).

Thus $8 \div 2 = 4$ $(+8) \div (-2) = (-4)$ or $(+8) \div (+2) = (+4)$ (or 4)

$(-8) \div (-2) = (+4)$ (or 4) $(-8) \div (+2) = (-4)$

Exercise 7.9

Calculate these and then check your answers with a calculator.

1. $16 \div 8$
2. $(-24) \div 8$
3. $36 \div (-9)$
4. $(+25) \div (-5)$
5. $12 \div (-3)$

6. $(-18) \div (-6)$
7. $(-24) \div (-6)$
8. $18 \div 2$
9. $(-72) \div 9$
10. $35 \div (-7)$

11. $(-64) \div 8$
12. $(+45) \div 9$
13. $32 \div (-8)$
14. $(-28) \div 7$
15. $36 \div (-4)$

16. $(-12) \div (-1)$
17. $(-15) \div 3$
18. $20 \div (-4)$
19. $(-24) \div (-12)$
20. $(-100) \div (-10)$

Exercise 7.10: Mixed examples

You may need to remember the BIDMAS rule (see page 23 if you need reminding):

1. $8 \times (-2)$
2. $-4 + 7$
3. $-3 - 6$
4. $14 \div (-2)$
5. $(-3) - (-4)$

6. $35 \div (-5)$
7. $-4 - (-7)$
8. $-3 + 9$
9. $(-3) \times (-6)$
10. $5 + (-10)$

11. $(-6) \times 12$

12. $24 \div 8$

13. $-6 + (-4)$

14. $(-4) \times (-6)$

15. $-7 - 3$

16. $5 + 3$

17. $(-4) \times (-9)$

18. $20 - (-4)$

19. $(-3) \times (-12)$

20. $(-36) \div (-9)$

21. $16 - 8 - 4$

22. $(-24) + 8 - (-3)$

23. $36 \div (-9) \times (-3)$

24. $(+5) - (-5) + (-10)$

25. $12 \times (-3) \div 4$

26. $(-12) \div (-6) \times (-3)$

27. $(-2) + (-6) - (-3)$

28. $18 \div 2 \times (-3)$

29. $(-7) - 9 - (-2)$

30. $5 + (-7) - (-3)$

Substitution

Example: If $x = 3$

(i) $x + 2 = 3 + 2$
$= 5$

(ii) $x - 1 = 3 - 1$
$= 2$

(iii) $2x + 4 = (2 \times 3) + 4$
$= 6 + 4$
$= 10$

In these examples we replaced the letter x with the number 3

This is called **substitution**. It is very important to show this substitution stage in your working out:

First write the **expression**
then show the **substitution**
then do the **working**
and finally **write the** answer.

If x is negative, then take care to remember the rules you learnt about negative numbers above.

Exercise 7.11

1. If $a = 4$, find the value of:
   (a) $a - 2$
   (b) $2a$
   (c) $6 + a$
   (d) $3a - 5$

2. If $b = -3$, find the value of:
   (a) $2b$
   (b) b^2
   (c) $2b^2$
   (d) $(2b)^2$

3. If $x = 5$, find the value of:
   (a) $2x - 2$
   (b) x^2
   (c) $x^2 + 1$
   (d) $3x + 5$

4. If $y = 0$, find the value of:
   (a) $2y$
   (b) y^2
   (c) $y + 4$
   (d) $15 - 3y$

5. If $a = 1$ and $b = 2$, find the value of:
   (a) $a + b$
   (b) $b - a$
   (c) $2a + 3b$
   (d) ab

6. If $x = 2$ and $y = -4$, find the value of:
   (a) $x - y$
   (b) $x + y$
   (c) xy
   (d) $\frac{y}{x}$

7. If $a = 3$ and $b = -2$, find the value of:
   (a) $a + b$
   (b) $a^2 + b^2$
   (c) $2a + 3b$
   (d) ab

8. If $x = 5$ and $y = -3$, find the value of:
   (a) $2x - y$
   (b) $\frac{3y}{x}$
   (c) $x^2 - y^2$
   (d) $3x + 5y$

Remember to do the calculation in the brackets first:

Example: If $a = 3$ and $b = -5$, find the value of $a(b + a)$:
$$a(b + a) = 3(-5 + 3)$$
$$= 3 \times -2$$
$$= -6$$

---

9. If $x = 4$ and $y = -4$, find the value of:
   (a) $x(y + x)$
   (b) $2x(3y - x)$
   (c) $(2x + y) - (x - y)$

10. If $a = -3$, $b = 0$ and $c = 4$, find the value of:
    (a) $b(a + c)$
    (b) $2a(3a + c)$
    (c) $(2b + 3c) - (2a + c)$

11. If $x = 4.5$, $y = 0.2$ and $z = 3.1$, find the value of:
    (a) xy
    (b) $2xz$
    (c) $x(2y + z)$

12. If $r = 30$, $s = 10$ and $t = 5$, find the value of:

    (a) $\frac{rs}{2}$
    (b) $\frac{r}{3} + \frac{t}{2}$
    (c) $\frac{t(r + s)}{2}$

Formulae

We have been substituting values into expressions. Now we are going to look at formulae. A **formula** is like an expression but, like an equation, it **contains** an **equal** sign:

Average: $\text{Mean} = \dfrac{\text{total}}{\text{number of items}}$

Area: $A = bh$

Perimeter: $P = 2a + 2b$

Exercise 7.12: Substituting into formulae

1. Consider the formula $P = 2a + 2b$
    (a) Find P when $a = 2$ and $b = 6$
    (b) Find P when $a = 100$ and $b = 50$
    (c) Find P when $a = 0.6$ and $b = 1.4$
    (d) Find a when $P = 10$ and $b = 3$
    (e) Find b when $P = 120$ and $b = 45$

2. Consider the formula $A = \dfrac{ab}{2}$
    (a) Find A when $a = 4$ and $b = 5$
    (b) Find A when $a = 100$ and $b = 80$
    (c) Find A when $a = 0.4$ and $b = 1.5$
    (d) Find a when $A = 10$ and $b = 4$
    (e) Find b when $A = 150$ and $a = 30$

3. Consider the formula $A = \dfrac{h(a+b)}{2}$
    (a) Find A when $a = 4$, $b = 5$ and $h = 8$
    (b) Find A when $a = 20$, $b = 50$ and $h = 40$
    (c) Find A when $a = 0.3$, $b = 0.55$ and $h = 1.8$
    (d) Find a when $A = 20$, $h = 10$ and $b = 3$
    (e) Find b when $A = 150$, $a = 30$ and $h = 5$

4. Consider the formula $X = v^2 - u^2$
    (a) Find X when $v = 10$ and $u = -8$
    (b) Find X when $v = 0.4$ and $u = 0.4$
    (c) Find v when $X = 9$ and $u = 4$
    (d) Find u when $X = 25$ and $v = 13$

Exercise 7.13: Writing formulae

We can use more than one letter when writing a formula. This is extremely useful when you are writing a formulae which represents a story puzzle. See what we mean below.

Example: If I have £a and I am given £b, find P, if P is the number of pounds I have now.

$P = a + b$

---

1. My brother's age is x years and my age is y years. Write a formula for S, the sum of our ages.

2. I have a piece of string s metres long and I cut off t metres. If L metres are left, write a formula for L.

3. There are m families in our road and each family has n children. Write a formula for C, the total number of children in the road.

4. On Monday I collect c conkers from each of t trees. On Tuesday I go to all the same trees but collect one fewer from each. I collect C conkers in total. Write a formula for C.

5. On my paper round I visit 50 houses. x houses have one paper every day of the week, but the rest of the houses have a total of y papers over the whole week. I deliver P papers over the week. Write a formula for P.

6. In my class of 24, g boys wear glasses all the time and s boys wear glasses some of the time. b boys do not wear glasses. Write a formula for b.

7. (a) What is the total cost, c pence, of y ice creams at x pence each?
    (b) What is the total cost, C pounds, of y ice creams at x pence each?

8. I grew a centimetres last year and b centimetres this year. I am now 1.6 metres tall. Two years ago I was T m tall. Write a formula for T.

9. I buy m magazines costing p pence each. Write a formula for F, where F is the change that I get from £5.

10. The total cost of a school trip is £150 for the coach hire plus £4.50 per child.
    (a) Write a formula for C_1, the total cost, of taking p pupils.
    (b) Write a formula for C_2, the cost per child, of taking p pupils.

11. In a class of 24 children p pupils have 2 pets, q pupils have 1 pet and the rest have no pets.

(a) Write a formula for p, the total number of pets the pupils in the class have altogether.

(b) What would the formula be if p pupils had no pets, q pupils had 1 pet and the rest had 2 pets?

12. Do you remember the man going to St Ives with his wives? Suppose that man had x wives, each wife had y cats and each cat had z kits, then T in total were going to St Ives. Write a formula for T.

Exercise 7.14: Shape formulae

Looking at diagrams can help us to write a formula:

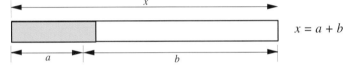

$x = a + b$

1. Write a formula for x for each of these diagrams:

(a)

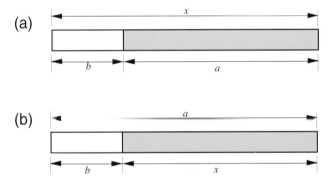

(b)

(c)

2. Write a formula for x for each of these diagrams:

(a)

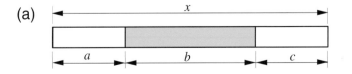

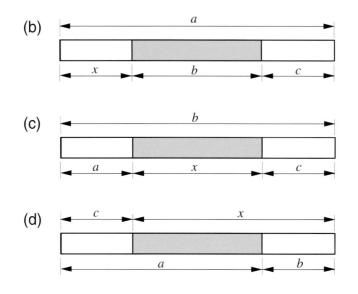

(b)

(c)

(d)

3. Write a formula for (a) A, the area and (b) P, the perimeter of this rectangle:

4. Write a formula for (a) P, the perimeter and (b) A, the area of this shape:

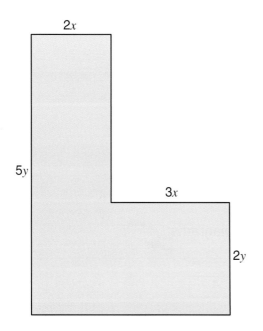

5. Write a formula for (a) *P*, the perimeter and (b) *A*, the area of this shape:

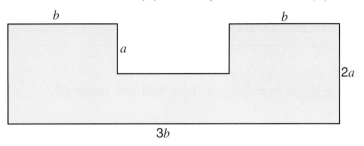

6. Write a formula for (a) *P*, the perimeter and (b) *A*, the area of this shape:

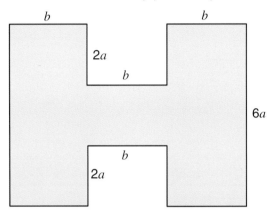

7. Write a formula for (a) *P*, the perimeter and (b) *A*, the area of this shape:

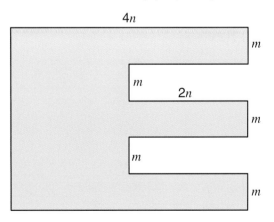

8. Draw a shape of your own that has an area of $20ab$. Write a formula for its perimeter.

9. Draw a shape of your own that has a perimeter of $8a + 10b$. Write a formula for its area.

Exercise 7.15: Extension questions- Harder substitution

Substitute fractions into these expressions:

Example:

If $x = \dfrac{1}{2}$, $y = \dfrac{2}{3}$, $z = 1\dfrac{1}{5}$, find the value of $\dfrac{x+y}{z}$

$$\frac{x+y}{z} = \frac{\frac{1}{2} + \frac{2}{3}}{1\frac{1}{5}}$$

First substitute the fractions into the expression.

$$= \frac{\frac{3+4}{6}}{\frac{6}{5}}$$

Then simplify.

$$= \frac{7}{6} \div \frac{6}{5}$$

$$= \frac{7}{6} \times \frac{5}{6}$$

$$= \frac{35}{36}$$

1. If $x = \dfrac{1}{2}$, $y = \dfrac{1}{3}$, $z = \dfrac{1}{5}$, find the value of:

(a) $x + y + z$

(d) $\dfrac{x^2 + y^2}{z^2}$

(b) $2z + (x + y)$

(e) $z(2x + y)$

(c) $x^2 + y^2 - z^2$

(f) $\dfrac{xz}{2y}$

2. If $a = \dfrac{3}{5}$, $b = \dfrac{2}{3}$, $c = \dfrac{1}{4}$, find the value of:

(a) $a^2 + bc$

(d) $\dfrac{bc}{a+b}$

(b) $a - \dfrac{c}{b}$

(e) $\dfrac{a+b}{b+c}$

(c) $\dfrac{2bc}{a^2}$

(f) $2ab - bc$

Now substitute decimals. Remember it is important to show every stage of your working:

3.   If $s = 2.5$, $t = 0.4$, $u = 0.7$, $v = 0.9$ find the value of:

(a) $\dfrac{v - u}{t}$

(d) $\dfrac{u + v}{2s}$

(b) $u^2 + st^2$

(e) $\dfrac{st}{v - u}$

(c) $\dfrac{v^2 - u^2}{2s}$

(f) $\dfrac{s(v - u)}{u + t}$

Exercise 7.16: Summary exercise

1.   Simplify: (a) $m + m + m + m - m$ (b) $4a + 3b - 2a - 4b$

2.   Simplify: (a) $b^2 + 2b^2 - b^2$ (b) $b^2 \times 2b^3 \times b$

3.   Simplify: (a) $\dfrac{3ab}{a}$ (c) $\dfrac{p^2}{p}$

(b) $\dfrac{2xy}{12x}$ (d) $\dfrac{8n^3}{n}$

4.   Simplify: (a) $(3a)^2$ (b) $3 \times (2a^2)$

5.   Calculate the answer to:
(a) $9 - 4$ (d) $(-2) \times (-4)$ (g) $(-4) \div (-4)$

(b) $-8 - 3$ (e) $36 \div (-4)$ (h) $6 \times (-4)$

(c) $-4 + (-3)$ (f) $(-8) \times (+3)$ (i) $(-2) - (-4)$

6.   (a) If $x = 5$, find: (i) $2x$ (ii) x^2 (iii) $2x^2$ (iv) $(2x)^2$

(b) If $x = -3$, find: (i) $2x$ (ii) x^2 (iii) $2x^2$ (iv) $(2x)^2$

7.   If $a = 2$ and $b = -6$, find:
(a) $a + b$ (b) $a - b$ (c) $2ab$ (d) $\dfrac{a - b}{4a}$

8.   Consider the formula $P = 2a(a - b)$
(a) Find P when $a = 10$ and $b = 5$
(b) Find P when $a = 0.6$ and $b = -0.4$
(c) Find b when $P = 2.8$ and $a = 1.4$

9. Write a formula for N, the total number of legs on h hens and c cows.

10. All three sides of an equilateral triangle have length a cm.
(a) Write a formula for P, the perimeter of the triangle in cm.
(b) Write a formula for Q, the perimeter of the triangle in metres.

11. Write a formula for P, the perimeter of this shape:

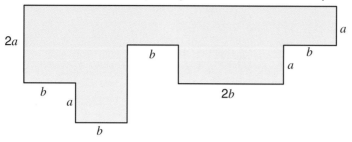

End of chapter 7 activity: Maths from stars 1 – Symmetry

1. (a) Copy and complete this pattern so that it has the two lines of symmetry shown:

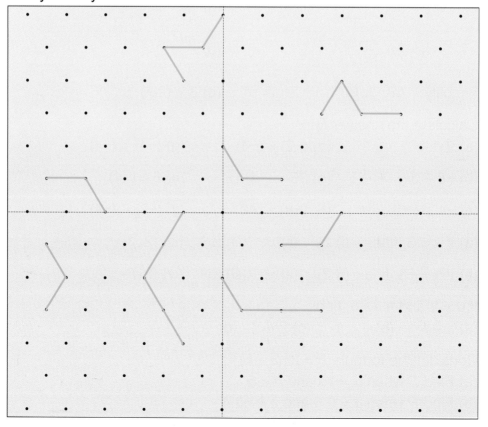

(b) Colour it so that the whole design still has two lines of symmetry.

2. Now design some star patterns of your own on triangular spotted paper.

3. (a) Copy and complete this pattern so that it has the two lines of symmetry shown:

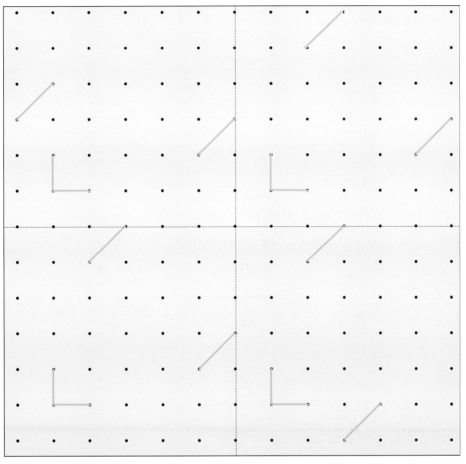

(b) Colour it so that the whole design still has two lines of symmetry.

4. Design some star patterns of your own on square spotted paper.

5. This design came from the Alhambra Palace. Investigate some more of its tiling patterns.

Chapter 8: Angles and polygons

An angle is formed when two straight lines meet at a point. Angles can be acute, right, obtuse or reflex:

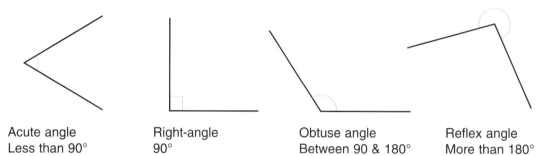

Acute angle
Less than 90°

Right-angle
90°

Obtuse angle
Between 90 & 180°

Reflex angle
More than 180°

Let us remind ourselves about what else we already know about angles:

Angles in a circle (at a point) add up to 360°

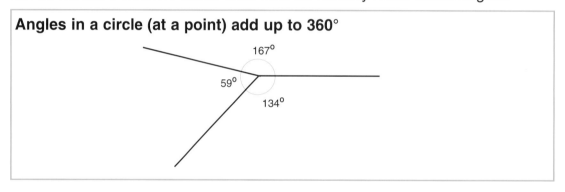

Angles on a straight line add up to 180°

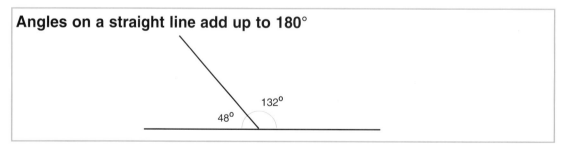

Angles in a triangle add up to 180°

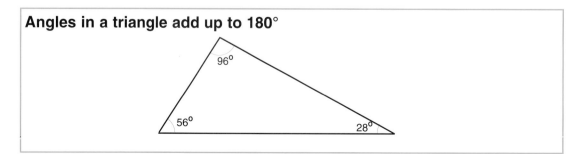

Vertically opposite angles are equal

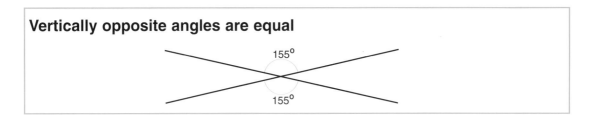

Base angles of an isosceles triangle are equal
Angles in an equilateral triangle all equal 60°

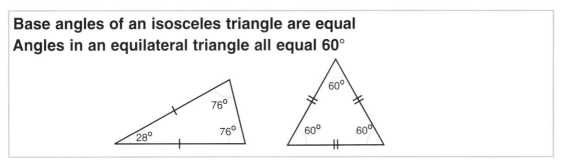

If we only know some of the angles in a figure, we can use these facts to calculate others:

Exercise 8.1

Example:

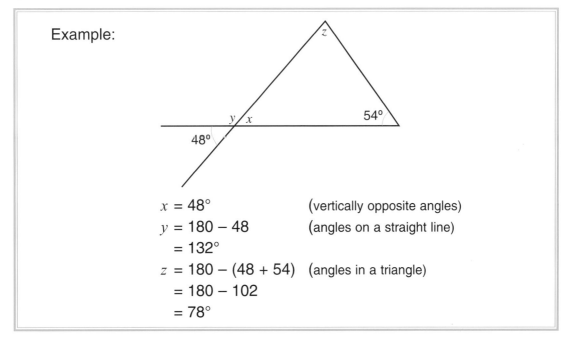

$x = 48°$ (vertically opposite angles)

$y = 180 - 48$ (angles on a straight line)

   $= 132°$

$z = 180 - (48 + 54)$ (angles in a triangle)

   $= 180 - 102$

   $= 78°$

Follow these four rules when answering the following questions:

1. Draw the diagram.
2. Write down each angle fact, stating the reason you have done so.
3. Work down the page, equals signs going under each other.
4. Show all your calculations, however simple.

Find all the numbers marked by letters in these questions, following the rules:

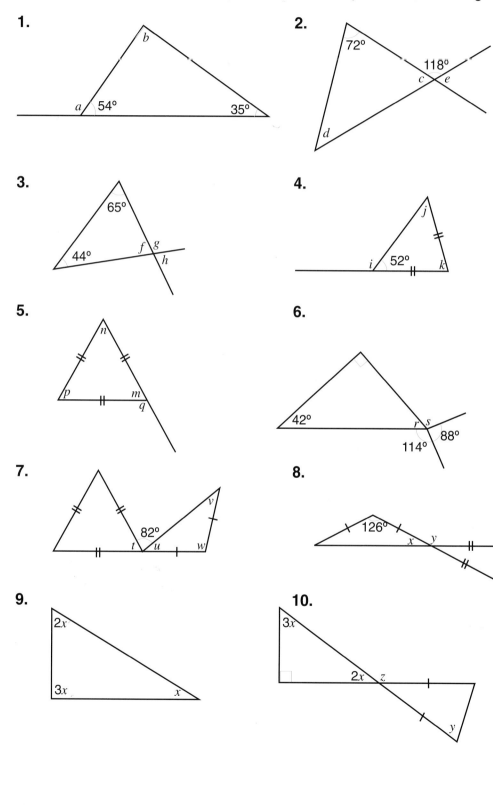

1.

2.

3.

4.

5.

6.

7.

8.

9.

10.

11.

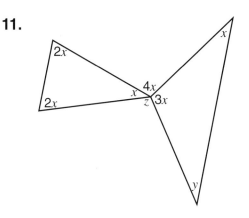

Parallel lines

Two lines are parallel if, however far you extend them, they will never meet and they remain the same distance apart.

These two lines are parallel:

If you cut parallel lines with another line, you produce some angles. Some of these angles are equal:

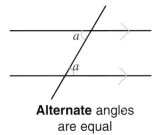

Alternate angles
are equal

Corresponding angles
are equal

The angles are either acute or obtuse. You can see that the four obtuse angles are all equal and that the four acute angles are all equal. Because the obtuse angle and the acute angle are adjacent angles on a straight line, they must add up to 180°. This gives us a third pair of angles special to parallel lines:

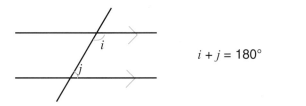

$i + j = 180°$

Co-interior angles
add up to 180°

These angles are sometimes called **supplementary angles**, which actually means that they add up to 180°, and sometimes **allied angles**. Nowadays they are usually known as interior or **co-interior**. We will refer to them as co-interior so as not to confuse them with interior angles of a polygon.

Exercise 8.2

1. State whether these pairs of angles are alternate, corresponding, co-interior, or none of these:

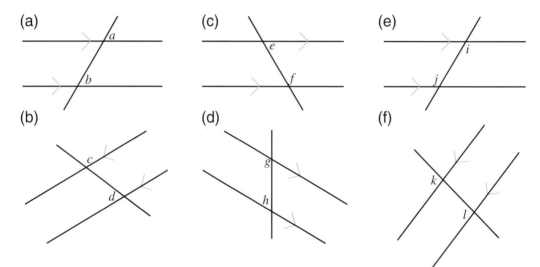

2. Find the lettered angle in each of these diagrams and say whether it is alternate to, corresponding to or co-interior with the other angle given:

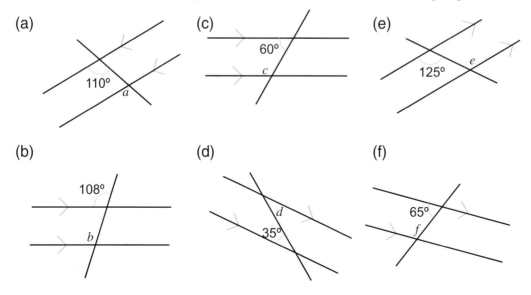

3. In this diagram find as many pairs of equal angles as you can. For each pair say why they are equal (e.g. corresponding angles or alternate angles).

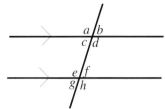

4. Use the same diagram as in q.3 but, this time, find as many pairs of angles as you can that add up to 180°. For each pair give the angle reason for their relationship (e.g. angles on a straight line or co-interior angles).

5. Find the lettered angles in this diagram. Write your answers in the order that you calculate the angles, which will not necessarily be in the order a, b, c etc. Give the reason for each answer. (You may need **vertically opposite angles** and **angles on a straight line** in addition to the three special cases for parallel lines.)

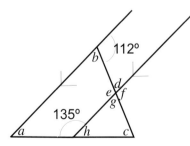

6. Repeat q.5 for the angles in this diagram:

Naming angles

In the exercises you have done so far the missing angles have been marked by letters. In more complicated diagrams it is customary to mark the corners or vertices with capital letters. Angles can then be described by the two lines that join at the point:

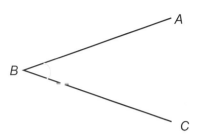

This is the angle *ABC*.
It is the angle at point *B*,
where *AB* meets *BC*.

Look at this triangle; three angles meet at point *A*:

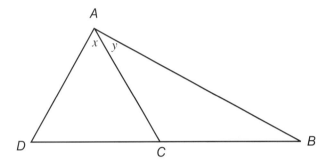

Run your finger over to diagram to make sure that you understand that:

Angle *BAC* is marked y
Angle *DAC* is marked x
Angle *BAD* is $x + y$

Exercise 8.3

1. Copy the diagram above:
    (a) Colour angle *ACD* red.
    (b) Colour angle *BCA* blue.
    (c) Colour angle *CBA* yellow.

2. Copy this diagram:

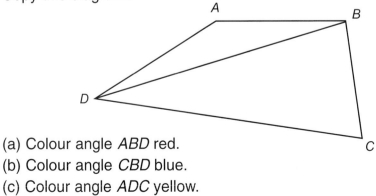

    (a) Colour angle *ABD* red.
    (b) Colour angle *CBD* blue.
    (c) Colour angle *ADC* yellow.

In Exercise 8.1 you saw that by knowing only one or two angles in a diagram you actually know enough about angles to find many, or even all, of the other angles. Now you know about parallel lines you can find even more angles. In mathematics we have to be able to justify our statements. In your answers to the following angle questions give the **reasons** for your answers:

Exercise 8.4

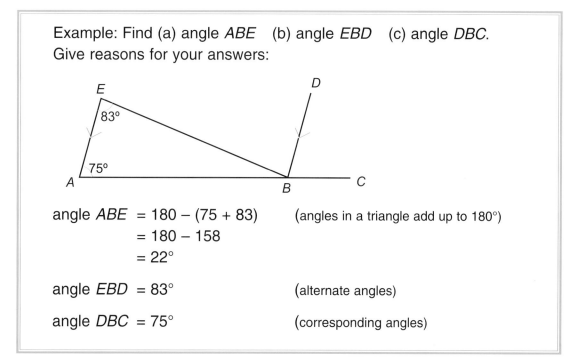

Example: Find (a) angle *ABE*   (b) angle *EBD*   (c) angle *DBC*.
Give reasons for your answers:

angle *ABE* = 180 − (75 + 83)   (angles in a triangle add up to 180°)
           = 180 − 158
           = 22°

angle *EBD* = 83°   (alternate angles)

angle *DBC* = 75°   (corresponding angles)

1.   In this diagram *AB* is parallel to CE and angle *ABD* = 72°:

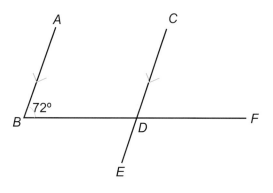

Find, giving reasons:
(a) angle *CDF*   (b) angle *CDB*   (c) angle *FDE*

2. In this diagram *AB* is parallel to *CD*, *AD* = *CD* and angle *BAD* = 32°:

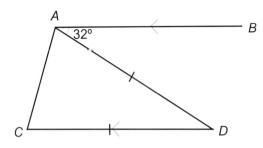

Find, giving reasons: (a) angle *ADC*   (b) angle *DCA*

3. In this diagram *AD* is parallel to *EH*, angle *DCH* = 65° and angle *BFH* = 80°:

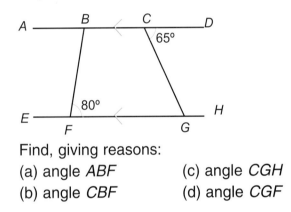

Find, giving reasons:
(a) angle *ABF*   (c) angle *CGH*
(b) angle *CBF*   (d) angle *CGF*

4. In this diagram *AB* is parallel to *DE*, angle *BAC* = 44° and angle *EDC* = 87°:

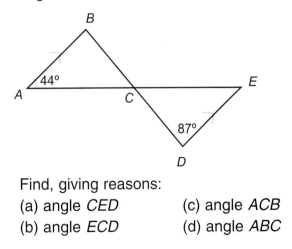

Find, giving reasons:
(a) angle *CED*   (c) angle *ACB*
(b) angle *ECD*   (d) angle *ABC*

5. In this diagram *ABC* is an equilateral triangle and *AB* is parallel to *DC*:

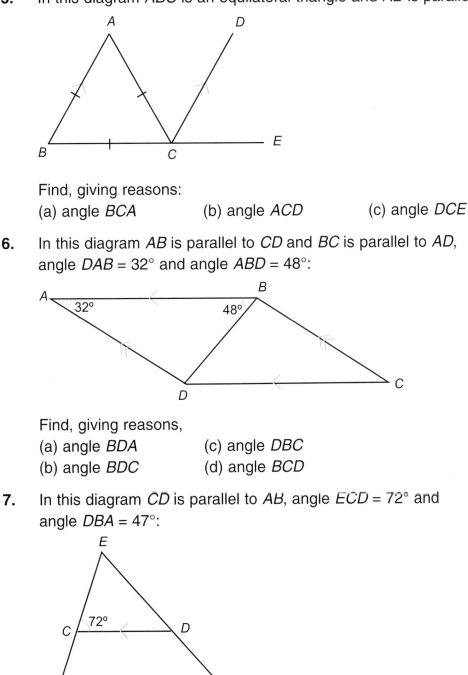

Find, giving reasons:

(a) angle *BCA* (b) angle *ACD* (c) angle *DCE*

6. In this diagram *AB* is parallel to *CD* and *BC* is parallel to *AD*, angle *DAB* = 32° and angle *ABD* = 48°:

Find, giving reasons,

(a) angle *BDA* (c) angle *DBC*
(b) angle *BDC* (d) angle *BCD*

7. In this diagram *CD* is parallel to *AB*, angle *ECD* = 72° and angle *DBA* = 47°:

Find angle *CED*. Clearly show your working and state any other angles that you have had to find first. Give reasons for all your calculations.

8. In this diagram *AE* is parallel to *FK,* angle *BGI* = 74° and angle *DJK* = 105°:

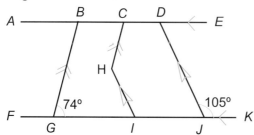

Find, giving reasons, and stating any other angles that you may have to find first:

(a) angle *GBC*   (c) angle *BCH*

(b) angle *CDJ*   (d) obtuse angle *CHI*

Polygons

Polygons are multi-sided shapes. The name comes from the Greek *poly* meaning 'many' and *gonia* meaning 'angles'. We frequently meet the prefix *poly* in words such as polyglot (a person who speaks many languages), polychrome (having several colours) and of course polygon (a shape with many angles / sides).

Polygons can be either regular or irregular. Regular polygons have all their sides the same length and all their interior angles equal:

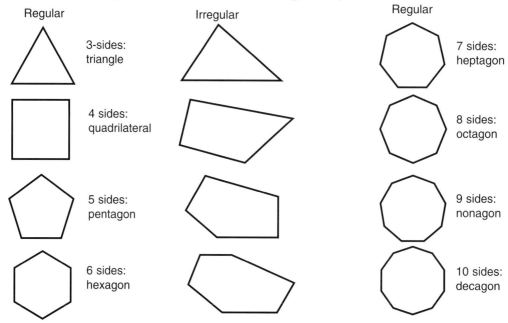

There are three angles that are of particular interest in a polygon:

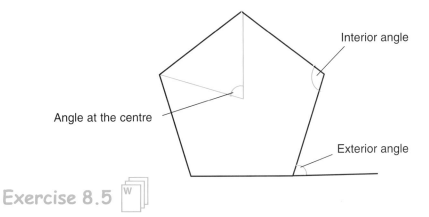

Interior angle

Angle at the centre

Exterior angle

Exercise 8.5

1.   On the worksheet for Exercise 8.5 you will find several polygons. On each one mark an exterior angle, an interior angle and the angle at the centre. Give each polygon its correct name and state whether it is regular or irregular.

2.   On the same worksheet you will see several polygons with all their exterior angles drawn. For each polygon measure each exterior angle and add them up. What do you notice ?

     Complete the word formula: Sum of exterior angles of any polygon = ...

The above formula works for any polygon, but for a **regular polygon all the angles**, and thus **all the exterior angles**, are **equal**.

So we can say: exterior angle $= \dfrac{360°}{n}$ (where n is the number of sides)

You can use the above formula to find the size of one exterior angle of a regular polygon.

Example:

Find the exterior angle of a regular nonagon.

   $n = 9$

Exterior angle $= \dfrac{360°}{n}$

$= \dfrac{360°}{9}$

$= 40°$

---

3. Give the size of an exterior angle for a regular:
    (a) pentagon   (d) hexagon
    (b) octagon   (e) heptagon
    (c) 18 sided polygon   (f) 20 sided polygon

You can rearrange the formula to find the number of sides of a regular polygon if you know the exterior angle:

> If   exterior angle $= x$
>
> Then it follows that $n = \frac{360}{x}$ (where n is the number of sides)

Example:

If the exterior angle of a regular polygon is 72°, how many sides has the polygon?

$$n = \frac{360}{\text{ext.angle}}$$

$$= \frac{360}{72}$$

$$= 5 \text{ sides. It is a pentagon.}$$

---

4. Find the number of sides in these regular polygons:

    (a) exterior angle is 40°
    (b) exterior angle is 60°
    (c) exterior angle is 30°
    (d) exterior angle is 90°
    (e) exterior angle is 20°
    (f) exterior angle is 15°

5. Why can a regular polygon not have an exterior angle of 65°?

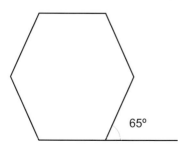

65°

6. Can a regular polygon have an exterior angle that is an obtuse angle?

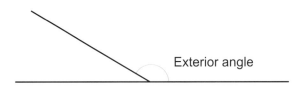

Exterior angle

Sum of interior angles of a polygon

Having found a formula for the angle sum of the exterior angles, we are now going to try and find a similar rule for the interior angles. Let's start by reminding ourselves what we have already discovered about interior angles.

We know that the angle sum of a triangle is 180°. So a good place to start is to divide the other polygons into triangles and then try and find a rule:

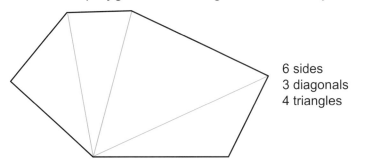

6 sides
3 diagonals
4 triangles

By the end of the next exercise you will have discovered the rule for interior angles.

Exercise 8.6

1. On the worksheet you will see several polygons. The first two have been divided into triangles. Divide the remaining polygons into triangles in the same way.

2. Fill in the table on the worksheet. What relationship do you notice between the number of triangles and the number of sides of the polygons?

You should have seen that:

Sum of interior angles of any polygon = $180°(n - 2)$

(where n is the number of sides)

Example: Find the sum of the interior angles of an octagon.

$n = 8$

Sum of interior angles $= 180\,(n - 2)$
$= 180\,(8 - 2)$
$= 180 \times 6$
$= 1080°$

3. Write down the sum of the interior angles of a:
(a) pentagon   (d) heptagon
(b) nonagon   (e) 18 sided polygon
(c) decagon   (f) 20 sided polygon

Finding the interior angle of a regular polygon

The formula, sum of interior angles $= 180°\,(n - 2)$, is true for all polygons, but **regular** polygons have all their angles equal. You can use the formula below to find the interior angle of a regular polygon:

Interior angle $= \dfrac{180\,(n - 2)}{n}$ (Remember that n is the number of sides.)

In practice it is easier to remember that the interior and exterior angles are on a straight line and therefore add up to 180°.

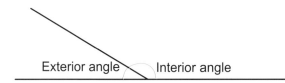

Exterior angle   Interior angle

So in fact what you can do is use the formula for finding an exterior angle and then subtract the answer from 180°. This will give you the interior angle.

Exterior angle $= \dfrac{360°}{n}$ (where n is the number of sides)

Interior angle $= 180° -$ exterior angle

Exercise 8.7

Example: What is the interior angle of a regular nonagon?

$$n = 9$$

$$\text{Exterior angle} = \frac{360}{n}$$

$$= \frac{360}{9}$$

$$= 40°$$

$$\text{Interior angle} = 180 - 40$$

$$= 140°$$

1. Give the interior angle of a regular:
   (a) hexagon
   (b) nonagon
   (c) heptagon
   (d) dodecagon
   (e) 16 sided polygon
   (f) 15 sided polygon

2. Here is a diagram showing part of a regular polygon:

   (a) The interior angle is five times as large as the exterior angle. How many sides has the polygon?

   (b) If the interior angle were 11 times the size of the exterior angle, how many sides would the polygon have?

To find the number of sides in the following questions, first find the exterior angle and then use the formula to find n.

3. Give the number of sides a regular polygon has if:
   (a) the interior angle is 140°
   (b) the interior angle is 156°
   (c) the interior angle is 90°
   (d) the interior angle is 150°

4.   Give the number of sides a regular polygon has if:
      (a) the interior angle is twice times the exterior angle.
      (b) the interior angle is three times the exterior angle.
      (c) the interior angle is four times the exterior angle.
      (d) the interior angle is seven times the exterior angle.

5.   The angles at the centre of a regular polygon will all be equal. Because
      they are angles at a point they must add up to 360°. Give the size of an
      angle at the centre of a regular:
      (a) octagon   (d) decagon
      (b) pentagon   (e) dodecagon
      (c) 20 sided polygon   (f) 24 sided polygon

Finding angles in polygons

We can use the information we have learnt about polygons to solve even more
angle problems. We will now look at isosceles triangles. A good starting point is
to recall that all the sides of a regular polygon are equal.

Remember, where n is the number of sides of the polygon:

> **Sum of interior angles** of any polygon = 180° $(n - 2)$
> **Sum of exterior angles** of any polygon = 360°

For a regular polygon we also know the following formulae:

Exterior angle = $\dfrac{360°}{n}$ **Interior** angle = 180° − ext. angle

Number of sides (n) = $\dfrac{360}{\text{exterior angle}}$ Angle at the **centre** = $\dfrac{360°}{n}$

It is also worth noting that a regular polygon **can** have some diagonals
parallel to its sides.

This one is parallel   This one is not parallel

So, equipped with all this information, you should now be able to tackle the
next exercise with ease.

Exercise 8.8

Find all angles in these diagrams involving polygons. Give reasons for all your calculations:

Here's a clue: It is a good idea always to start by finding the exterior and interior angles.

Example: *ABCDEFGH* is a regular octagon.

Find: (a) angle *GFE*   (b) angle *FGE*   (c) angle *GHA*   (d) angle *HGB*

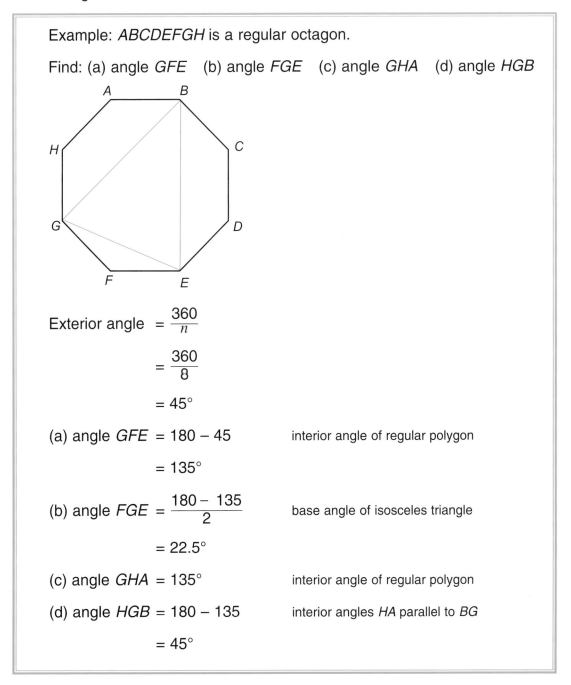

Exterior angle $= \dfrac{360}{n}$

$$= \dfrac{360}{8}$$

$$= 45°$$

(a) angle *GFE* $= 180 - 45$ interior angle of regular polygon

$$= 135°$$

(b) angle *FGE* $= \dfrac{180 - 135}{2}$ base angle of isosceles triangle

$$= 22.5°$$

(c) angle *GHA* $= 135°$ interior angle of regular polygon

(d) angle *HGB* $= 180 - 135$ interior angles *HA* parallel to *BG*

$$= 45°$$

Look carefully at the working in the example on page 163. This is how your answers should look.

The calculations are not difficult but working out which calculation is which is important. That is why you should write down each step carefully.

1. *ABCDE* is a regular pentagon:

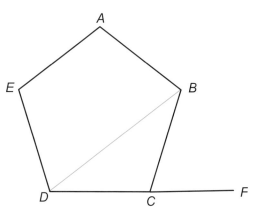

Find: (a) angle *BCF*
(b) angle *BCD*
(c) angle *CBD*
(d) angle *ABD*

2. *BCDEFG* is a regular hexagon:

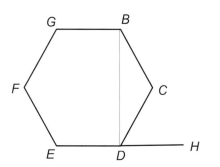

Find: (a) angle *CDH*
(b) angle *BCD*
(c) angle *CDB*
(d) angle *BDE*

3. *ABCDEF* is a regular hexagon, with centre *O*:

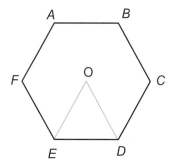

Find: (a) angle *EOD*
(b) angle *ODE*
(c) angle *ABC*
(d) angle *CDO*

4. *ABCDEFGH* is a regular octagon with centre *O*:

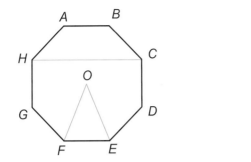

    Find: (a) angle *COD*
          (b) angle *FEA*
          (c) angle *ABC*
          (d) angle *BCO*

5. *ABCDE* is a regular pentagon with centre *O*:

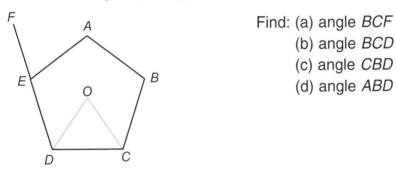

    Find: (a) angle *BCF*
          (b) angle *BCD*
          (c) angle *CBD*
          (d) angle *ABD*

Exercise 8.9: Maths from Stars 2 – Calculating angles

Earlier in Chapter 7 we found a tessellating pattern of stars and hexagons. Now we know how to calculate angles of a regular hexagon, we can look more closely at the angles:

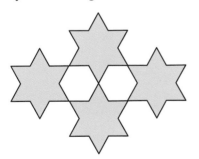

1. What is the interior angle of a regular hexagon?

2. Look at the middle of the pattern above. Calculate the size of the acute angle inside the six-pointed star.

3. The six-pointed star is an irregular dodecagon. What is the interior angle sum of a dodecagon?

4. Calculate the reflex angle inside the six-pointed star.

5. Draw a six-pointed star on triangular spotted paper and check that your answers are correct.

Here is a regular pentagon with all its diagonals drawn in. This design is known as a pentagram and has been linked with magic for centuries:

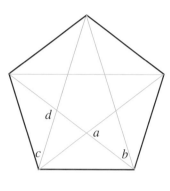

The pentagram from the *Transendental Magic* of Eliphas Levi (1810–1875)

6. What is the interior angle of a regular pentagon?

7. Now calculate the angles *a*, *b*, *c* and *d* in the pentagram above.

This eight-pointed star is an important part of Islamic tiling patterns. It is made from two squares and in its centre is a regular octagon:

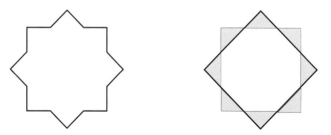

8. What is the interior angle of a regular octagon?

9. Look at the eight-pointed star pattern on the the right. Calculate all the angles in one of the green isosceles triangles.

10. The eight-pointed star is an irregular 16-sided figure. What is the interior angle sum of a 16-sided figure?

11. Calculate the size of the reflex angle in the eight-pointed star.

Eight-pointed stars can be put together to make a pattern of tiles. Here is a part of a tiling pattern from the Alhambra Palace in Spain:

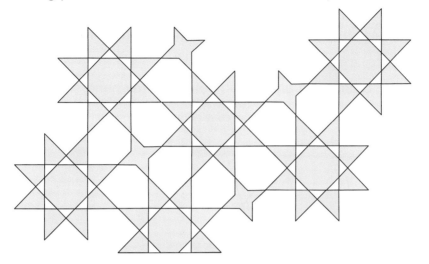

12. The new eight-pointed star has eight kites forming its eight points. Calculate the angles in the kites.

13. Between the four eight-pointed stars there are four irregular hexagons that meet and form an irregular octagon. Calculate all the angles in the hexagon and the octagon.

Exercise 8.10: Extension questions

1. To cover a room with tiles the angles at the corners must add up to 360°.

Squares are obvious shapes for tiles because their corners are 90°.

(a) What other regular polygons could be used for tiles?
(b) There is no reason why you could not tile a room with 2 different tiles.

Here is a common pattern:

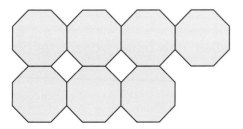

Explain, using the rules you know about angles of a polygon, why the octagon and the square can be used together to tile an area.

(c) Can you find three tiles, which are all regular polygons, and which fit together exactly around a point? Could you tile an area with these three tiles? Is there more than one combination? (The worksheet for Exercise 8.6 q.2 may help you with this.)

2. I was drawing a hexagon on my computer and my hand slipped with the drawing tool:

Instead of this: I drew this:

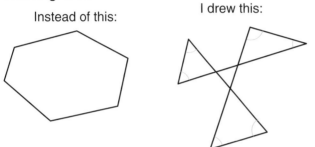

(a) What is the sum of the interior angles of the proper hexagon? What is the sum of the exterior angles?

(b) Can you work out the sum of the marked angles in the figure that I actually drew?

(c) Draw similar figures with eight lines, ten lines and twelve lines. Mark the equivalent angles. Can you work out the sum of those angles in each figure?

(d) What can you deduce from your answers?

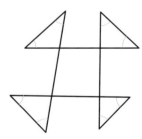

3. Three regular polygons meet like this:

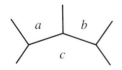

If *a* and *b* have the same number of sides, how many sides does polygon *c* have? Is there more than one answer?

4. Hexagons are fascinating because they tessellate. Honeybees use them to make their honeycomb. They are made out of six equilateral triangles. Let us look at patterns of hexagons:

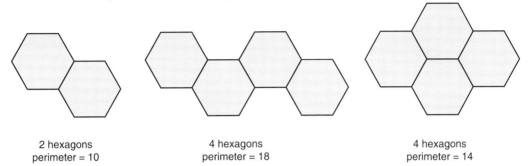

2 hexagons
perimeter = 10

4 hexagons
perimeter = 18

4 hexagons
perimeter = 14

There should be a connection between the number of hexagons and the perimeter of the whole shape. However, the four hexagons have two different perimeters. What else is different about them? The shape with the larger perimeter is in a row, while the shape with the smaller perimeter is in a block with two points completely enclosed in the shape. Let us look at some more:

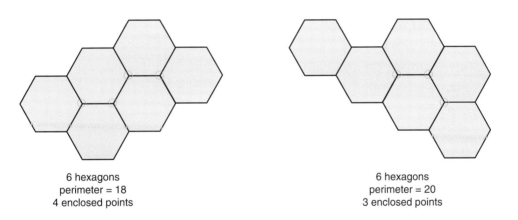

6 hexagons
perimeter = 18
4 enclosed points

6 hexagons
perimeter = 20
3 enclosed points

(a) On triangular spotted paper draw as many groups of four hexagons as you can. Which has the shortest perimeter?

(b) Now draw as many different combinations of five hexagons as you can. Which has the shortest perimeter?

(c) Draw some more hexagon combinations. Count the perimeter and the enclosed points for each.

(d) Put your results in a table.

(e) If n is the number of hexagons, and p is the number of enclosed points, can you write a formula for the perimeter in terms of n and p?

Exercise 8.11 : Summary exercise

1. Copy this diagram 3 times and mark a pair of alternate angles on the first diagram, a pair of corresponding angles on the second and a pair of co-interior angles on the third:

2. Find the angles marked by the letters in this diagram and give reasons for your answers:

3. In this diagram *AB* is parallel to *CD* and *BCE* is a straight line. We also know that angle *BAC* = 44° and angle *DCE* = 118°:

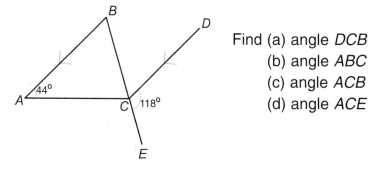

Find (a) angle *DCB*
(b) angle *ABC*
(c) angle *ACB*
(d) angle *ACE*

4. (a) What is the exterior angle of a regular 9-sided polygon?
(b) What is the interior angle of regular 15-sided polygon?

5. Write down the number of sides these regular polygons have with:
(a) an exterior angle equal to 36°
(b) an interior angle equal to 160°

6. What is the sum of the interior angles of a 13-sided polygon?

7. *ABCDE* is a regular pentagon.
Find (a) angle *CDF*
(b) angle *BCD*
(c) angle *ADE*
(d) angle *CDA*

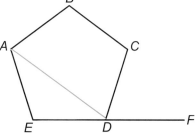

8. In this diagram *AE* is parallel to *BD*, *AB* = *EB*, angle *EBD* = 54° and angle *DCB* = 37°:

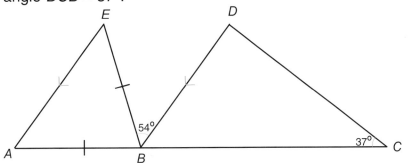

Find, giving reasons, and stating any other angles that you have had to find first:

(a) angle *BEA*   (c) angle *ABE*

(b) angle *DBC*   (d) angle *BDC*

9. In this diagram *AC* is parallel to *DH* and angle *BEF* = 54°, angle *BFG* = 73° and *BF* = *FG*

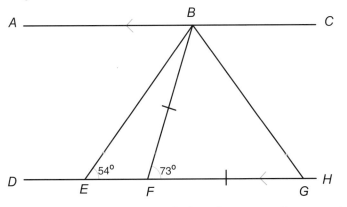

Find, giving reasons and showing any other angles that you have to find:

(a) angle *ABE*   (b) angle *FBE*   (c) angle *GBC*

End of chapter 8 activity: Nets of prisms

In *So you really want to learn Maths* Book 1 we looked at the nets of a cube and cuboid. In this activity we are going to construct the nets of some prisms. A prism is a solid object with a constant cross section (that means it can be cut into equal shaped slices). You are probably familiar with a triangular prism from your science lessons.

Hexagonal prism of edge 2 cm and height 4 cm.

First we need to draw the top of the prism; look on the next page for instructions. We know that a hexagon is made of six equilateral triangles. Draw the triangles with sides of 2 cm.

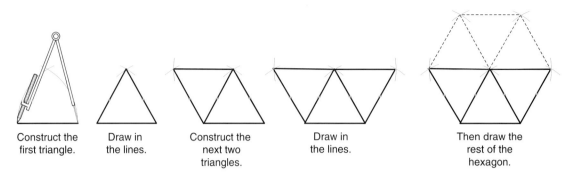

Construct the first triangle.   Draw in the lines.   Construct the next two triangles.   Draw in the lines.   Then draw the rest of the hexagon.

The sides of the prism will all be rectangles of width 2 cm and height 4 cm. The bottom of the prism will be another hexagon. Your net should end up looking like this:

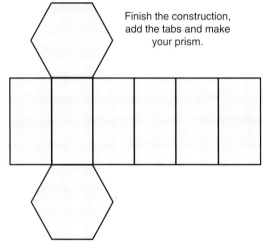

Finish the construction, add the tabs and make your prism.

Rhomboid

A rhomboid is a prism with a cross section that is a rhombus. Constructing the rhombus is similar to constructing the hexagon, except that you only need two triangles. A net for a rhomboid of side 3 cm and height 4 cm looks like this:

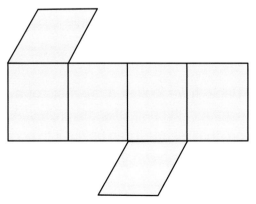

Construct the net and make your rhomboid.

Chapter 9: Percentages

Fractions, decimals and percentages

When we looked at fractions and decimals in chapter 3, we also looked at percentages. We saw that values can be written as fractions, decimals or percentages. For example:

$$\frac{1}{2} = 0.5 = 50\%$$

Here's a very useful little reminder about how to do this:

Rules of conversion	Examples

- **To turn fractions to decimals:**

    Divide the top number (numerator) by the bottom number (denominator)

$$\frac{3}{8} = 3 \div 8$$
$$= 0.375$$

- **To turn decimals or fractions into percentages:**

    Multiply by 100

$$0.125 = 0.125 \times 100\%$$
$$= 12.5\% \text{ or } 12\frac{1}{2}\%$$

$$\frac{1}{2} = \frac{1}{2} \times 100\%$$
$$= 50\%$$

- **To turn percentages into decimals:**

    Divide by 100

$$85\% = 85 \div 100$$
$$= 0.85$$

- **To turn percentages into fractions:**

    Write as a fraction with 100 as the denominator and simplify if possible.

$$72\% = \frac{72}{100}$$
$$= \frac{18}{25}$$

- **To turn decimals into fractions:**

    Write a fraction with the correct denominator (10,100 ,1000 etc.) and simplify if possible.

$$0.64 = \frac{64}{100}$$
$$= \frac{16}{25}$$

Exercise 9.1

1. Write these fractions as decimals and then as percentages:

   (a) $\frac{7}{10}$ (c) $\frac{2}{3}$

   (b) $\frac{2}{5}$ (d) $\frac{3}{8}$

2. Write these decimals as percentages and then as fractions:

   (a) 0.27   (c) 0.65

   (b) 0.7   (d) 0.6

3. Write these percentages as decimals and then as fractions:

   (a) 40%   (c) 84%

   (b) 55%   (d) 24%

4. Write these fractions as decimals and then as percentages:

   (a) $\frac{4}{25}$ (c) $\frac{37}{40}$

   (b) $\frac{9}{20}$ (d) $1\frac{1}{5}$

5. Write these decimals as percentages and then as fractions:

   (a) 1.19   (c) 2.6

   (b) 0.325   (d) 0.77

6. Write these percentages as decimals and then as fractions:

   (a) 43%   (c) $37\frac{1}{2}\%$

   (b) $66\frac{2}{3}\%$ (d) $112\frac{1}{2}\%$

A percentage of an amount

Although a percentage is equivalent to a fraction or a decimal, there is a difference. When looking at problems, a percentage is always a percentage of **something.**

If I get 63% in an exam, I then have 63% of the total marks.
If VAT is 17.5%, that is 17.5% of the price before VAT.
If I have grown by 12%, that is 12% of my old height.

A percentage of an amount can be calculated by thinking of the 'of' as 'multiplied by':

$$50\% \text{ of } 80 = \frac{1}{2} \times 80$$
$$= 40$$

In the above example we found a percentage of an amount by turning the percentage into a fraction and then multiplying.

This is the method to use if the **fraction is simple** and if you do **NOT have a calculator**.

Exercise 9.2

Find these amounts, without using a calculator:

Example:

$$72\% \text{ of } 80 \text{ cm} = \frac{72}{100} \times 80$$
$$= \frac{576}{10}$$
$$= 57.6 \text{ cm}$$

1.	25% of 80 cm	**6.**	64% of £5
2.	40% of £200	**7.**	28% of 5 kg
3.	35% of 500 g	**8.**	35% of 8 km
4.	60% of £1000	**9.**	85% of £300
5.	80% of 4 m	**10.**	12% of 20m

There are other times when the fraction is not simple. This is when you could use a calculator. Often calculators have buttons marked %, but in fact it is as easy, and good practice, to turn the percentages into decimals and then do the calculation, using the calculator.

Example: Find 37% of £6.35

$$37\% \text{ of } £6.35 = 0.37 \times 6.35$$
$$= 2.3495$$
$$= £2.35 \text{ (to 2 d.p.)}$$

Exercise 9.3

Use a calculator to find these amounts. Remember that money is always given to the nearest penny:

1. 27% of 250 cm

2. 18% of £22

3. 7% of 250 g

4. 63% of £150

5. 41% of 5 m

6. 78% of £6.50

7. 124% of 6.2 kg

8. 3% of 8.7 km

9. 89% of £324

10. $17\frac{1}{2}$% of 6 m

Now solve some problems

Remember: if the question is a sentence, you should make sure you write your answer as a phrase or sentence that relates to the original question. Here's what we mean:

Example:

45% of Year 7 boys do Latin. If there are 20 boys in Year 7 how many do not do Latin?

$$45\% \text{ of } 20 = \frac{45}{\underset{5}{100}} \times \cancel{20}$$

$$= \frac{45}{5}$$

$$= 9$$

You write your answer as:
9 boys do Latin and therefore 11 boys do not do Latin.

Exercise 9.4

1. 48% of the pupils in our school are boys. If there are 300 children in the school, how many are boys and how many are girls?

2. The price of hiring a video has gone up by 15%. If the price used to be £1.60, by how many pence has it risen?

3. In a sale prices are down by 20%. I want to buy a watch that was marked at £20 before the sale. How much cheaper will the watch be in the sale?

4. In a test I scored 65%. If the test was marked out of 80, how many marks out of 80 did I get?

5. There are 30 trees in our road and 40% of them are now in blossom. How many trees is that?

6. A service charge of 12% is added to our bill. What is the value of the service charge on a bill of £48?

7. In a recent survey we found that 30% of the school went to France last year. If there are 480 children in the school, how many went to France?

8. $12\frac{1}{2}$% of the houses in our road have white front doors. If there are 80 houses in the road, how many do not have white front doors?

9. In a recent leaflet from our local council we were told that 40% of the people in our borough were in employment. If there are 240 000 people in the borough, how many are unemployed?

10. In a recent election 48 000 people voted. 25% of the people voted for Mr Smith. How many people did not vote for him?

Calculating the percentage

When I get 45 marks out of 60 for a test, I write my marks like this: $\frac{45}{60}$, expressing them as a fraction. I can change a fraction to a percentage by multiplying by 100:

$$\frac{45}{60} \times 100\% = 75\%$$

We can turn the information into a percentage by making a fraction and multiplying by 100.

When making the fraction, the **denominator** (bottom number) is important because it shows what the percentage is a percentage **of**:

i.e.   16 out of a **class of 24** is $\frac{16}{24}$ to find a percentage **of the class**.

£12 from a **price of £15** is $\frac{12}{15}$ to find a percentage **of the price**.

Example:

In my class of 24 there are 15 boys. What percentage of the class are girls?

No. of girls $= 24 - 15 = 9$

Percentage $= \frac{9}{24} \times 100$

$= 37\frac{1}{2}\%$

The above calculation could be done without a calculator by cancelling:

$$\text{Percentage} = \frac{\overset{3}{\cancel{9}}}{\underset{2}{\cancel{24}_6}} \times \cancel{100}^{\,25}$$

$$= \frac{75}{2}$$

$$= 37\frac{1}{2}\%$$

Or by using a calculator: $\frac{9}{24} \times 100 = 9 \div 24 \times 100$

$= 37.5\%$

Exercise 9.5

Take care to read the question carefully to make sure that you answer the question. Answer these without using a calculator:

1. In my school there are 240 pupils. 144 of these are girls. What percentage of the pupils are boys?

2. Last year I received £2.40 per week pocket money. This year I am getting 30 pence extra. What percentage increase is this in my pocket money?

3. I am growing a bean plant. Last week it was 1.6 m tall and this week it is 2 m tall. What is its growth as a percentage of its previous height?

4. This term I have read 40 books. 5 of them were science fiction. What percentage of the books were science fiction?

5. I am 12 years old and I have spent 8 of those years going to school. What percentage of my life so far have I spent as a school child?

6. I have £4 pocket money each week, and I put £1.50 into my piggy bank. What percentage of my pocket money do I **not** put in my piggy bank?

7. I have to write a 400-word essay. I have just counted up the words that I have written so far and they total 320. What percentage of my essay have I left to write?

Use a calculator for these questions; give any non-exact answers to one decimal place:

8. What is 45 marks out of 65 as a percentage?

9. £4 service is added to our bill of £32. What percentage increase is this?

10. Trainers normally cost £39.99 but in the sale they cost £29.99 What percentage saving is this?

11. In a 3 kg cake there is 210 g of dried fruit. What percentage of the cake is this?

12. 18 of the 23 books that I have just read are non fiction. What percentage of the books is this?

13. In a class of 19 pupils, 4 of them have red hair. What percentage of the pupils do not have red hair?

14. In a science experiment I mix 45 mg of chemical A with 120 mg of chemical B. What percentage of the total mix is chemical A?

These last few are harder. Use whichever method you prefer to answer them:

15. For my exams I got 60 out of 75 for French, 52 out of 70 for Maths, 80 out of 110 for English, 45 out of 65 for History and 63 out of 80 for Geography. If I add all my marks up, what percentage of the total possible marks did I get?

16. In my maths exam I scored 60 marks out of a possible 75. How many more marks would I have had to get to have scored over 90%?

17. When we bought a litre of cleaning fluid, we were told to leave the top on or as much as 15% of the liquid could evaporate overnight. My mother forgot and the next morning there were only 850 cubic millimetres of fluid left in the bottle. How accurate were the manufacturer's claims?

18. For a maths project we decided to test an advertiser's claim that over 65% of people had eaten a McJimmy's hamburger. Between us we interviewed 300 people and 124 of them had **not** eaten a McJimmiburger. Does that mean that the advertising claim was correct or not?

Profit and loss

When manufacturers, wholesalers and shopkeepers work out the price to sell their goods at, they usually work in percentages.

The **manufacturer** adds a percentage on to the manufacturing cost and sells to the **wholesaler**.

The **wholesaler** adds a percentage on to his total purchase and transport costs and sells to the **shopkeeper**.

The **shopkeeper** adds a percentage on to his costs, and then he has to add on VAT before he can fix a price to sell to the public.

Use this information to answer the questions in the next exercise.

Exercise 9.6

Example: A shopkeeper buys pencils at £7.50 per 100 and sells them for 12p each. What is his percentage profit?

Cost price : £7.50   Selling price: £12.00

$$\text{Profit} = £12.00 - £7.50$$

$$= £4.50$$

$$\text{Percentage profit} = \frac{\text{profit}}{\text{cost price}}$$

$$= \frac{^{15}\cancel{450}}{\cancel{750}_{\cancel{5}}} \times \cancel{100}^{4}$$

Use pence for your calculations so that you can cancel common factors without worrying about decimals.

$$= 15 \times 4$$

$$= 60$$

The shopkeeper's percentage profit is 60%.

1. Find the percentage profit for these transactions:
   (a) Trainers bought for £12 and sold for £15
   (b) A loaf of bread is sold for 64p a loaf when manufacturing costs are 40p a loaf.
   (c) A cake is made with ingredients costing £1.25 and is then sold at the fete for £2.50
   (d) I bought a book for £2.50 and then sold it to my teacher for £4

2. Find the percentage loss for these transactions:
   (a) A book was bought for £5 and sold for £3
   (b) Potatoes are bought from the farm for £5 for 20kg, and sold for 80p for 5kg.
   (c) Black bin liners are bought from the factory at £4 for 100 and sold in the market at £1 for 20
   (d) I bought a CD for £8 and sold it to my sister for £6

Example: In a sale all prices are marked down by 20%. If a camera normally costs £35, what does it cost in the sale?

Selling price = 80% of normal price

$$= \frac{\overset{4}{\cancel{80}}}{\underset{5}{\cancel{100}}} \times \overset{7}{\cancel{35}}$$

$$= £28$$

---

3. Find the selling price for each of these transactions:
   (a) A shopkeeper adds 17.5% VAT to his own price of £10.00
   (b) A manufacturer adds 20% profit to his costs of £8.00
   (c) A shop is having a sale with all prices marked down 25%. A jacket normally costs £40
   (d) A wholesaler adds 15% to his own costs of £20

4. A manufacturer works out that his total costs for 100 floppy discs are £150   If he sells boxes of 100 discs at £175, what is his percentage profit? Is this the same if you calculate on 1 disc or on 100 discs?

5. A shopkeeper has to add VAT at 17.5% to his price of £60.
   How much money is the VAT?

6. A wholesaler sells trainers for £12 a pair. He paid £15 for each pair. What was his percentage loss?

7. A market trader buys in potatoes at £50 for 200kg and sells them in 5 kg bags for £2   What percentage profit does he make?

8. I make 8% per year by investing my money in a National Savings account.
    (a) If I started with £125, how much interest will I have earned in one year?
    (b) How much money will I then be able to reinvest?

9. A jacket was being sold for £24.50 but has been marked down by 40% in a sale. What price can I buy it for now?

10. A manufacturer's total costs on 1000 print cartridges are £5000   At what price should he sell a box of 5 cartridges in order to make a 20% profit?

11. A car devalues by 20% of its original price in its first year, and from then on it devalues each year at 12% of its price at the beginning of that year. If a car cost £9000 in January 1992:
    (a) What was its value in January 1993?
    (b) What was its value in January 1994?
    (c) What is the total percentage devaluation of the car from January 1992 to January 1994?

12. A salesman claims that if you let him invest your money it will appreciate (grow) by at least 10% per annum. You invest £2000 with his fund. At the end of the year you have lost 8%.
    (a) How much money would you have made if his claims were true?
    (b) How much money have you lost?
    (c) If you had invested the money elsewhere it would have made the 10% growth, so what is your actual percentage loss?

13. A 20kg bag of potatoes costs £5 from the farm shop. At what price should I sell 2.5 kg bags in order to make 30% profit?

14. I buy some ingredients from the supermarket for £4.50 and then I make 48 little cakes. I sell the cakes for 24p each. What percentage profit or loss do I make?

15. In Charity Week my form decides to wash teachers' cars. We buy some cleaning materials that cost a total of £9.50
    There are 32 teachers' cars in the car park.
    (a) If we wash all the cars, what should we charge so that we cover our expenditure?
    (b) We only got to wash 28 of the cars, but we made a 490% profit. What did we charge per car?

16. A videotape costs 80p to manufacture. The manufacturer adds 40% to the costs when he sells to the wholesaler. The wholesaler adds 50% to his purchase price to cover his overheads as he sells the tape to the shopkeeper. The shopkeeper adds 50% to his purchase price in order to make a profit, and to that price he adds 17.5% VAT. At what price does the shopkeeper sell the videotape?

Exercise 9.7: Extension questions

Some percentages include fractions. Some of these are in the common fraction families, but some are not.

It is a good idea if we can recognise common percentage and fraction equivalents.

For example: $12\frac{1}{2}\% = 0.125 = \frac{1}{8}$ and $66\frac{2}{3}\% = 0.66666... = \frac{2}{3}$

If you are not using a calculator, then turn the percentage into a fraction by:

first making it **top heavy**
then **dividing by 100**

Here's what we mean:

$36\frac{1}{2}\% = \frac{73}{2}\% = \frac{73}{200}$

We get the top heavy fraction by multiplying 2 × 36 to get 72 and then adding the 1 to get 73.

You then make it a fraction by dividing by 100.

Example:

First turn the mixed fraction into a proper fraction percentage

$$12\frac{1}{2}\% \text{ of } 80 \text{ cm} = \frac{25}{\underset{5}{\cancel{200}}} \times \cancel{80}^{\,2}$$

Then cancel by 10 and by 4

$$= \frac{\cancel{25}^{\,5} \times 2}{\cancel{5}}$$

Finally cancel by 5

$$= 10 \text{ cm}$$

1. $12\frac{1}{2}$ % of 120 g

2. $37\frac{1}{2}$ % of £200

3. $33\frac{1}{3}$ % of 66 m

4. $66\frac{2}{3}$ of 144 litres

5. $87\frac{1}{2}$ % of 240 grams

6. $16\frac{2}{3}$ % of £30

7. $83\frac{1}{3}$ % of £6

8. $12\frac{1}{2}$ % of 2 km

9. $33\frac{1}{3}$ % of 12 g

10. $16\frac{2}{3}$ % of 3 litres

If you are using a calculator, turn the percentage into a decimal as we did before:

$$36\frac{1}{2}\% = 36.5\% = 0.365$$

$$72\frac{1}{5}\% = 72.2\% = 0.722$$

Remember: You cannot calculate with recurring decimals. You must work with their fraction equivalents.

Use a calculator to find these:

11. $65\frac{1}{2}$ % of £3.20

12. $16\frac{1}{6}$ % of 450 m

13. $25\frac{1}{5}$ % of 5 kg

14. $42\frac{2}{5}$ % of £1725

15. $33\frac{1}{3}$ % of 4.7 km

16. $17\frac{1}{2}$ % of £35

17. $68\frac{3}{5}$ % of £6.40

18. $24\frac{1}{2}$ % of 65 tonnes

19. $65\frac{1}{4}$ % of 12 kg

20. $2\frac{3}{4}$ % of 35 litres

Exercise 9.8: Summary Exercise

Do NOT use a calculator for questions 1 to 6:

1. Write these as fractions:
   (a) 0.35
   (b) 0.12
   (c) 42%
   (d) $12\frac{1}{2}\%$

2. Write these as decimals:
   (a) 82%
   (b) $\frac{3}{8}$
   (c) $87\frac{1}{2}\%$
   (d) $\frac{7}{25}$

3. Write these as percentages:
   (a) 1.5
   (b) 0.125
   (c) $\frac{1}{3}$
   (d) $\frac{6}{25}$

4. Find these amounts:
   (a) 25% of £14
   (b) 14% of 500 g
   (c) 80% of 1200 people
   (d) 45% of 500 km
   (e) $12\frac{1}{2}\%$ of £400
   (f) $33\frac{1}{3}\%$ of 900 miles

5. There are 240 children in the school and 5% of them have chicken pox. How many children is that?

6. I scored 42 out 60 in my French test. What is that as a percentage?

You may use a calculator for the following questions, if you wish, but **do write down your working out**!

7. Of the 24 people in my class, $37\frac{1}{2}\%$ are going on the school ski trip. How many of us are not?

8. Last year, which was not a leap year, there were 146 days when it rained for more than one hour. For what percentage of the year did it rain for more than one hour a day?

9. I wanted a new game for my computer but last week it cost £28
   In the sale today it is marked down by 35%. What could I buy it for now?

10. In my school tuck shop we buy boxes of 50 packets of potato crisps for £4.20 and we sell the crisps for 12p per packet. What is our percentage profit?

11. An old wives' tale says that the height you are on your second birthday is exactly half the height you will be when fully grown. My mother's baby book says that a baby will grow 40% of its height at birth in its first year, while in its second year it will grow to 20% of its height at the beginning of the year. The height of my new baby sister is 50 cm. How tall will she be:
    (a) on her first birthday?
    (b) on her second birthday?
    (c) as an adult?

12. A market trader bought some bunches of daffodils. He paid £15 for a hundred daffodils and hoped to make a fortune on Mother's Day. Unfortunately it rained that day and he ended up selling his flowers at 50p per bunch of 10. What percentage profit or loss did he make?

End of chapter 9 activity: Tormenting tessellations

The word tessellation comes from *tessella,* the Latin for 'little tile'.

If you look at bathroom walls or kitchen floors, they are often covered in tiles. These tiles are generally square. This is because a square is the easiest shape to cover a whole area without leaving any gaps.

Use the 'nibble' technique described below to design your own tessellations. These instructions are given for using paper and card, but if you have a good computer graphics programme then you can make some fantastic patterns using that. However, try this method first:

Step 1

Draw a square and make sure it is the same size as the square on the worksheet where you are going to draw your tessellation.

Step 2

Start at the top corner and draw an outline of the piece you are going to cut out or 'nibble'.

Step 3

Cut out the nibbled piece and stick it back on either the opposite side, as in the example, or on an adjacent side if you prefer.

Step 4

Do the same thing again but this time, go from top to bottom **or** bottom to top **or** a different pair of adjacent sides.

Step 5

Decorate your shape. Stick it on to card and draw round it carefully. Cut it out. This is now your tessellating template.

Step 6

Position the card on the worksheet. Line up the corners very carefully. Trace round it. Now reposition your template so that it notches into the first figure. Trace round it again. Keep going!

When you have finished, decorate the whole design:

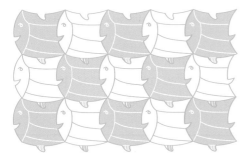

Chapter 10: Ratio and enlargement

You have probably made yourself the sort of drink where you add water to concentrated fruit cordial. Buying it in this concentrated form is quite useful because you can make up quite a lot of drink from just a small bottle by adding water to dilute it.

The instructions on the bottle usually say something like:

'Mix one part cordial with 4 parts water.'

In Maths we say that the **ratio** of **cordial to water** is **1 : 4**

Ratio

A ratio is a comparison of numbers. We generally separate the numbers in the ratio with a colon (:). It is important to get the quantities the right way round. For example, if you mixed your fruit cordial in the ratio 4 : 1 it would be far too strong.

Exercise 10.1

1. A blackcurrant fruit cordial needs to be mixed with water, with one part cordial to five parts water.
   (a) Write the mix as the ratio of cordial to water.
   (b) Write the mix as the ratio of water to cordial.
   (c) I carefully measure 100 ml of cordial. How much water will I need?
   (d) I carefully measure 100 ml of cordial. How many millilitres of mixed drink do I have?
   (e) I pour a litre of water into a jug. How much cordial do I need?
   (f) I have a bottle containing 750 ml of cordial. How much water do I need if I want to mix the bottle up in the correct proportions?

2. Orange fruit cordial is to be mixed with water, with one part cordial to three parts water.
   (a) Write the mix as the ratio of cordial to water.
   (b) Write the mix as the ratio of water to cordial.
   (c) I carefully measure 100 ml of cordial. How much water will I need?
   (d) I carefully measure 100 ml of cordial. How many millilitres of mixed drink do I have?
   (e) I pour a litre of water into a jug. How much cordial do I need?
   (f) I have a bottle containing 750 ml of cordial. How much water do I need if I want to mix the whole bottle up in the correct proportions?

3. Weedkiller is to be mixed with water, with one part weedkiller to twenty parts water.
   (a) Write the mix as the ratio of weedkiller to water.
   (b) Write the mix as the ratio of water to weedkiller.
   (c) I carefully measure 100 ml of weedkiller. How much water will I need?
   (d) I pour a litre of water into a jug. How much weedkiller should I add?
   (e) I have a bottle containing 400 ml of weedkiller. How much water do I need in order to mix the whole bottle?

Simplifying the ratio

There would be no point in saying 'mix 2 parts cordial with 8 parts water' because that is just the same as adding 1 part cordial to 4 parts of water.

Just as we saw with fractions, ratios need to be expressed in their lowest terms. As we did with fractions, we can also cancel ratios by dividing both parts by the same number, i.e. by a common factor.

Example:

(a) Simplify the ratio 3 : 6

   3 : 6 = 1 : 2   We divide both 3 and 6 by 3

(b) Simplify the ratio 20 : 30

   20 : 30 = 2 : 3   We divide both 20 and 30 by 10

Exercise 10.2

1. Simplify these ratios:
   (a) 8 : 2   (b) 2 : 8   (c) 5 : 10   (d) 10 : 5

2. Simplify these ratios:
   (a) 8 : 6   (b) 6 : 8   (c) 15 : 10   (d) 10 : 15

3. Simplify these ratios:
   (a) 18 : 12   (b) 12 : 18   (c) 25 : 10   (d) 10 : 25

4. Simplify these ratios:
   (a) 15 : 25   (b) 20 : 8   (c) 50 : 35   (d) 10 : 55

If you are comparing **quantities**, first make sure that they are in the **same units** and **leave the units out** of your final answer:

Example: Simplify the ratio 60 cm to 1.2 m

60 cm to 1.2 m = 60 cm : 120 cm
= 6 : 12
= 1 : 2

---

5. Simplify these:
   (a) 1.2 m : 1.4 m   (b) 3.2 km : 2.4 km   (c) £ 2.20 : £ 1.80

6. Simplify these:
   (a) 70p : £1.20   (b) 350 g : 1.25 kg   (c) 1.4 km : 600m

7. Copy and complete these, replacing the stars to make the ratios equivalent:
   (a) 2 : 3 = * : 60   (b) 2 : 7 = 14 : *   (c) 5 : 8 = 25 : *

8. Copy and complete these, replacing the stars to make the ratios equivalent:
   (a) 22 : 33 = * : 3   (b) 21 : 7 = * : 1   (c) 25 : 80 = 5 : *

9. These ratios have been written **incorrectly** and are **not equal**. Find the mistake and write them correctly (there may be more than one correct answer):
   (a) 2 : 3 = 21 : 14   (b) 15 : 40 = 3 : 5   (c) 35 : 70 = 7 : 10

Finding the ratio

When finding the ratio there are three important points to remember:

Point 1. Make sure the ratio is the right way round:

> If A is 4 m and B is 5 m then:
> The ratio of A : B = 4 : 5
> The ratio of B : A = 5 : 4

Point 2. The ratio should be expressed in its lowest terms without decimals or fractions:

> If A = 1.2 m and B = 1.5 m then:
> The ratio of A : B = 1.2 : 1.5
> = 12 : 15
> = 4 : 5

Point 3. The dimensions of the various parts must be expressed in the same units before the ratio is simplified:

> If A = 70 cm and B = 1.4 m then
> The ratio of A : B = 70 cm : 1.4 m
> = 70 : 140
> = 1 : 2

Exercise 10.3

Example:

If I am 12 years old and my brother is 15 years old, what is the ratio of my age to my brother's?

My age : My brother's age = 12 : 15
= 4 : 5

---

1. I am 12 years old and my brother is three years younger than I am. What is the ratio of my age to my brother's age?

2. Look at this pattern:

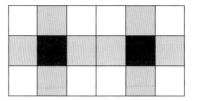

    (a) What is the ratio of black squares to grey squares?
    (b) What is the ratio of white squares to grey squares?
    (c) What is the ratio of black squares to the total number of squares?

3. If there are 240 boys in my school and 360 girls, what is the ratio of boys to girls?

4. I earn £120 per week and my sister earns £30 more than I do. What is the ratio of my sister's earnings to mine?

5. I mix 50 ml blackcurrant concentrate with 200 ml of water to make blackcurrant squash:
    (a) What is the ratio of concentrate to water?
    (b) What is the ratio of concentrate to diluted squash?

6. Look at this pattern:

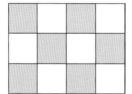

    (a) What is the ratio of white squares to grey squares?
    (b) What is the ratio of white squares to the total number of squares?

7. I have saved up £25 and my brother has saved up £40
    What is the ratio of our savings?

8. I mix 500 grams of flour with 350 grams of butter. What is the ratio of flour to butter?

9. Look at this pattern:

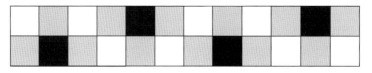

    (a) What is the ratio of grey squares to black squares?
    (b) What is the ratio of white squares to the total number of squares?

10. To blend MacTavish whisky, mix 50 litres of GlenTav whisky with 350 litres of GlenVish whisky.
(a) What is the ratio of GlenTav whisky to GlenVish whisky?
(b) What is the ratio of GlenTav whisky in the blended MacTavish whisky?

Ratio as a fraction

Suppose we want to write the ratio of 8 to 12

We can write this as 8 : 12 or like a fraction $\frac{8}{12}$, and we say the ratio is 'eight to twelve'.

This simplifies to 2 : 3 or $\frac{2}{3}$

A ratio can be written without the colon like a fraction:

$$1 : 2 = \frac{1}{2}$$

Exercise 10.4

1. Copy and complete these, replacing the stars to make the ratios equivalent:

(a) $\frac{14}{8} = \frac{*}{4}$

(b) $\frac{16}{12} = \frac{4}{*}$

(c) $\frac{15}{45} = \frac{*}{9}$

2. Copy and complete these, replacing the stars to make the ratios equivalent:

(a) $\frac{14}{*} = \frac{1}{4}$

(b) $\frac{*}{72} = \frac{2}{9}$

(c) $\frac{*}{144} = \frac{5}{9}$

3. The ratio of tin to zinc in a toy solder is 60 : 40
(a) What is the ratio of tin to zinc?
(b) What is the ratio of zinc to tin?
(c) What fraction of the mix is zinc?
(d) What fraction of the mix is tin?

4. In a recipe for fruit cake you need 200 g of raisins, 150 g of currants and 100 g of sultanas:
(a) What is the ratio of currants to raisins?
(b) What fraction of the dried fruit is sultanas?
(c) What is the ratio of sultanas to raisins?
(d) What is the ratio of raisins : currants : sultanas?
(e) Why can't you write the ratio in (d) as a fraction?

Ratio as parts of a whole

Sometimes we need to divide an amount up into a number of parts. Look at these lines:

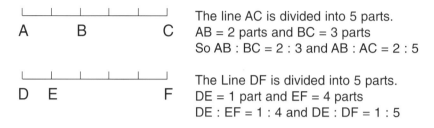

The line AC is divided into 5 parts.
AB = 2 parts and BC = 3 parts
So AB : BC = 2 : 3 and AB : AC = 2 : 5

The Line DF is divided into 5 parts.
DE = 1 part and EF = 4 parts
DE : EF = 1 : 4 and DE : DF = 1 : 5

Both these lines have been divided into five parts, but the first has been divided in the ratio 2 : 3, and the second in the ratio 1 : 4

Exercise 10.5

In each question B is a point on AC. Draw a line ABC and then answer the questions:

1. Draw a line AC 6 cm long. Mark a point B such that AB : BC = 1 : 2

2. Draw a line AC 10 cm long. Mark a point B such that AB : BC = 2 : 3

3. Draw a line AC 8 cm long. Mark a point B such that AB : BC = 1 : 3

4. Draw a line AC 12 cm long. Mark a point B such that AC : AB = 6 : 1

5. Draw a line AC 12 cm long. Mark a point B such that AC : AB = 3 :1

6. Draw a line AC 12 cm long. Mark a point B such that AC : AB = 3 : 2

Answer these questions without drawing:

7. AB = 20 cm, BC = 40 cm. Find the ratio of:
   (a) AB : BC   (b) BC : AB   (c) AB : AC   (d) BC : AC

8. AB= 40 cm and BC = 1.2 m. Find the ratio of:
   (a) AB : BC   (b) BC : AB   (c) AB : AC   (d) BC : AC

9. I have to draw a line AC and mark a point B such that AB : BC = 2 : 5 If AB is 4 cm, how long are AC and BC?

10. If XY : YZ = 4 : 7 and XZ is 22 cm long, how long is (a) XY and (b) YZ?

Solving problems with ratio
Exercise 10.6

Make sure that you show all your working clearly.

> Example: My uncle gives my brother and me £50 to be divided in the ratio of our ages. My brother is 9 and I am 11
> How much do we each get?
>
> $$\text{No. of parts} = 9 + 11$$
> $$= 20$$
>
> $$\text{One part} = £50 \div 20$$
> $$= £2.50$$
>
> $$\text{My brother has 9 parts} = 9 \times 2.50$$
> $$= £22.50$$
>
> $$\text{I have 11 parts} = 11 \times 2.50$$
> $$= £27.50$$

1. £100 is shared between two sisters in the ratio of their ages. The elder sister is 13 years old and the younger is 7 years old. How much money does each sister receive?

2. I need to make 140 kg of mortar. The ratio of cement to sand is 1 : 6
   How much cement and sand will I need?

3. Molotov is making explosives. He mixes 75 ml of chemical A with 120 ml of chemical B, and then blows his eyebrows off. What ratio of chemical A to chemical B caused this explosion?

4. I mix orange squash by mixing orange juice concentrate and water in the ratio 3 : 7
   If I want to make 5 litres of orange squash, how many litres of orange juice concentrate will I need?

5. Garden fertiliser is made from a mixture of the chemical concentrate and water in the ratio 2 : 25
   If I need 1 litre of water, how much concentrate must I add?

6. My father likes his gin and tonic with gin and tonic in the ratio 2 : 5
    (a) If I put in 50 ml of gin, how much tonic do I need?
    (b) How many millilitres was his drink in total?
    (c) In fact I made a mistake and gave him his drink In the ratio 2 : 5 but
        with 50 ml of tonic. How many millilitres was this drink?

7. I am making some rectangular invitation cards where the ratio of width to
    height is 3 : 5. If the width is 9 cm what is the area of the card?

8. I am painting my bedroom green. To make just the right shade I have to
    mix yellow and blue in the ratio 2 : 7. If I have 6 litres of yellow paint, how
    many litres of blue will I need and how many litres of green paint will I
    make?

9. I am going to paint another room pale yellow and I must mix lily white
    and buttercup in the ratio 2 : 5. If I need 28 litres of paint altogether, how
    many litres each of lily white and buttercup will I need?

10. To cause an explosion chemical A is mixed with chemical B in the ratio
    2 : 13. If I have 390 mg of chemical B, how many mg of explosive will
    I have?

11. The angles in a triangle are in the ratio 1 : 2 : 3. What are the angles and
    what is the name of the triangle?

12. The angles of a triangle are in the ratio 1 : 2 : 2. What are the angles and
    what special triangle is this?

Scale drawings

It is often impossible to draw objects, diagrams or plans to their full size and
so we draw them to scale:

Model   **Imagine this as full size!**

If the model is 10 cm long and the real train is 10 metres long, then the scale
is 10 cm to 10 m, or 1 cm to 1 m.

Firstly, we have to make sure the ratio is expressed in the same units and then write it in its lowest terms: Scale → 10 cm : 10 m

→ 1 cm : 1 m

→ 1 cm : 100 cm

→ 1 : 100

Exercise 10.7

1. If a map is drawn so that 1 cm represents 1 km, what is the scale as a ratio?

2. If a plan is drawn so that 1 cm represents 1 m, what is the scale as a ratio?

3. If a map is drawn so that 1 cm represents 500 m, what is the scale as a ratio?

4. If a diagram is drawn so that 2 cm represents 10 cm, what is the scale as a ratio?

5. If a plan is drawn so that 1 cm represents 5 m, what is the scale as a ratio?

6. If a map is drawn so that 1 cm represents 5 km, what is the scale as a ratio?

7. If a diagram is drawn so that 2 cm represents 1 m, what is the scale as a ratio?

Using scale

Think back to our trains:

The scale is 1 : 100, where 1 cm represents 100 cm (1 m).

Therefore: If the train is 15 m long, the model will be 15 cm long.
        If the model is 3 cm high, then the train will be 3 m high.

But, remember, there are some things that don't change. For example, if the model has eight wheels, then the train will also have eight wheels!

Exercise 10.8

When you do this next exercise, it will help if you start by finding out what 1 cm represents. Make sure you set out your working carefully, as shown in the example below:

Example:

I am drawing a plan of my classroom to a scale of 1 : 50
(i) If my classroom is 5 m wide, what will this be on the plan?
(ii) I have to fit in a teacher's desk that is 4 cm long on the plan.
　　How long is a real desk?

　　　Scale = 1 : 50　　　　　　　　　　First find out what 1 cm represents.
　　　　　　1 cm represents 50 cm

(i) Width of classroom is 5 m (500 cm)
　　Scaled length of classroom is　500 ÷ 50
　　　　　　　　　　　　　　　　　= 10 cm

(ii) Desk scaled length is 4 cm
　　　　Real length = 4 × 50　　　　　Multiply by 50 because we know
　　　　　　　　　 = 200 cm　　　　　that 1 cm represents 50 cm,
　　　　　　　　　 = 2 m　　　　　　　therefore 4 cm must be 4 x 50 cm.

1.　A model train has been built to a scale of 1:100
　　(a) What is the length of a real carriage if a model carriage is 12 cm long?
　　(b) What is the length of the real goods van if the model is 20 cm long?
　　(c) What is the length of the model engine if the real engine is 15 m long?
　　(d) What is the diameter of a model wheel if the real wheels are 1 m in diameter?
　　(e) If the model has four carriages, how many does the real train have?

2. I have drawn a plan of my bedroom to a scale of 1 : 50

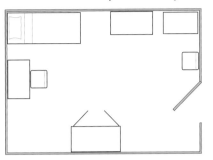

(a) What does 1 cm on my plan represent?
(b) My bed is 2 m long. What length is it on my plan?
(c) On my plan, my desk is 1.2 cm wide. How wide is it really?
(d) My plan is 10 cm by 14 cm. What are the actual measurements of my bedroom?
(e) I have two chairs in my bedroom. How many chairs are on my plan?

3. This seed is drawn to a scale of 5: 1
Measure the diameter of the drawing and find the diameter of the real seed.

4. This is a hair from an insect's body enlarged to a scale of 20 : 1
Measure the length of the drawing of the hair and calculate its real length in millimetres.

5. A map is drawn to a scale of 1 : 10 000
(a) What does 1 cm on the map represent?
(b) What distance in the map represents 4 km?
(c) The distance from the church to the post office on the map is 3.2 cm. What is this distance on the ground?
(d) On Monday we walked for 2.4 km. What distance on the map is this?
(e) There are two churches on the map. How many are there in reality?

6. I want to draw a map of a field 600 m by 1.4 km on a piece of paper 20 cm by 30 cm. What scale should I use? (You will need to try a few scales before you get your answer!)

7. I am building a model boat to a scale of 1 : 20
   (a) What does 1 cm on the model represent?
   (b) What length on the model represents 1 metre on the real boat?
   (c) The masts are 6 m and 7.5 m tall. How long are they on my model?
   (d) There are two masts on the model. How many are there on the real boat?

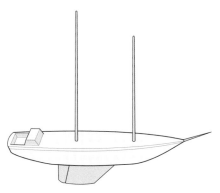

8. Another boat was built some time ago and was therefore built in Imperial units. I find that a scale of 1 : 24 makes more sense because there are 12 inches in a foot.
   (a) What does 1 inch on the model represent?
   (b) If the boat was 20 feet long what length is my model?
   (c) If the model is 4 inches wide, how wide is the actual boat?
   (d) One mast was 15 feet high. How tall will the model's mast be?

Proportional division: The unitary method

Consider the problem:

If eight mega gobstoppers cost 44p, what will 6 mega gobstoppers cost?

We can solve this either by using ratios like this:

$\frac{8}{44} = \frac{6}{?}$ which does not give us a simple answer (we will come back to this later on page 209) or by using the **unitary method**.

The unitary method is a method where we work out the **value of one unit** (unit = one). Here's an example to show you what we mean:

Example:

If 8 gobstoppers cost 44p

$$(\div 8)$$

1 gobstopper costs $\dfrac{44}{8}$

$$(\times 6)$$

Then 6 gobstoppers cost $\dfrac{44}{8} \times 6p = 33p$

Exercise 10.9

Solve these problems using the unitary method but, be warned, some questions may not be quite as they seem! Leave your answer as a fraction when necessary:

1. If my car travels 84 miles on 14 litres of petrol, how far will it travel on 21 litres of petrol?

2. If I can buy 12 bars of Candynut for 80p, how much will it cost me to buy 9 bars?

3. If a bricklayer, on average, lays 84 bricks in 2 hours, how many bricks could he lay in five hours?

4. My cat eats 18 tins of cat food in two weeks. How many tins of cat food would she eat in three weeks?

5. Two of my class took 40 minutes to complete the school cross-country course. How long will it take 18 of my class to complete the same course?

6. An electric golf caddie can travel 2 miles in 50 minutes. How long would it take to travel three miles?

7. In four weeks my bean plant has grown 1.2 m. How high might it grow in 7 weeks?

8. A car travels 122 miles on 4 gallons of petrol. How many miles will it travel on 9 gallons of petrol?

9. Mrs Smith can type 12 pages in 45 minutes. If she keeps typing at the same rate, how long will it take her to type 20 similar pages?

10. I read three books in five days. How many books will I read in nine days?

If you check back over your answers to q.5, 7, and 10, you will notice something interesting:

> The time it takes one person to run a race is different from the time that it takes anyone else.
> Bean plants do not grow at a steady rate.
> Books can be different lengths.

You can use ratio methods only when the amounts are proportional. This means that they increase or decrease at the same rate. Now try these:

11. 91 litres is equal to 20 gallons. How many gallons are there in 70 litres?

12. Water can be added to 5 tins of concentrated soup to make 2.2 litres of diluted soup. How many tins of concentrated soup will I need to make 3.5 litres of diluted soup?

13. 5 bags of cement weigh 560 lb. How much will 3 bags of cement weigh?

14. If three men can, on average, shift 90 bags of cement in one hour, how many men would I need to shift 150 similar bags of cement in one hour?

15. Here is a recipe for making 16 Scotch pancakes:
    250 g of self-raising flour
    250 ml water
    4 tablespoons of milk
    1 egg
    Rewrite the recipe so
    that you can make 24
    Scotch pancakes.

Ratio and enlargement

If we look at a line:

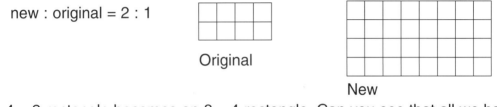

We can say the ratio of AB : BC = 1 : 3
We can also say that AB : AC = 1 : 4
This tells us therefore that AC is 4 times as long as AB

Now let's look at enlarging a rectangle.

Here is a 4 × 2 rectangle and we want enlarge it in the ratio of:

new : original = 2 : 1

Original

New

The 4 × 2 rectangle becomes an 8 × 4 rectangle. Can you see that all we have done is multiplied the original rectangle's dimensions by 2?

When we enlarge by the ratio 2 : 1, the length of the enlargement is twice the length of the original, so we can say that the enlargement has **scale factor 2.**

Now consider another example. A 4 x 2 rectangle is to be enlarged in the ratio:

new : original = 1 : 2

Original

New

This time we are dividing by 2 and so the 4 x 2 rectangle becomes a 2 x 1 rectangle.

When we enlarge by the ratio 1 : 2, the length is half the length of the original, so we can say that the enlargement has **scale factor** $\frac{1}{2}$.

Any enlargement has to be defined by a scale factor. Each **length** in the **object** is multiplied by the scale factor to give the length in the **image**.

Exercise 10.10

1. Draw a line 2 cm long.
   Draw the enlargement of that line by scale factor 3

2. Draw a line 2 cm long.
   Draw an enlargement of that line by scale factor 2

3. Draw a line 4 cm long.
   Draw an enlargement of that line by scale factor 1.5

4. Copy these rectangles on to squared paper.

   (a)   (b)

   Enlarge them both in the ratio 2 : 1

5. Copy this shape on squared paper:

   Draw the enlargement by scale factor 3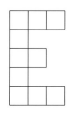

6. Look at this picture:

   The picture is to be reduced in the ratio 1 : 2
   Draw the shape after the reduction.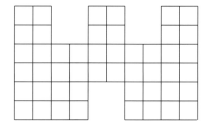

7. Copy this shape on squared paper and label it A.
   Draw the following enlargements of A:
   (a) Scale factor 2: label the enlargement B.
   (b) Scale factor 3: label the enlargement C.
   (c) In the ratio 3 : 2, label the enlargement D.

8. Calculate the areas of the shapes A, B, C and D that you drew in q.7.
   Calculate these ratios:
   (a) Area A: Area B
   (b) Area A : Area C
   (c) Area A : Area D
   What do you notice about the relationship between the areas?

Exercise 10.11:Enlargement on a grid

Finding the centre of enlargement and the scale factor

When an object drawn on a co-ordinate grid is to be enlarged, we must know where to draw the enlargement.

1. Look at these two diagrams. They are also on the worksheet:

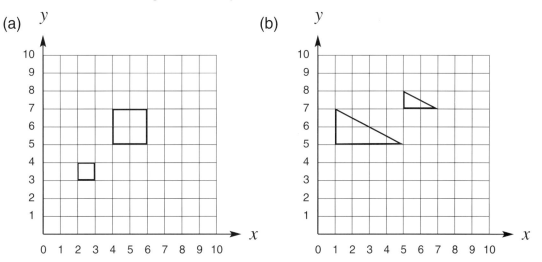

(a)   (b)

To find the centre of enlargement, we need to join the corresponding points together with a long line, and see where the long lines cross. Do this on the worksheet.

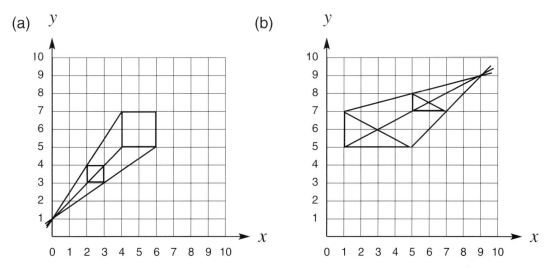

(a)   (b)

By doing this we have now found the centre of enlargement:

Centre of enlargement is (0, 1)   Centre of enlargement is (9, 9)
Scale factor 2   Scale factor 2

(c) – (f) Now find the centres of enlargement and the scale factor for the next four diagrams on the worksheet.

In the following q.2 – 7, the co-ordinates of the two shapes have been given to you. On the worksheet draw and label each shape and then find the centre of enlargement and the scale factor for each.

To make it easier to join the correct points, look carefully at the letters:

If Δ *ABC* is enlarged to Δ *DEF* then

$A \rightarrow D$ *A* **maps** on to *D*

$B \rightarrow E$ *B* **maps** on to *E*

$C \rightarrow F$ *C* **maps** on to *F*

N.B. The expression '**maps on to**' means that the two are not equal but the first point is '**transformed to**' the second. We cannot say *A* equals *D* and so it is written →.

2.   (a) Draw Δ *ABC* such that *A*(3, 4), *B*(5, 4) and *C* (4, 5) and Δ *DEF* such that *D*(2, 7), *E*(6, 7) and *F*(4, 9).
     (b) Find the centre of enlargement and the scale factor for the enlargement that maps Δ *ABC* to Δ *DEF*.

3.   (a) Draw Δ *GHI* such that *G*(3, 5), *H*(3, 4) and *I*(4, 4) and Δ *JKL* such that *J*(5, 9), *K*(5, 6) and *L*(8, 6).
     (b) Find the centre of enlargement and the scale factor for the enlargement that maps Δ *GHI* to Δ *JKL*.

4.   (a) Draw Δ *LMN* such that *L*(6, 6), *M*(5, 5) and *N*(6, 3) and Δ *PQR* such that *P*(3, 8), *Q*(1, 6) and *R*(3, 2).
     (b) Find the centre of enlargement and the scale factor for the enlargement that maps Δ *LMN* to Δ *PQR*.

5.   (a) Draw a square *ABCD* such that *A*(7, 4), *B*(7, 3), *C*(8, 3) and *D*(8, 4) and a square *EFGH* such that *E*(5, 7), *F*(5, 5), *G*(7, 5) and *H*(7, 7).
     (b) Find the centre of enlargement and the scale factor for the enlargement that maps *ABCD* to *EFGH*.

6.   (a) Draw a square *PQRS* such that *P*(4, 3), *Q*(4, 2), *R*(5, 2) and *S*(5, 3) and a square *WXYZ* such that *W*(5, 8), *X*(5, 5), *Y*(8, 5) and *Z*(8, 8).
     (b) Find the centre of enlargement and the scale factor for the enlargement that maps *PQRS* to *WXYZ*.

7. (a) Draw a square *ABCD* such that *A*(5, 6), *B*(5, 5), *C*(6, 5) and
        D(6, 6) and a square *EFGH* such that *E*(2, 9), *F*(2, 5), *G*(6, 5) and
        H(6, 9).
    (b) Find the centre of enlargement and the scale factor for the
        enlargement that maps *ABCD* to *EFGH*. (You will notice that points *C*
        and *F* are the same – which should give you a clue!)

Drawing the enlargement

For each of the next set of questions in Exercise 10.12, you are given the co-
ordinates of the object, the centre of enlargement and the scale factor. You
then have to draw and label the enlargement.

Here's an example to show you what we mean:

Draw *EFG*, the enlargement of *ABC* by scale factor 3 and centre of
enlargement (1, 1) where *A*(2, 3), *B*(2, 4) and *C*(4, 3).

Step 1.   Draw the object (e.g. *ABC*) (see below)

Step 2.   Mark the centre of enlargement X.

Step 3.   Draw and extend X*A*, X*B*, X*C*:

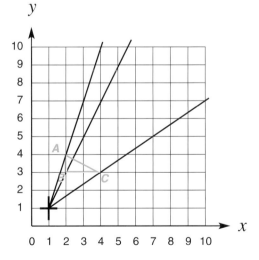

Step 4.   X*D* is 3 times as long as X*A*; mark *D*

Step 5.   Similarly mark *E* and *F*

Step 6.   Draw triangle *DEF*

Step 7. Check *AB* : *DE* and *BC* : *EF* and *AC* : *DF* are all in the ratio 1 : 3

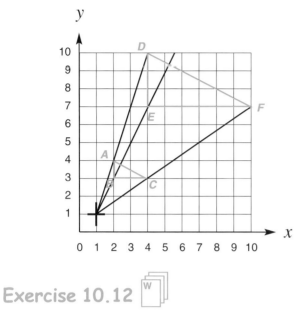

Exercise 10.12

1. (a) Draw the enlargement, *EFG*, of *ABC* by scale factor 3, with centre of enlargement (0, 0), where *A*(1, 2), *B*(2, 1) and *C*(3, 2).
    (b) What is the ratio area *EFG* : area *ABC* ?

2. (a) Draw the enlargement, *XYZ*, of *UVW* by scale factor 2, with centre of enlargement (9, 2), where *U*(6, 4), *V*(6, 2) and *W*(7, 2).
    (b) What is the ratio area *XYZ* : area *UVW* ?

3. (a) Draw the enlargement, *EKL*, of *EFG* by scale factor 3, with centre of enlargement (2, 2), where *E*(2, 2), *F*(4, 2) and *G*(4, 3).
    (b) What is the ratio area *EKL* : area *EFG* ?

4. (a) Draw the enlargement, *EFGH*, of *ABCD* by scale factor 3, with centre of enlargement (1, 8), where *A*(2, 7), *B*(2, 6), *C*(3, 6) and *D*(3, 7).
    (b) What is the ratio area *EFGH* : area *ABCD* ?

5. (a) Draw the enlargement, *JKLM*, of *PQRS* by scale factor 2, with centre of enlargement (3, 1), where *P*(3, 4), *Q*(3, 2), *R*(5, 2) and *S*(5, 4).
    (b) What is the ratio area *JKLM* : area *PQRS* ?

6. (a) Draw the enlargement, *AFGH*, of *ABCD* by scale factor 2, with centre of enlargement (3, 2), where *A*(3, 2), *B*(5, 2), *C*(5, 4) and *D*(3, 4).
    (b) What is the ratio area *AFGH* : area *ABCD* ?

7. Write a rule about the ratio of the areas when you know the scale factor.

Exercise 10.13: Extension questions 1

These are similar to the questions you have met before, but a little harder. As always make sure you read the questions carefully and show all your working:

1. I have to make a bar of an alloy. I do this by mixing up copper and zinc in the ratio 3 : 8. If my finished bar has to have a mass of 187 kg, how many kg each of copper and zinc will I require?

2. James and Jane mixed up jugs of orange squash for sports day. Each jug contained 2 litres. The orange concentrate and water were supposed to be mixed in the ratio 1 : 7. Jane mixed her squash correctly but James did not read the instructions and mixed his in the ratio 1 : 4. If the concentrate came in bottles of 1.5 litres, how many more jugs did Jane make from one bottle of concentrate than James?

3. My bicycle is geared in the ratio 2 : 3, so two turns of the pedals turns the wheel three times. If the circumference of the wheel is 1.2 m, how many turns of the pedals will I need to go one kilometre?

4. The angles of a quadrilateral are in the ratio 1 : 2 : 3 : 4
    What are the angles?

5. The angles of a quadrilateral are in the ratio 2 : 3 : 3 : 4
    What are the angles and what special quadrilateral could this be? (Could it be any other quadrilateral?)

6. Colonel Mustard likes his gin and tonic in the ratio 2 : 3 of gin to tonic.
    His wife, Mrs Mustard, likes hers in the ratio 1 : 5
    If they both have 200 ml of drink, how much gin do they each have?

Exercise 10.14: Extension questions 2
Ratio and algebra

On page 193 we looked at how some ratios may be written as fractions
$1 : 2 = \dfrac{1}{2}$

and how you could end up with having to try to find the missing value in a calculation that looked like:

$$\frac{15}{25} = \frac{3}{x}$$

We then went on to learn about and to use the unitary method.

However, as we hinted earlier on, we can solve these sorts of questions, and indeed more complicated ones, by carefully calculating the missing value like this:

Notice that if $\frac{15}{25} = \frac{3}{x}$ then $\frac{x}{3} = \frac{25}{15}$

(We want to try to find the value of x, so the first thing to do is to get the x on its own by multiplying both sides of the equation by 3.)

$$\cancel{3} \times \frac{x}{\cancel{3}} = \frac{25}{\cancel{15}5} \times \frac{\cancel{3}}{1}$$

$$x = \frac{25}{5}$$

$$x = 5$$

1.   Calculate x in each of these ratios:

(a) $24 : 81 = 8 : x$ (b) $125 : x = 500 : 164$ (c) $432 : 240 = x : 90$

2.   Calculate x in each of these ratios:

(a) $\frac{455}{x} = \frac{195}{21}$ (b) $231 : 385 = x : 45$ (c) $561 : 385 = 153 : x$

When solving ratio questions, it can be useful to call the unknown quantity x, then form an equation in x and finally solve it.

3.   Consider this enlargement:

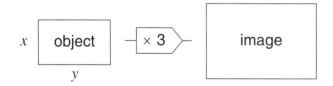

(a) What is the height of the image, in terms of x?
(b) What is the length of the image, in terms of y?
(c) What is the ratio   Height of object : Length of object?
(d) What is the ratio   Height of image : Length of image?
(e) What is the ratio   Height of object : Height of image?
(f) What is the ratio   Length of object : Length of image?

(g) Is it always true that $\dfrac{\text{height of object}}{\text{height of image}} = \dfrac{\text{length of object}}{\text{length of image}}$?

4.   Find x and y in this enlargement:

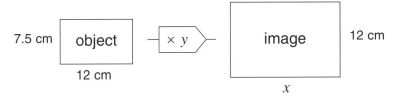

5.   In this enlargement the area of the object is given. This should help you
     to find the missing dimensions:

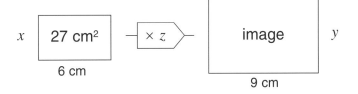

     What is the ratio of the area of the object to the area of the image?

You should notice that the ratio of the areas is equal to the ratio of the squares
of the sides.

6.   In this enlargement we know the areas of the object and the image and
     some dimensions:

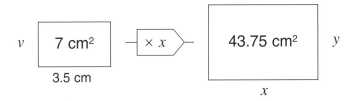

     Find: (a) the scale factor. (b) the missing dimensions.

Exercise 10.15: Summary exercise

1.   I have 4 tins of white paint and 7 tins of red paint.
     (a) What is the ratio of white paint to red paint?
     (b) What is the ratio of red paint to white paint?
     (c) What is the ratio of red paint to the total number of tins of paint?

2.   Simplify these ratios:
     (a) 12 : 24   (b) 32 : 144   (c) 108 : 45

3. A map is drawn to a scale of 1 : 50 000
    What does 4 cm on the map represent on the ground?

4. Draw a line AC 5 cm long.
    Mark a point B so that AB : BC = 2 : 3

5. Draw a line AC 12 cm long.
    Mark a point B so that AB : BC = 1 : 2

6. Replace the x in these ratios:
    (a) 34 : x = 2 : 1   (b) 24 : 8 = 6 : x (c) 2 : 7 = 34 : x

7. A piece of string 1.2 m long is cut into two pieces in the ratio 3 : 5
    How long was each of the two pieces?

8. I need 12 litres of fertiliser to treat 30 m² of lawn. How many litres will I
    need to treat a lawn that measures 8 m by 6 m?

9. In two hours we received 2.3 cm of rain. How many centimetres of rain
    would we receive in 3 hours?

10. On a grid with a pair of axes numbered from 1 to 10, draw triangle A with
    vertices at (2, 3), (3, 3) and (3, 5). Draw the triangle B, which is the
    enlargement of A by scale factor 3 with centre of enlargement at (1, 4).

End of chapter 10 activity: Christmas lunch investigation

It is Christmas day in Acacia Avenue and here at number 12 Mum is trying to
draw up the table plan. Freddy, Sally, Vinnie and I are coming for lunch as well
as Mum, Dad, Granny and Grandpa, Aunt Ethel and Uncle Bert, and cousins
Cynthia and Sonnie.

How many different ways of arranging the Christmas lunch table are there?

After spending several hours on this, Dad suggests that we make it easier by
trying to find the answer for tables of fewer people. If we can find a pattern
then we might be able to use that to solve the problem.

At number 1 Acacia Avenue lives Stan. He will have Christmas lunch on his
own, so there is only one way to arrange his table.

At number 2 Acacia Avenue live Dot and Doris. The two of them always eat together. Of course, Dot sits next to Doris and Doris next to Dot, so there is only one way their table can be arranged.

At number 3 Acacia Avenue live Mr and Mrs Blott and their son, Inky Blott. Whichever way their table is arranged, Inky sits between his Mum and Dad, and his Mum sits between Inky and Mr Blott and his Dad sits between Inky and Mrs Blott, only one arrangement again! How easy life must be in the Blott household!

At number 4 Acacia Avenue live the Whites. There is Chalky White and his sisters, Pearl and Ivory, and their dog, Snowy. Snowy always sits down for Christmas Lunch too. These are the different arrangements for the table at number 4:

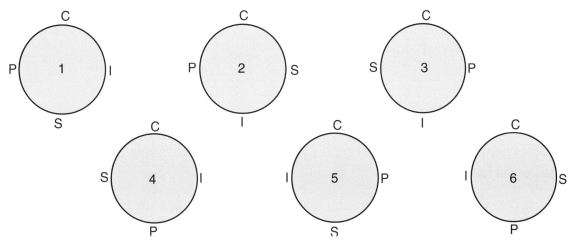

This looks like 6 arrangements, but if you look carefully you will see that arrangement 1 is the same as 5, 2 is the same as 3 and that 4 is the same as 6, so there are only three different arrangements.

You can see from number 4 Acacia Avenue that we think of a table arrangement by considering who sits next to whom. Although arrangement 1 looked different from arrangement 5, Chalky was still opposite Snowy and next to Pearl and Ivory. Remember this definition when you work out the next few answers.

At number 5 Acacia Avenue live Mr and Mrs Cake and their children, Pan, Fairy and Sponge. Can you work out the 12 different ways in which they can arrange their table?

At number 6 Acacia Avenue live the Gone family. As well as Mum and Dad there are the twins, Octa and Nona, and Uncle Penta and Aunt Polly. How many ways can their table be arranged?

Working out the arrangements for the seven people at number 7 might be quite hard. First copy and complete this table, and then see if you can spot a pattern:

House number	Arrangements
1	1
2	1
3	1
4	3
5	12
6	

Check your pattern is correct by drawing all the arrangements for the family of seven at number 7.

Now can you work out how many arrangements there are for our family of 12 at number 12? (Please remember that Dad refuses to sit next to Aunt Ethel, no two boys can sit next to each other as they fight, nor two girls as they argue. Have a happy Christmas lunch yourself!)

Chapter 11: Algebra 2 – Equations and brackets

The toy shop is having a sale. It is selling bundles of toys at special discount prices.

One bundle is of three lorries and two spiders (🚛 🚛 🚛 🕷 🕷)

I buy two of these bundles:

(🚛 🚛 🚛 🕷 🕷)   (🚛 🚛 🚛 🕷 🕷)

In the **two** bundles I have **twice** the number of lorries and **twice** the number of spiders.

I could write this as: 2 (🚛 🚛 🚛 🕷 🕷) = (🚛 🚛 🚛 🚛 🚛 🚛 🕷 🕷 🕷 🕷)

In the same way we put these little pictures in brackets, we can also put numbers in brackets. When we have a calculation with brackets in it, we normally do the calculation inside the brackets first:

$$2(7 + 2) = 2 \times 9$$
$$= 18$$

We do, however, get the same answer if we multiply out the brackets like this:

$$2(7 + 2) = 2 \times 7 + 2 \times 2$$
$$= 14 + 4$$
$$= 18$$

If there is an x term inside the brackets, we can in fact only multiply out the brackets. Here's an example:

$$2(x + 2) = 2 \times x + 2 \times 2$$
$$= 2x + 4$$

Exercise 11.1

Multiply out the following brackets:

1. $3(x + 1)$
2. $2(x + 3)$
3. $2(x - 3)$
4. $4(3 + x)$
5. $2(5 - a)$

6. $3(2b + 1)$
7. $2(4x + 3)$
8. $2(5 + 2a)$
9. $5(2y + 3)$
10. $3(7 - 3a)$

11. $4(6 + 3a)$
12. $2(2x - 3y)$
13. $3(4a - b)$
14. $5(2x + 1)$
15. $3(b - 5a)$

16. $3(7 - 2x)$
17. $2(6a - 3b)$
18. $6(4 - 3x)$
19. $8(2n - 4m)$
20. $5(3p - q)$

Sometimes we can combine terms:

Example: $3x + 4(2x + 3)$ $= 3x + 8x + 12$ Multiply out the brackets as
$= 11x + 12$ we did above and then add
the like terms together.

Exercise 11.2

Multiply out these brackets and simplify the following calculations:

1. $2 + 3(x + 2)$
2. $4x + 2(x - 1)$
3. $2x + 5(x - 3)$
4. $x + 2(2x + 5)$
5. $3(x + 2) - 3$

6. $3(4 - 2x) + 3x$
7. $2 + 3(4 - 2x)$
8. $4(3x - 4) - 12x$
9. $4 + 4(2x - 1)$
10. $3x + 5(2 + 3x)$

The next ten questions have two sets of brackets. Here's an example to show you how to deal with this:

Example: $2(3x - 3) + 3(x + 4)$ $= 6x - 6 + 3x + 12$ Simply multiply out the
$= 9x + 6$ brackets and combine
like terms.

11. $2(4x + 3) + 3(2x - 4)$ **16.** $2(4x - 3) + 3(5 - x)$

12. $3(x + 2) + 2(2x + 1)$ **17.** $5(2 + 3x) + (5x + 6)$

13. $4(3 + x) + 3(5 - 2x)$ **18.** $4(5 - 3x) + 2(4 - 6x)$

14. $2(1 + 2x) + 3(x + 2)$ **19.** $3(7 + 3x) + 2(5 - x)$

15. $3(2x + 4) + (5x + 3)$ **20.** $2(6 - x) + (3 - 2x)$

Brackets and minus signs

If there is a minus sign before the bracket, then you have to **change the sign of everything inside the brackets**:

Example:

(i) $6x - 2(2x + 1)$ $= 6x - 4x - 2$ (ii) $5 - 3(x - 2)$ $= 5 - 3x + 6$
$= 2x - 2$ $= 11 - 3x$

If there is **no number** in front of the brackets, just **multiply by one** and **change the signs** as before:

Example:

(i) $5x - (3 + 2x)$ $= 5x - 3 - 2x$ (ii) $5 - (3x - 1)$ $= 5 - 3x + 1$
$= 3x - 3$ $= 6 - 3x$

Exercise 11.3

Multiply out these brackets and simplify:

1. $4 - 2(x + 1)$
2. $3x - 2(2 + x)$
3. $5x - 2(5 + 2x)$
4. $8 - 3(3x + 2)$
5. $3 - (2x + 1)$

6. $8x - (4 + 5x)$
7. $10x - 3(2 + 3x)$
8. $8 - 4(3x + 2)$
9. $12 - (2 + x)$
10. $3x - 2(5x - 1)$

And now let's do the same thing but where there are two sets of brackets:

$$\text{Example: } 2(3x - 3) - 3(x + 4) = 6x - 6 - 3x - 12$$
$$= 3x - 18$$

11. $2(4x + 3) - 3(x - 1)$
12. $3(x + 2) - 2(2x + 1)$
13. $4(2 + 2x) - 3(4 - 2x)$
14. $2(1 + 3x) - 3(x + 1)$
15. $3(2x + 2) - (3x + 3)$

16. $2(x + 3) - 3(3x - 4)$
17. $5(2 + x) - (5x + 1)$
18. $4(3 - 2x) - 2(6 - 6x)$
19. $4(5 + 3x) - 2(5 + 6x)$
20. $2(3 - x) - (6 - 2x)$

Sometimes you may find that your answers come out like this:

(i) $-6x + 7$ (ii) $-2x - 12$

We should, if we can, avoid beginning with a negative number.

So it would be better to give the expression in (i) above as: $7 - 6x$

There is nothing we can do about the answer for (ii), so we leave it as it is.

Remember this when you do the next exercise.

Exercise 11.4

These questions are mixed. Multiply out the brackets and then simplify. Be careful to notice the minus signs and deal with them correctly. Don't let them catch you out!

1. $8 + 3(2x - 4)$

2. $10 - 2(2x + 1)$

3. $3(3 + x) - 2(5 - 2x)$

4. $2(1 + x) + 3(x + 2)$

5. $3(3x + 4) - (5x + 4)$

6. $12 - (2x - 4)$

7. $5(2 + 3x) - 8x$

8. $3(3 - 4x) + 2(6x - 1)$

9. $3(6 + 3x) - 2(9 - x)$

10. $2(7 + x) - (3 + 5x)$

11. $2(4x + 3) - 6$

12. $4x - 2(2x + 1)$

13. $4(3 + 6x) - 3(5 - 8x)$

14. $4(1 + 2x) - 2(x + 2)$

15. $15x - 5(5x + 3)$

16. $2(4x + 6) + 3(2x - 4)$

17. $6(2 + 3x) - 3(5x + 6)$

18. $12x - 2(4 - 6x)$

19. $3(7 + 3x) - 21$

20. $4(6 - 3x) - 3(8 - 4x)$

Making bundles or factorising

Some of the expressions we had in the last exercise had the same numbers or letters in both parts. We call this a **common factor** in the same way that 2 is a common factor of 4 and 6

Finding the common factor and taking it outside the brackets is called **factorising**. You can always check that your factorising is correct by multiplying out the brackets.

> Example: Factorise $2ab + 6$
> $$2ab + 6 = 2 \times a \times b + 3 \times 2$$
> $$= 2(ab + 3)$$
>
> Check: $2(ab + 3) = 2ab + 6$

Exercise 11.5

Factorise these expressions:

1. Copy and complete these: the factors have already been taken out for you:
   (a) $2x + 6 = 2(x + *)$
   (b) $3x + 12 = 3(x + *)$
   (c) $4x - 8 = 4(* - 2)$
   (d) $3x + 6 = 3(x + *)$
   (e) $6x + 8 = 2(*x + 4)$
   (f) $14 - 8x = 2(* - 4x)$

2. Copy and complete these; the common factor needs to be written in each time:
   (a) $3x + 12 = *(x + 4)$
   (b) $6x - 3 = *(2x - 1)$
   (c) $4x + 2y - 6 = *(2x + y - 3)$
   (d) $15 - 3x = *(5 - x)$
   (e) $8x + 2 = *(4x + 1)$

3. This time the common factors have been taken out and you have to fill in the brackets:
   (a) $4x + 6 = 2(** + *)$
   (b) $3x - 15 = 3(* - *)$
   (c) $6x + 9y - 12 = 3(** + ** - *)$
   (d) $12 + 9x = 3(* + **)$
   (e) $24 + 16x = 8(* + **)$

There is no reason why the common factor cannot be a letter:

Example: Factorise $ab + 6a$
$$ab + 6a = a \times b + 3 \times 2 \times a$$
$$= a(b + 6)$$

Check: $a(b + 6) = ab + 6a$

4. Copy and complete these; the common factor needs to be written in each time:
   (a) $3x + xy = *(3 + y)$
   (b) $ab - 7a = *(b - 7)$
   (c) $15p - 7pq = *(15 - 7q)$
   (d) $3abc - 4b = *(3ac - 4)$

5. Copy and complete these; here the factors have been taken out for you:
   (a) $2x + xy = x(2 + *)$
   (b) $ab + 12a = a(b + *)$
   (c) $5ab + a = a(** + 1)$
   (d) $pq + 6q = q(* + *)$
   (e) $5y - 3xy = y(* - **)$
   (f) $4ab - a = a(** - *)$

Sometimes there are two common factors:

Example: Factorise $2ab + 6a$

$$2ab + 6a = 2 \times a \times b + 3 \times 2 \times a$$
$$= 2a(b + 3)$$

Check: $2a(b + 3) = 2ab + 6a$

---

6. Copy and complete these; the common factor needs to be written in each time:

(a) $3x + 6xy = **(1 + 2y)$
(b) $21ab - 7a = **(3b - 1)$
(c) $15p - 3pq = **(5 - q)$
(d) $3abc - 12b = **(ac - 4)$

7. Copy and complete these; the factors have been taken out for you:

(a) $2x + 6xy = 2x(* + **)$
(b) $3ab + 12a = 3a(* + *)$
(c) $12pq + 6q = 3q(** + *)$
(d) $15y - 25xy = 5y(* - **)$

8. Factorise these; the common factor is a number:

(a) $4x + 8$
(b) $3y - 6$
(c) $12 + 18y$

9. Factorise these; the common factor is a letter:

(a) $4x + xy$
(b) $3ab - 7a$
(c) $3x + 14\,xy + xz$

10. Factorise these; there are two common factors:

(a) $8x + 2xy$
(b) $12ab$ $8a$
(c) $3x + 9xy + 6xz$

11. Factorise these; note that you may need to leave the number 1 inside the bracket:

(a) $15y + 5$
(b) $24a - 16ab$
(c) $16x - 20xy + 4$
(d) $16x - 20xy$
(e) $8a + 4ab - 6ac$
(f) $8x + 4y - 12xy$

12. Factorise these, if possible:

(a) $2x + 8$
(b) $17x + 14xy$
(c) $12a + 5$
(d) $15 - 21x$
(e) $9a + 16b$
(f) $18a + 16ab$
(g) $8a + 16b - 24ab$
(h) $18abc + 6ab$
(i) $9a^2 + 16a$
(j) $18a^2 + 16ab$
(k) $4x^2 + 16xy$
(l) $8pq + 16p^2$

(m) $16ab - 4a$
(n) $24a - 15ab$
(o) $18 + 12a$
(p) $14xy + 15y$
(q) $15x + 24 - 9y$
(r) $12a - 5b + 10ab$

(s) $25x - 26y$
(t) $12pq - 3p + 9ps$
(u) $15x + 9xy^2$
(v) $12a - 5b^2 + 10ab$
(w) $24x^2 - 9xy + 18x$
(x) $15a^2 - 5ab^2 + 10ab$

Equations

In *So you really want to learn Maths* Book 1 we learned to solve simple equations.

Remember that an equation is like a balance and in order to keep it balanced we must do the same thing to both sides:

Example:

(i) $x + 3 = 9$
$\qquad\qquad (-3)$
$\qquad x = 6$

(ii) $3x = 6$
$\qquad\qquad (\div 3)$
$\qquad x = 2$

It is good practice to **check** your answer by **substituting** the value you found into the original equation:

(i) $6 + 3 = 9$ We were right!

Exercise 11.6

Solve these equations; remember to check your answers in your head:

1. $x + 4 = 6$
2. $a - 6 = 3$
3. $4b = 8$
4. $2c = 10$
5. $p + 8 = 4$

6. $4x = 12$
7. $m - 4 = 7$
8. $3d = 12$
9. $7 + x = 6$
10. $6 - m = 5$

Sometimes we need to go through two or more stages:

Example:

(i) $2x + 3 = 9$

$\qquad\qquad\qquad$ $(- 3)$

$\qquad 2x = 6$

$\qquad\qquad\qquad$ $(\div 2)$

$\qquad x = 3$

(ii) $7 - 3x = 6$

$\qquad\qquad\qquad$ $(+ 3x)$

$\qquad 7 = 6 + 3x$

$\qquad\qquad\qquad$ $(- 6)$

$\qquad 1 = 3x$

$\qquad\qquad\qquad$ $(\div 3)$

$\qquad x = \dfrac{1}{3}$

In example (ii) the unknown term is negative, so we add it to both sides. This way it appears on the other side of the equals sign, but is now positive. It is important to keep the unknown term positive:

11. $2a + 4 = 8$

12. $3m - 1 = 5$

13. $5 + 4p = 13$

14. $1 - 3n = 7$

15. $2x + 14 = 9$

16. $3s + 7 = 16$

17. $2t - 4 = 10$

18. $7 + 3q = 13$

19. $6x + 1 = 7$

20. $9 - 4n = 1$

21. $5 + 3b = 8$

22. $6 = 2 + 3x$

23. $11 = 2 - 3b$

24. $1 + 4b = 6$

25. $5 - 2c = 8$

26. $5 = 2 - 3n$

27. $7 = 8 - 2b$

28. $9 = 1 + 2x$

29. $7 = 2 - 5c$

30. $3 = 8 + 5a$

Squares and square roots

If x^2 is the square of x, we say that x is the **square root** of x^2

1 is the square of 1 and −1	1 and −1 are the square roots of 1
4 is the square of 2 and −2	2 and −2 are the square roots of 4
9 is the square of 3 and −3	3 and −3 are the square roots of 9
16 is the square of 4 and −4	4 and −4 are the square roots of 16

We write 'square root' like this: $\sqrt{}$ and therefore the square root of 4 is $\sqrt{4}$

$\sqrt{4} = 2$ or −2   We can write 2 or −2 like this: ±2

Exercise 11.7

Find these squares and square roots:

1. $\sqrt{16}$

2. $\sqrt{25}$

3. $\sqrt{10\,000}$

4. 0.4^2

5. 1.2^2

6. $\sqrt{0.25}$

7. $\sqrt{144}$

8. 100^2

9. 0.1^2

10. $\sqrt{121}$

11. $\left(\dfrac{1}{2}\right)^2$

12. $\sqrt{\dfrac{1}{9}}$

13. $\left(\dfrac{1}{10}\right)^2$

14. $\sqrt{\dfrac{1}{25}}$

15. $\sqrt{0.0036}$

16. $\left(\dfrac{2}{3}\right)^2$

Exercise 11.8: Solving equations with x^2

We know that $3 \times 3 = 9$ and also that $-3 \times -3 = +9$

Therefore we can see that equations with x^2 do in fact have **two** solutions.

Example: If $x^2 = 9$
$$x = 3 \text{ or } -3$$

Solve these equations:

1. $x^2 = 1$

2. $a^2 = 100$

3. $b^2 = 49$

4. $c^2 = 81$

5. $y^2 = 4$

6. $a^2 = 64$

7. $x^2 = 0.09$

8. $c^2 = 1600$

9. $b^2 = 0.16$

10. $y^2 = 400$

Write an equation and solve it to find the answers to these questions:

11. The area of a square is 144 m². What is the length of one of its sides?

12. The area of a square is 1.44 m². What is the length of one of its sides?

13. The area of a square is 0.64 cm². What is the length of one of its sides?

14. The area of a square is 0.04 cm². What is its perimeter?

Equations with brackets

As we have seen throughout this chapter, we sometimes need brackets in an equation.

For example:

Two of my friends are having a birthday. I have £10 to spend. Birthday cards cost £1. Assuming I spend the same amount on each friend, how much can I spend on each present?

I could write the puzzle like this:

$$(\blacksquare + £1) + (\blacksquare + £1) = 10$$

But it is easier to say: 'let the present cost £x', and then form an equation in x which can be solved:

Example:

$$(x + 1) + (x + 1) = 10$$
$$2(x + 1) = 10 \qquad \text{(brackets)}$$
$$2x + 2 = 10$$
$$\qquad\qquad\qquad (- 2)$$
$$2x = 8$$
$$\qquad\qquad\qquad (\div 2)$$
$$x = 4$$

Each present costs £4

(Note that we leave the units **out** of the equation – i.e. the £ in this case – until we have solved the equation. We then give the answer to the question, including the units, after the calculation.)

It is good practice to **check** your answer by **substituting** it back into the original equation:

$$2(4 + 1) = 2 \times 5$$
$$= 10 \qquad \text{So the answer is correct!}$$

Exercise 11.9

Solve these equations; remember to multiply out the brackets first and to write down what you are doing at each stage; do check your answers in your head:

1. $3(x + 1) = 12$

2. $2(x - 3) = 10$

3. $4(3 + x) = 16$

4. $3(2 + x) = 15$

5. $2(2x - 1) = 18$

6. $15 = 3(2x + 3)$

Remember that there is no reason why an answer cannot be a negative number or a fraction:

7. $2(2x + 3) = 8$

8. $2(2x - 3) = 8$

9. $16 = 3(4 + 2x)$

10. $4(2x + 5) = 3$

11. $5(x - 4) = 6$

12. $2(5 + 3x) = 1$

If an x term is negative, remember to add it to both sides:

13. $2(3 - x) = 9$

14. $3(4 - x) = 6$

15. $14 = 3(3 - 5x)$

16. $4(2 - 3x) = 6$

17. $11 = 2(1 - 3x)$

18. $3(2 - 3x) = 3$

19. $2(x - 1) = 8$

20. $12 = 4(x + 2)$

21. $2(4 + 3x) = 2$

22. $4 = 3(2 + 2x)$

23. $4(2 - 3x) = 16$

24. $2(2 + 3x) = 22$

25. $3(2x - 1) = 8$

26. $4(3 - x) = 8$

Fractions and equations

If the equation involves a fraction, then multiply both sides by the denominator (the bottom number) first:

Example:

(i) $\dfrac{x}{3} = 4$

$\qquad$ ($\times$ 3)

$\quad x = 12$

(ii) $\dfrac{(x - 4)}{3} = 2$

$\qquad$ ($\times$ 3)

$\quad x - 4 = 6$

$\qquad$ (+ 4)

$\quad x = 10$

You can see that by multiplying by three first, in both these examples, we were able to multiply out the fraction. The equation then becomes simple.

Exercise 11.10

Solve these equations:

1. $\dfrac{x}{5} = 2$

2. $\dfrac{a}{2} = 7$

3. $9 = \dfrac{m}{3}$

4. $\dfrac{b}{4} = 5$

5. $\dfrac{3a}{2} = 9$

6. $\dfrac{4a}{3} = 12$

7. $\dfrac{3n}{4} = 1$

8. $\dfrac{(x+5)}{2} = 3$

9. $\dfrac{(a-4)}{3} = 5$

10. $\dfrac{(2x+4)}{5} = 2$

Exercise 11.11

Here are some more complicated equations; in these questions you have to multiply out the brackets first and then simplify before solving the equation:

Example:

$$2(3x - 1) + 4x = 10 \quad \text{(brackets)}$$
$$6x - 2 + 4x = 10 \quad \text{(simplify)}$$
$$10x - 2 = 10$$
$$10x = 12 \quad \text{(+ 2)}$$
$$\qquad\qquad\qquad \text{(÷ 10)}$$
$$x = \frac{12}{10} = \frac{6}{5} = 1\frac{1}{5}$$

1. $3(2x - 2) + 4 = 8$

2. $2(3 + 2x) - 1 = 12$

3. $5 + 2(x - 2) = 7$

4. $3(1 + 2x) + 5 = 8$

5. $3 - 2(x + 4) = 6$

6. $4 - 3(2x + 1) = 7$

7. $12 = 3 - 4(2 + x)$

8. $9 = 4 - 2(3x + 1)$

9. $2(4x - 1) - 3x = 8$

10. $6 - (2x + 5) = 7$

11. $3x + 4(2x - 3) = 21$

12. $4x - 3(2 + 3x) = 36$

13. $3(x + 3) + 2(x + 4) = 22$

14. $3(3 - 2x) - 4(4 + 3x) = 6$

15. $2(x - 1) + 3(x - 4) = 1$

16. $4(2 + 3x) - 4(3 + 2x) = 11$

17. $3(2 + x) - (4x + 1) = 8$

18. $3(x + 3) - 2(x + 4) = 12$

19. $2(3x + 2) + 5(3x - 3) = 22$

20. $2(x + 2) - (x - 1) = 4$

Writing story puzzles with brackets

It can be difficult to decide whether or not to use brackets in a story problem. In our original story on page 215 we had two 'bundles' of the same size:

(🎁 + 1) and (🎁 + 1)

We used brackets because '1' was added to the unknown quantity 🎁.

Then the (🎁 + 1) was multiplied by 2 because there were 2 presents to be bought.

It is a good idea to use brackets round two amounts added or subtracted, even if you are not sure if they are really necessary.

Exercise 11.12

Write equations for these story puzzles and then solve them to find the solution to the puzzles:

Example: If you double the age that I will be in five years time, you will get my mother's age now. My mother is 38. How old am I?

Let my age be x years.
In five years time I will be $(x + 5)$ years.
Double $(x + 5)$ is my mother's age, so we write:

$2(x + 5) = 38$ (brackets)

$2x + 10 = 38$ (− 10)

$2x = 28$ (÷ 2)

$x = 14$

I am 14 years old   Remember to write out the answer with the correct units.

1.   I think of a number, add 5, double the result and I get 30.
     What was my number?

2.   I think of a number, double it, add 5 and I get 25.
     What was my number?

3.   I think of a number, subtract 3, double the result and I get 14.
     What was my number?

4.   I think of a number, double it, subtract 3 and I get 17.
     What was my number?

5.   If you double the age that I will be in four years time, you will get 40.
     How old am I now?

6.   If you treble the age that I was 4 years ago, you will get 36.
     How old am I now?

7.   I am 5 years younger than my sister. My brother is twice as old as I am.
     (Note some of the answers will be expressions in terms of x.)
     (a) If my sister is x years old, how old am I?
     (b) How old is my brother?
     (c) Write an expression in x for the sum of our ages.
     (d) If the sum of our ages is 33, form an equation in x and solve it. How
         old is my sister?
     (e) How old am I? How old is my brother?

8.   My sister is three years younger than I am and my brother is three times
     as old as my sister.
     (a) If I am x years old how old is my sister?
     (b) How old is my brother?
     (c) Write an expression in x for the sum of our ages.
     (d) If the sum of our ages is 28, write an equation in x and solve it to find
         my age.
     (e) How old is my brother?

9.   Tom, Sally and I divide up a packet of sweets. Tom has the green ones,
     Sally has the orange ones and I have the rest. I have twice as many as
     Tom and 5 more sweets than Sally.
     (a) If Tom has x sweets, how many do I have?
     (b) How many does Sally have?
     (c) Write an expression in x for the total number of sweets.
     (d) If there were 15 sweets in total, write an equation in x and solve it to
         find how many sweets we each had.

Exercise 11.13: Extension questions

Working with fractions

In Exercise 11.10 we had equations with fractions. In these there was only one fraction and the first thing we did was to multiply both sides of the equation by the denominator, so that we could get rid of the fraction. These are the same, but with an extra stage.

Example:

$$\frac{2}{3}(x - 4) = 2 \qquad (\times 3)$$
$$2(x - 4) = 6 \qquad (\text{brackets})$$
$$2x - 8 = 6 \qquad (+ 8)$$
$$2x = 14 \qquad (\div 2)$$
$$x = 7$$

There are a lot of stages you have to go through in order to find the solution. But don't be put off: each stage is in fact very straightforward. Make sure you don't try to combine stages together. It's tempting but is likely to get you the wrong answers!

1. $\frac{1}{2}(x + 3) = 4$

2. $\frac{3}{4}(2x - 3) = 5$

3. $\frac{3x - 1}{2} = 4$

4. $\frac{1}{4}(3x + 4) = 5$

5. $\frac{1}{3}(4 - x) = 2$

6. $\frac{2(x + 3)}{5} = 4$

7. $\frac{2}{3}(2x - 5) = 4$

8. $\frac{1}{4}(x + 3) = 4$

9. $\frac{3(x + 2)}{4} = 2$

10. $\frac{3}{5}(2x - 1) = 4$

Exercise 11.14: Summary exercise

1. Multiply out these brackets:
   (a) $2(x + 1)$ (b) $3(2x - 4)$ (c) $4(5 + 3x)$

2. Multiply out these brackets and then simplify the expressions:
   (a) $2(x + 1) + 3x$ (c) $4x - 5(2x + 1)$
   (b) $3 + 2(2x - 1)$ (d) $6(3x + 4) - 20x$

3. Factorise the expressions, if possible:
   (a) $2a + 4$ (e) $24a + 15b - 21c$
   (b) $3b - 18c$ (f) $10xy - 5x^2$
   (c) $4x + xy$ (g) $5ab + -7b + 12c$
   (d) $4a + 5c$ (h) $8a + 16ab - 24a^2$

4. (a) $3x = 12$ (c) $m - 6 = 11$
   (b) $a + 4 = 7$ (d) $4s = 3$

5. Solve these equations:
   (a) $4x - 7 = 9$ (c) $3 - 2m = 11$
   (b) $2a + 3 = 7$ (d) $4 = 3 + 5t$

6. Solve these equations:
   (a) $\dfrac{x}{4} = 5$ (b) $\dfrac{(2x - 1)}{3} = 2$

7. Solve these equations:
   (a) $2(x + 3) = 5$ (c) $4x + 3(4 - 3x) = 7$
   (b) $3 - 2(3x + 2) = 5$

8. I think of a number, double it, add 7 and get the result 15
   What was my number?

9. Freddy, Henry and Casper are going on a sponsored walk. Henry walks 10 miles further than Casper, and 6 miles fewer than Freddy.
   (a) If Henry walks x miles, how far does Freddy walk?
   (b) How far does Casper walk?
   (c) Write an expression in x for the total distance the three children walk.
   (d) If they walk a total of 41 miles, write an equation in x and solve it to find how far each one walks.

End of chapter 11 activity: Dungeons and dragons

Dragons rule on the planet Trigon.

If you were unlucky enough to find yourself on the planet Trigon, you would probably be caught and thrown into a dungeon. Dragons guard the dungeons carefully. It is not an easy job and so the dragons have to be trained.

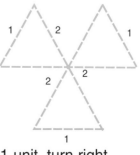

A learner dragon is known as a (1,1). 'Why?', I hear you ask.

Well, on the planet Trigon the dungeons are arranged on a triangular grid. The dragons are known by the instructions they are given, and because dragons are not very bright they repeat their instructions. Oh – and they can only turn right.

So a (1,1) dragon will go: 1 unit, turn right, 1 unit, turn right, 1 unit, turn right; or in other words it will walk round and round an equilateral triangle:

Once the dragon has mastered this patrol, he is promoted to a (1,2) dragon. He then has to patrol as follows:

1 unit, turn right, 2 units, turn right, 1 unit, turn right, 2 units, turn right, 1 unit, turn right, 2 units, turn right.

His patrol will look like this:

1 unit, turn right,
2 units, turn right.

1 unit, turn right,
2 units, turn right.

1 unit, turn right,
2 units, turn right.

So you can see the (1,1) dragon guards one dungeon and the (1,2) dragon guards 3 dungeons.

1. Applying the same principle as the one described above, use triangular isometric paper to draw the paths of:
(a) a (1,3) dragon
(b) a (1,4) dragon
(c) a (1,5) dragon
(d) a (1,6) dragon

(N.B. The dungeons are all 1 unit in length, so if a dragon walks round a triangle of sides 2 units, he is cleverly guarding 4 dungeons.)

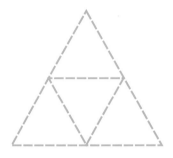

2. Copy and complete this table:

Dragon	Units walked in one circuit	Dungeons guarded
(1,1)	3	1
(1,2)	9	3
(1,3)		
(1,4)		
(1,5)		

3. Without drawing, try to work out the numbers in the next two lines.

4. Now draw and check your answers.

5.   To become a megadragon, you have to work out how many dungeons a (1,10) dragon will guard.

6.   That was easy! Now what is the formula to see how many a (1,*n*) dragon will guard?

7.   Once a dragon becomes a megadragon, his training follows the pattern described below:

First he is given the command (2,1).

When he has mastered that he becomes a (2,2) dragon

and then is promoted to (2,3) dragon and so on.

Just as before, draw the patrol for the first few commands. Now copy and complete the table below and fill in the results.

Dragon	Units walked in one circuit	Dungeons guarded
(2,1)	9	
(2,2)	6	
(2,3)		
(2,4)		
(2,5)		

8.   Work out the (2,10) results and then write the formula for a megadragon.

9.   Even dragons have ambition. To become a megamegadragon, you have to work out the formula that tells you how many dungeons an (*m,n*) dragon can patrol and how far he walks in one circuit.

Chapter 12: Scale drawing and bearings

In Chapter 8 we learnt many facts about angles and how to calculate missing angles in a diagram. In day to day life one can come across angles in many situations, for example navigation. The captain of a boat or a plane relies on navigation all the time.

The most useful tool in navigation is a simple instrument called a compass. Compasses come in many styles, but you will probably be most familiar with these:

Exercise 12.1: How to use a compass 1

Let's take a look at the type of compass often used by walkers:

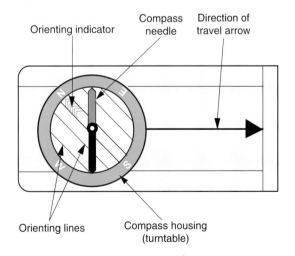

Step 1. Look at the red (in the picture above this is the grey end) and black needle. If you have a compass like this, hold it flat and move it around. What do you notice? You should see that the needle always points in the same direction. The red end points to the Earth's magnetic north pole.

Step 2. That is fine if you want to walk north, but suppose you want to go in another direction? Let us assume you want to go north west, that is the direction half way between north and west. If your compass has a turntable and a direction of travel arrow, turn the compass housing so that north west on the housing comes exactly where the large *direction of travel arrow* meets the housing.

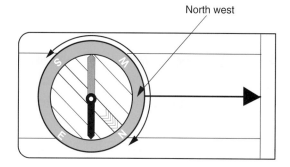

North west

Step 3. Hold your hand out flat and put the compass on your hand then turn yourself, your hand, and the compass, until the compass needle is aligned with the north south lines inside the compass housing (red end pointing north).

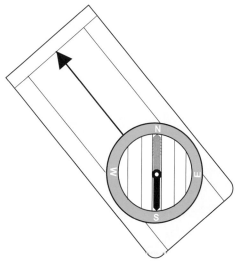

Step 4. Be careful!
It is *extremely* important that the red, north, part of the compass needle points at north in the compass housing. A very common mistake is to have the wrong end of the needle pointing at north. Then you would walk in the wrong direction, so check that it is right! Make sure that you are not standing beside anything metal that might attract your needle, so walk away from any buildings and check that the compass needle stays pointing in the same direction.

Step 5. When you are sure the compass is set correctly, walk in the direction the arrow is pointing. To avoid going off course, look at the compass quite frequently, but do not look at the compass all the time or else you will bump into something. Once you have the direction, fix your eyes on some point in the distance and aim for that, but look down at the compass from time to time.

Step 6. Something else to help you check is the Sun. At noon, the Sun is roughly in the south (or in the north if you are in the southern hemisphere). Work out where you expect the Sun to be and check that it is there.

Step 7. Try taking the following route:
Walk north west for 10 paces.
Turn and walk north east for 10 paces.
Turn and walk south east for 10 paces.
Turn and walk south west for 10 paces.
You have ended up where you started!

In between the four cardinal points, north, south, east and west are the four points north east (NE), north west (NW), south east (SE), south west (SW) and between them are the points NNE, ENE, SSE, ESE etc. Between these are even more points. We describe these using a three figure bearing, or angle:

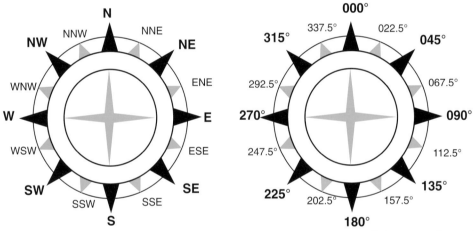

A full circle is 360°. As the north point is 0°, so then east will be 90°, but all bearings have three figures, and so we say 090° (oh-nine-oh). Note that bearings are measured clockwise from north.

Exercise 12.2: How to use a compass 2

Take some bearings

On a boat you will probably have a special compass designed to take bearings, but at school you will probably have to use the same sort of walkers' compass that you used in the first exercise.

Step 1. Turn the compass so the direction of travel arrow is pointing at the object you are looking at.

Step 2. Turn the compass housing so that north on the housing is lined up exactly with the north of the needle.

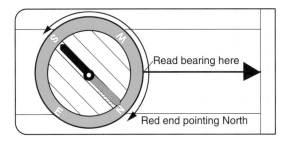

Read bearing here

Red end pointing North

Step 3. The bearing will be given where the direction arrow meets the housing. In the diagram above the direction arrow is pointing at NW or a bearing of 315°.

Step 4. Take some bearings of some objects that you can see.

Step 5. Swap your list of bearings with a friend. Check that you both find the same objects as each other.

Exercise 12.3: How to use a compass 3

Combine bearings and distance.

Step 1. Start at one corner of your playground or playing field. Work out a suitable series of distances and bearings. For example:

Walk 10 metres in direction 045°, alter course to 175° and walk for 25 metres, alter course to 215° and walk for 5 metres.

Step 2. Walk your course and leave a special marker where you end up.

Step 3. Swap instructions with a friend. Walk his or her course and you should be able to pick up his or her marker.

Exercise 12.4: Using bearings

The diagram represents a map showing yourself on your yacht in the middle of a bay. Around you are another boat, a tanker, a lighthouse and a hilltop. You have to find the bearing of each one from your own position.

You find the bearings by positioning your protractor as shown and read off the bearings:

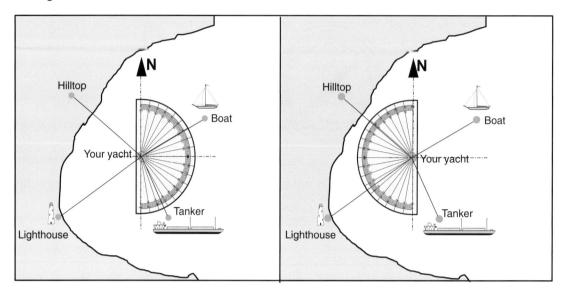

For the lighthouse and the hilltop you will have to put the protractor the other way round, as in the diagram on the right, and add 180° to the reading.

If you have a 360° protractor then you only have to carefully line up North with 0° and then you can read all four bearings without changing the position of the protractor.

Now complete the rest of worksheet.

Exercise 12.5

Using the scales stated draw diagrams to show these points:

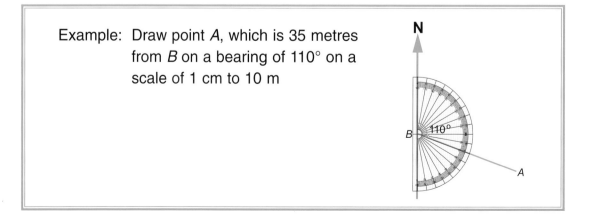

Example: Draw point *A*, which is 35 metres from *B* on a bearing of 110° on a scale of 1 cm to 10 m

1.   Draw a point *P* which is 7 m from *Q* on a bearing of 045° using a scale of 1 cm to 1 m.

2.   Draw a point *A* which is 800 m from *B* on a bearing of 127° using a scale of 1cm to 100 m.

3.   Draw a point *X* which is 120 m from *Y* on a bearing of 175° using a scale of 1cm to 10 m.

4.   Draw a point *M* which is 60 m from *N* on a bearing of 200° using a scale of 1cm to 10 m.

5.   Draw a point *A* which is 750 m from *B* on a bearing of 312° using a scale of 1:10000

6.   Draw a point *R* which is 6.5 m from *S* on a bearing of 163° using a scale of 1:100

7.   Draw a point *V* which is 72 m from *W* on a bearing of 035° using a scale of 1:1000

8.   Draw a point *P* which is 8.6 km from *Q* on a bearing of 287° using a scale of 1cm to 1 km.

9.   In q.1 and q.8 measure the bearings of *Q* from *P* and in q.2 and q.5 measure the bearings of *B* from *A*.

Calculating bearings

When we looked at angles we learnt that when lines are parallel we are able to find pairs of equal angles and pairs of angles that add up to 180°:

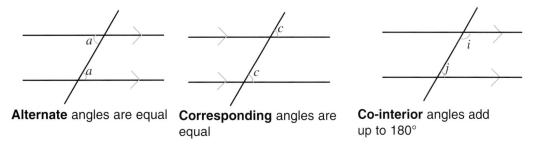

Alternate angles are equal   **Corresponding** angles are equal   **Co-interior** angles add up to 180°

We can use this fact to help us to calculate angles and bearings. We do this by drawing 'north' lines from each of the points. These two lines will be parallel which means we can use them to find pairs of equal angles and pairs of angles that add up to 180°.

This enables us to calculate previously unknown angles and bearings. Here's an example:

Example:

If the bearing of *A* from *B* is 140°, what is the bearing of *B* from *A*?

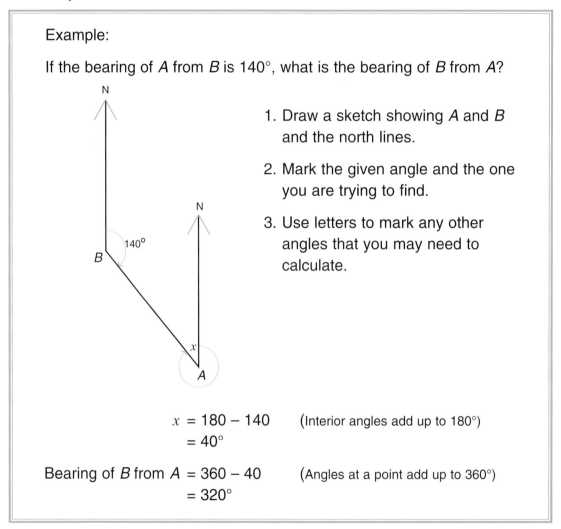

1. Draw a sketch showing *A* and *B* and the north lines.

2. Mark the given angle and the one you are trying to find.

3. Use letters to mark any other angles that you may need to calculate.

$$x = 180 - 140$$ (Interior angles add up to 180°)
$$= 40°$$

Bearing of *B* from *A* $= 360 - 40$ (Angles at a point add up to 360°)
$$= 320°$$

Exercise 12.6

1. If the bearing of *A* from *B* is 120°, what is the bearing of *B* from *A* ?

2. If the bearing of *P* from *Q* is 072°, what is the bearing of *Q* from *P* ?

3. If the bearing of *X* from *Y* is 213°, what is the bearing of *Y* from *X* ?

4. If the bearing of *M* from *N* is 298°, what is the bearing of *N* from *M* ?

5. A yacht race is in the shape of an isosceles triangle, with base angles equal to 63°, starting from point *P* :

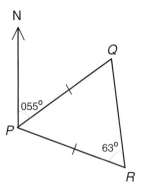

The first mark, *R* is on a bearing of 055° from *P*. Calculate the bearing of:
(a) *R* from *Q*
(b) *P* from *R*
(c) *R* from P

6. I have to run a square course starting from point *A*:

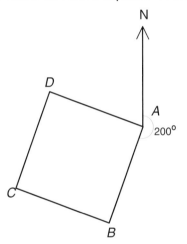

The first corner, *B*, is on a bearing of 200° from *A*.

(a) Calculate the bearing of:
    (i)   *C* from *B*
    (ii)   *D* from *C*
    (iii)   *A* from *D*

(b) I sprain my ankle when I get to *C* and hobble back to *A*. What is the bearing of *A* from *C* ?

7. Look at this plot of a ship's course, *PQ* is equal to *QR*:

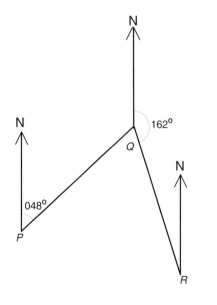

(a) Calculate the bearing of:
    (i)   *P* from *Q*
    (ii)   *Q* from *R*

The ship is in trouble when it reaches *R* and an emergency helicopter is sent out from *P*.

(b) What is the bearing of *R* from *P* ?

8. A ship sails from Ayport on a course of 127° to a point *B*, then turns 90° anticlockwise. What is its new bearing?

9. A plane flies WSW and then changes course to head NNW. Through how many degrees did it turn and in what direction?

10. I am on an expedition and set off from base on a bearing of 037°. I walk for 6 km, then turn 120° clockwise, walk another 6 km and turn 120° clockwise. What is my bearing and distance from the base camp now?

Measuring bearings

We now know that bearings must be measured from a north line. When you have one north line you can use a ruler and a set square to draw other north lines parallel to the first:

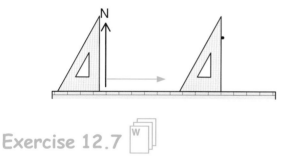

Exercise 12.7

Use the worksheets for this exercise.

1. You are given the bearings of four landmarks from a yacht on a lake. Using these you must find the position of the yacht. First mark a point for the bearing and then continue the line backwards as far as necessary,

Use the bearings for the boathouse and the rescue station to draw two lines. Where they cross will be the position of the boat. Check your position with the other two bearings.

2. This treasure map is drawn to a scale of 1 millimetre to one pace. You should not have too much trouble finding the buried treasure. The black dots in the towers mark the centres. Take your bearings and distances from these.

3. Here is a plan of Hazardous wood. You have been given a list of bearings and distances. If you follow these carefully you should get out of the wood without mishap.

4. Having finally found your way through the wood without mishap you find that you have left your lunch back at the start of your journey. You have to go back to get it, but you must not cross your original path or even go close to it because the gremlins may be lying in wait for you. Work out another path that will take you back to the beginning.

Copy out a table like the one on the sheet and fill in the instructions. Once you are sure that your route will keep you out of danger give it to a friend to test for you!

Exercise 12.8

Draw a scale drawing for each of these. Remember you will first have to draw a sketch. Mark your scale drawing with the given information and do not forget to answer the question. Here's an example:

Example:

I start from a point *A* and walk 100m on a bearing of 110° to *B*.
I then walk 75 m on a bearing of 040° to *C*.
Draw my journey to a scale of 1 cm to 10 m and from your drawing measure the distance and bearing of *C* from *A*.

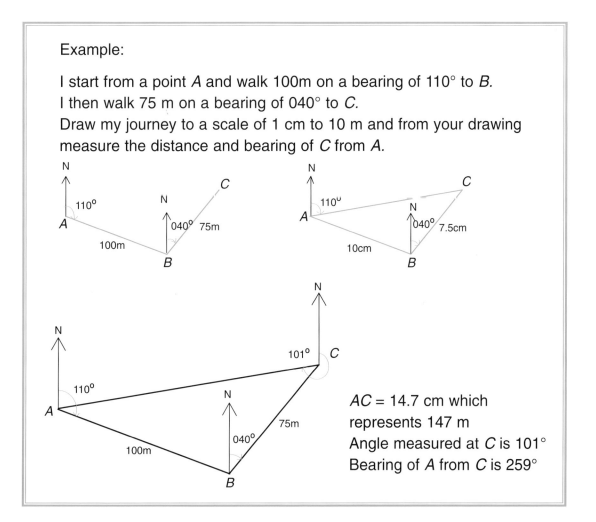

AC = 14.7 cm which represents 147 m
Angle measured at *C* is 101°
Bearing of *A* from *C* is 259°

1. Draw the sketch, and the scale drawing, for the last example. Check that your measurements agree.

2. A ship sails on a bearing of 125° from a port *A*. Another ship starts from port *B*, 15 km due south of *A* at the same time, and sails at a bearing of 070°.
   (a) Draw a sketch of the relative positions of the two boats.
   (b) Draw a line to the left of your page. Mark point *A* and then draw a line to show the first ship's journey.
   (c) Using a scale of 1 cm to 1 km plot point *B* on your drawing. Now draw a line to show the journey of the second ship.
   (d) By measuring the distance and the correct angle, find the distance and bearing from *A* of the point *P* where the two ships' paths pass.

3. I am standing by a tree *A* and I see a bird on a bearing of 210°. My friend is standing by tree *B*, 400 metres to the west of me, and he sees the bird on a bearing of 142°.
   (a) Draw a sketch of the relative positions of me, my friend and the bird.
   (b) Draw a line across the top of your page. Use a scale of 1 cm to 50 metres and mark points *A* and *B*.
   (c) Now draw the two lines from *A* and *B* to find the position of the bird.
   (d) By measuring, find the distance from the bird to point *B*. Remember to turn your measurement back into metres.

4. I walk 300 m from *A* on a bearing of 310° to a point *B*, and then I walk 400m on a bearing of 220° to point *C*.
   (a) Draw a sketch of the relative positions of *A*, *B* and *C*.
   (b) Draw a north line from point *A* to the right of your page. Use a scale of 1 cm to 50 metres and mark point *B*.
   (c) Draw a north line from point *B* mark point *C*.
   (d) Measure the distance *AC* then find the distance in metres for *A* to *C*.
   (e) Measure the appropriate angle and find the bearing of *C* from *A*.

For the next three questions use the information from your sketch to work out where to start your drawing.

5. The first leg of a yacht race is sailed from the start at *X* on a bearing of 072° for 4.5 km to a buoy *Y*. The next leg of the course is to a buoy at *Z*, a distance of 6.3 km from *X* on a bearing of 164°. Draw a plan of the course to a scale of 1 cm to 0.5 km. What is the length of the second leg and what is the bearing of *Z* from *Y*?

6. On our geography field trip, I left the base camp *B* and walked for 2.4 km. My friend Bert walked due south of the base camp for 2 km, then realised that he had gone wrong, and then walked for another 2 km and ended up in exactly the same place as me. Using a scale of 1 cm to 0.25 km, draw a scale drawing of our journeys. What is the bearing of our meeting point from the camp?

7. A yacht leaves Ayport and sails for 8 km on a bearing of 102°. It then changes direction and sails for 5 km on a bearing of 138°. Here it runs into difficulties. Beeport is 10 km due South of Ayport. A lifeboat leaves Beeport and heads for the yacht. How far does the lifeboat have to go and on what bearing should it travel?

Exercise 12.9: Extension questions – Angles and algebra

1. The hands of a 12-hour clock move at different speeds. In one hour the minute hand will have gone a full circle, i.e. 360°, but the hour hand will have gone through one twelfth of a full circle, i.e. 30°. At what times will the angle between the hands of the clock be exactly 90°?

2. The time is m minutes past four.
   (a) How many degrees round from 12 is the minute hand of the clock, in terms of m?
   (b) How many degrees round from 12 is the hour hand of the clock, in terms of m?
   (c) At m minutes past four, the hour and minute hand are in exactly the same place. Form an equation in m and solve it.
   (d) Give the time to the nearest minute.
   (e) What is the angle between the hands 15 minutes later?

3. (a) The bearing of point *X* from point *Y* is $b°$, and b is greater than 0 and less than 90. What is the bearing of *Y* from *X* in terms of b?
   (b) Is your answer the same if b lies between 090° and 180°? Explain your answer carefully.
   (c) What is the bearing of *Y* from *X* if b lies between 180° and 270°?
   (d) What is the bearing of *Y* from *X* if b lies between 270° and 360°?

4. The bearing of *A* from *B* is $x°$ and the bearing of *C* from *B* is $y°$.
   Both x and y lie between 000° and 180° and y is greater than x.
   AB is equal to *BC*.
   Find the bearing of *C* from *A* in terms of x and y.

5.

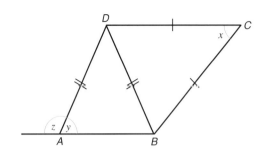

ABD is an isosceles triangle with base angles equal to $y°$.
BCD is an isosceles triangle with the angle at the apex equal to $x°$.
(a) Write angle *CBD* in terms of x.
(b) Write angle *ADB* in terms of y.
(c) If *AB* is parallel to *CD* write a simple formula for y in terms of x.
(d) If *AD* is parallel to *BC* write a formula for x in terms of y.
(e) If *AD* is parallel to *BC* write a formula for z in terms of x.

6. *ABCDEF* is a semi-regular hexagon. The sides are equal but not the angles:

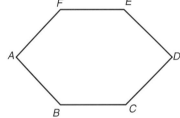

(a) If angle *FAB* is 80° find:
   (i) angle *ABF*   (ii) angle *ABC*   (iii) angle *ABD*

(b) If angle *FAB* is 100° find:
   (i) angle *ABF*   (ii) angle *ABC*   (iii) angle *ABD*

(c) If angle *FAB* is $x°$ find:
   (i) angle *ABC*   (ii) angle *ABF*   (iii) angle *ABD*

Exercise 12.10: Summary exercise

1. (a) Using a scale of 1 cm to 1 km, draw point *Q*, 7.5 km from point *P* on a bearing of 127°.
   (b) Measure the bearing of *P* from *Q*.

2. If the bearing of *A* from *B* is 217°, what is the bearing of *B* from *A*?

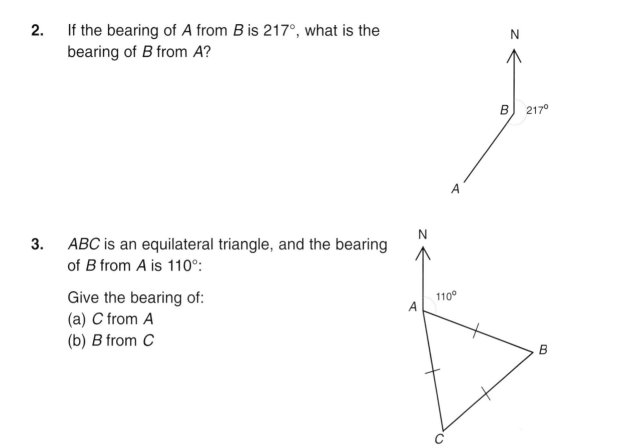

3. *ABC* is an equilateral triangle, and the bearing of *B* from *A* is 110°:

Give the bearing of:
(a) *C* from *A*
(b) *B* from *C*

4. On a geography field trip, we walked for 1.2 km on a bearing of 129° from the base camp. Simon wrote down the directions incorrectly. He walked for 2.1 km on a bearing of 192°.
(a) Draw a sketch to show the relative positions of the base camp, *B*, my group, *G*, and Simon, *S*.
(b) Using a scale of 5 cm to 1 km, draw an accurate scale drawing to show the positions of *B*, *G* and *S*.
(c) Simon has to come and find us. From your drawing measure *GS* and find out how far he has to walk.
(d) Measure the bearing of *G* from *S* to find the direction that Simon has to walk.

End of chapter 12 activity: Black-eyed Jack's treasure

Imagine that you are the pirate, Black-eyed Jack. You are going to bury your ill-gotten treasure on a desert island.

First you are going to have to draw a map of the island or use the worksheet. Put in lots of detail.

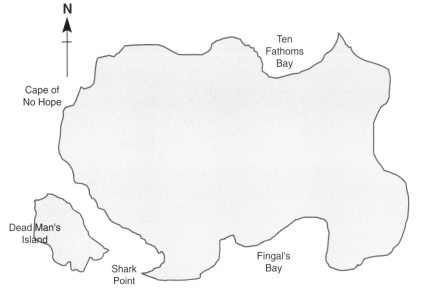

Now decide where your treasure is to be buried.

The next thing you have to do is to write some instructions so that Lucky Jim can discover the treasure. The instructions must not be too easy, and should use both bearings and compass directions. To follow the instructions, the map will need a scale (this could be in kilometres or leagues or even paces).

For example: Start at the stricken pine tree.

> Take forty paces on a bearing of 045°
> From there turn due east and take twenty paces.
> Walk fifteen paces on a bearing of 312°
> Walk north until you meet the coast.
> Turn south west and take five paces.
> There lies the treasure!

Once you are happy with your set of instructions, give them, with your map, to a friend. Can they find the treasure? (Or were your instructions not clear enough?)

Chapter 13: Area

This is a Chinese Tangram square:

The tangram is an ancient Chinese puzzle. The square is divided into 7 pieces and the pieces can be reassembled into other shapes.

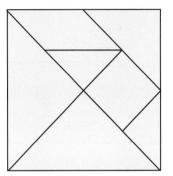

Exercise 13.1

On the worksheet you will find several copies of the tangram.

1. Take the first square and cut out the pieces. Now, rearrange the pieces to make this shape:

Stick your solution in your exercise book.

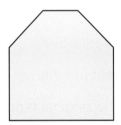

2. Take the second square and cut out the pieces. Now, rearrange the pieces to make this shape:

Stick your solution in your exercise book.

3. Take the third square and cut out the pieces. Now, rearrange the pieces to make this shape:

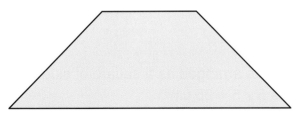

Stick your solution in your exercise book.

4. Take the fourth square and cut out the pieces. Now, rearrange the pieces to make this shape:

Stick your solution in your exercise book.

5. Use the next two squares to make up some designs of your own. Be as creative as you can.

Exercise 13.2

Use a set of tangram pieces to revise some basic geometry.

1. The original tangram set is arranged in a square, and one of the pieces is a square itself. Write down whether you can make a square using:
   (a) two tangram pieces
   (b) three tangram pieces
   (c) four tangram pieces
   (d) five tangram pieces
   (e) six tangram pieces

2. Write down whether it is possible to make these figures using all seven tangram pieces:
   (a) a trapezium (but not the one in Exercise 13.1)
   (b) a rectangle that is not a square
   (c) a parallelogram that is not a square
   (d) a triangle

The original set of tangram pieces was arranged as a square of side 5 cm.
The area of this square is therefore $5 \times 5 = 25$ cm².

What is the area of each of the shapes in Exercise 13.1?
What is the area of each of the shapes in Exercise 13.2 q.2?
They are all 25 cm² as well.

Just because we rearranged the pieces does not mean that the area changes.

We are going to use this fact to discover some more area formulae.

First, here are two that we know:

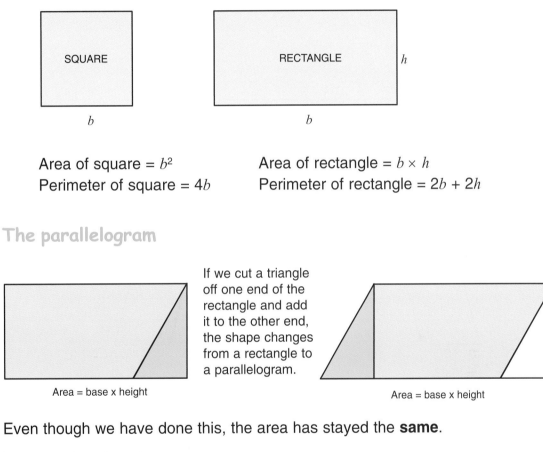

Area of square = b^2
Perimeter of square = $4b$

Area of rectangle = $b \times h$
Perimeter of rectangle = $2b + 2h$

The parallelogram

If we cut a triangle off one end of the rectangle and add it to the other end, the shape changes from a rectangle to a parallelogram.

Area = base x height

Area = base x height

Even though we have done this, the area has stayed the **same**.

It means therefore that we can say:
    Area of a parallelogram = base × height
                = $b \times h$

Exercise 13.3

Find the areas of these parallelograms:

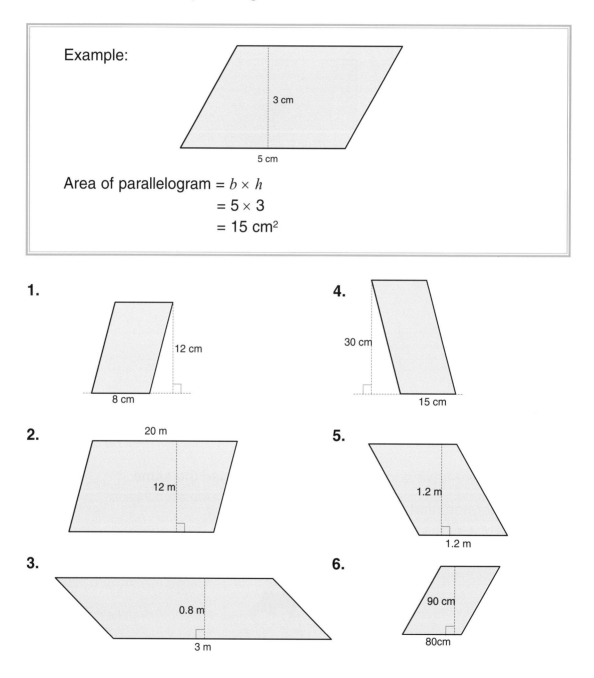

Example:

3 cm

5 cm

Area of parallelogram = $b \times h$
$$= 5 \times 3$$
$$= 15 \text{ cm}^2$$

1.

12 cm

8 cm

4.

30 cm

15 cm

2.

20 m

12 m

5.

1.2 m

1.2 m

3.

0.8 m

3 m

6.

90 cm

80cm

In these examples it was very easy to see which lines were the base and height. In other examples you have to look more carefully. Remember that whichever way round the parallelogram is on the page, the base and the height are **perpendicular** to each other.

Perpendicular means **at right-angles to.**

Axes are perpendicular: remember, you wake up –
horizontal – then you stand up – vertical:

Horizontal first, then ...   vertical.

So **horizontal** is **perpendicular** to **vertical**, but these lines are also
perpendicular:

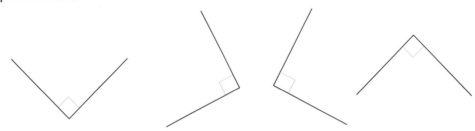

Note the little square where the lines meet; this shows the angle is a **right-
angle**.

Exercise 13.4

Calculate the area of each parallelogram. Be careful to substitute the correct
value for base and height:

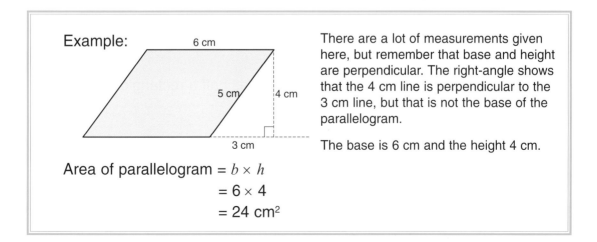

Example:

There are a lot of measurements given
here, but remember that base and height
are perpendicular. The right-angle shows
that the 4 cm line is perpendicular to the
3 cm line, but that is not the base of the
parallelogram.

The base is 6 cm and the height 4 cm.

Area of parallelogram = $b \times h$
$$= 6 \times 4$$
$$= 24 \text{ cm}^2$$

1.

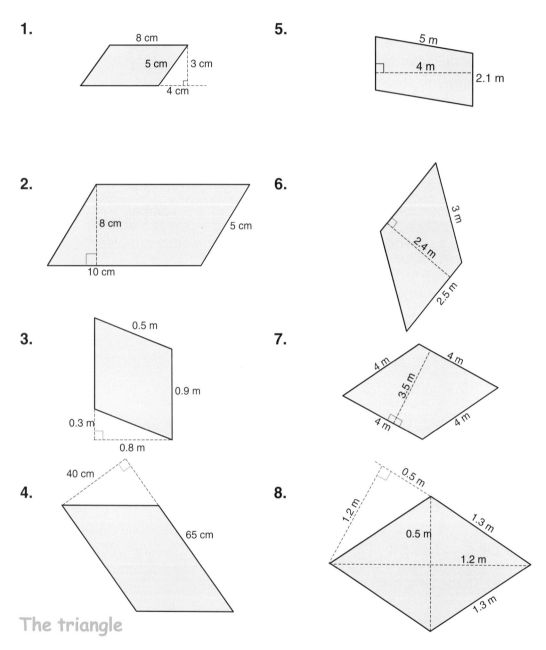

8 cm

5 cm | 3 cm

4 cm

2.

8 cm

5 cm

10 cm

3.

0.5 m

0.9 m

0.3 m

0.8 m

4.

40 cm

65 cm

5.

5 m

4 m

2.1 m

6.

3 m

2.4 m

2.5 m

7.

4 m

3.5 m

4 m

4 m

4 m

8.

0.5 m

1.2 m

0.5 m

1.3 m

1.2 m

1.3 m

The triangle

In Book 1 we saw that a right-angled triangle was half a rectangle:

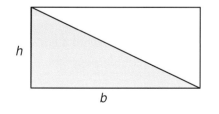

h

b

Area of a right-angled triangle $= \dfrac{1}{2} b \times h$

But what about other triangles?

If you **divide a parallelogram in half**, what do you get? **A triangle!**

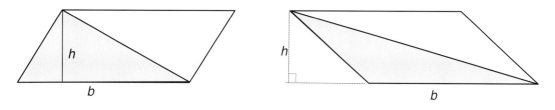

Area of any triangle = $b \times h$

But, again, you must remember that the height is perpendicular to the base.

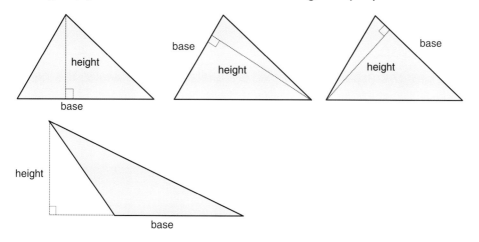

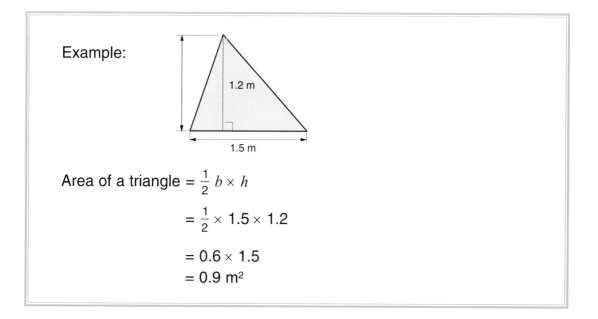

Example:

Area of a triangle $= \frac{1}{2} b \times h$

$= \frac{1}{2} \times 1.5 \times 1.2$

$= 0.6 \times 1.5$

$= 0.9 \text{ m}^2$

Exercise 13.5

1. You will need to use the worksheet for this exercise. On the worksheet you will see several triangles. Each has one has a base or a height marked on it. Give the corresponding height or base on each triangle.

2. Now calculate the area of each triangle.

A note about the formula

We discovered that the formula for the area of a triangle is half the area of a parallelogram, and that the area of a parallelogram is the same as the area of a rectangle.

Using the formula for the area of a triangle, calculate the answers to the next exercise.

$$\text{Area of a triangle} = \frac{1}{2}\, b \times h$$

Exercise 13.6

If $b = 4$ and $h = 5$, work out the answers to these:

1. $\frac{1}{2}\, bh$

2. $\frac{b \times h}{2}$

3. $b \times h \div 2$

4. $\frac{b}{2} \times h$

5. $b \times \frac{h}{2}$

6. $\frac{1}{2}\,(b \times h)$

You can see that you get the same answer every time. All the above formulae mean the same. It does matter which way you think of the formula but the most usual way to see it written is:

$$\frac{bh}{2}$$

Exercise 13.7

1. Calculate the areas of these triangles; all dimensions are in centimetres:

(a)

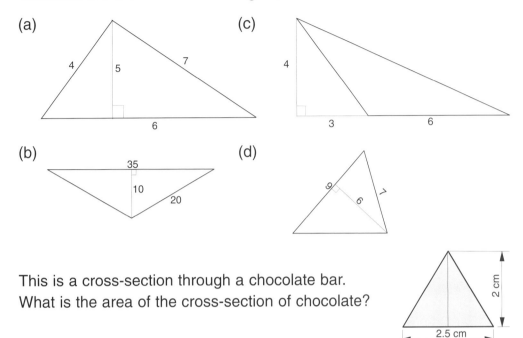

(c)

(b)

(d)

2. This is a cross-section through a chocolate bar.
   What is the area of the cross-section of chocolate?

   2 cm

   2.5 cm

3. Our garden has some triangular flower beds. Here is a plan of the garden:

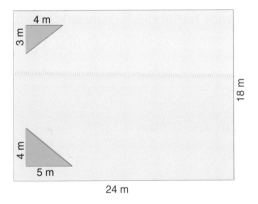

4 m

3 m

18 m

4 m

5 m

24 m

   (a) Calculate the total area of the two flower beds.
   (b) Calculate the grassed area.

4. A hexagon is made up of 6 triangles, all of base 2cm and height 1.73 cm.
   (a) What is the area of one triangle?
   (b) What is the area of the hexagon?

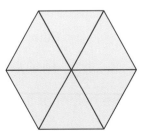

5. Two isosceles triangles, each of base 5 cm and height 3 cm, are joined together along a side to make a new shape.
    (a) How many new shapes can be made with the two triangles? (The triangles must touch each other at at least one vertex.)
    (b) Draw a sketch of each.
    (c) What are their names and what are their areas?

6. 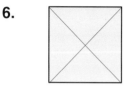 This square is 2 cm by 2 cm
    (a) How many triangles in total can you find in the square?
    (b) What is the sum of their areas?
    (c) What is the area of the square?
    (d) How many times greater is your answer to (b) than your answer to (c)?
    (e) Why?

Finding the height

In the problems we have just looked at, the base and height were used to find the area. However, there are times when we know the area and one of the dimensions and we need to find the missing dimension.

This process becomes more complicated with a triangle. To understand it, we must think about how we worked puzzles backwards in the Chapter 11 on algebra:

Example: If a triangle has base = 8 cm and area = 40 cm², what is the height?

$$A = \frac{b \times h}{2}$$

$$40 = \frac{8 \times h}{2} \qquad (\times\ 2)$$

$$80 = 8 \times h \qquad (\div\ 8)$$

$$10 = h$$

The height of the triangle is 10 cm.

Exercise 13.8

1. A triangle has an area of 10 cm² and a base of 5 cm. What is the height?

2. What is the base of this triangle:

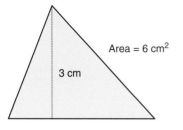

Area = 6 cm²

3 cm

3. The area of a triangle is 60 cm² and its base is 20 cm. What is the height?

4. Triangle *ADC* has an area of 12 cm².

   AD = 4 cm   *BD* = 6 cm

   Find: (a) *CD*
   (b) Area of triangle *BCD*
   (c) Area of triangle *ABC*

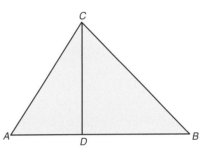

5. A triangle of height 8 cm and base 12 cm is equal in area to a triangle with a base of 6 cm. What is the height of this triangle?

Some other quadrilaterals

We can use the method of taking a formula we know and adding, or subtracting, areas to find the areas of some other quadrilaterals. Let's start by looking at the trapezium.

The trapezium

A trapezium has one pair of parallel sides but, because these sides are not equal, it is quite hard to describe them. Let us call them 'top' and 'bottom' for the moment:

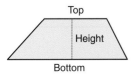

Top

Height

Bottom

It is not obvious what the formula for this area is, so we are going to rotate a copy of the trapezium and then join the two together.

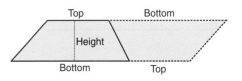

Top   Bottom

Height

Bottom   Top

Now the two trapezia have a combined area the same as that of a parallelogram with a base length of 'top + bottom' and a height which is the same height as the trapezium. We can write a formula to represent this:

$$\text{Area of trapezium} = \frac{1}{2} \, height \, (top + bottom)$$

$$= \frac{1}{2} \, h \, (a + b) \quad \text{or} \quad \frac{h \, (a + b)}{2}$$

Exercise 13.9

Find the area of these trapezia (trapezia is the plural of trapezium):

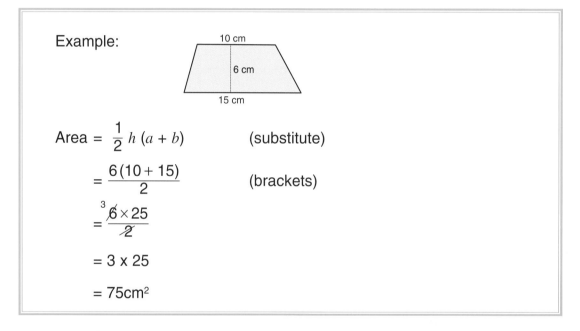

Example:

10 cm

6 cm

15 cm

$$\text{Area} = \frac{1}{2} \, h \, (a + b) \qquad \text{(substitute)}$$

$$= \frac{6 \, (10 + 15)}{2} \qquad \text{(brackets)}$$

$$= \frac{\overset{3}{\cancel{6}} \times 25}{\cancel{2}}$$

$$= 3 \times 25$$

$$= 75 \text{cm}^2$$

1.

12 cm

8 cm

18 cm

2.

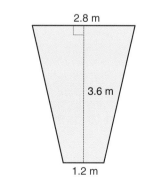

2.8 m

3.6 m

1.2 m

3.

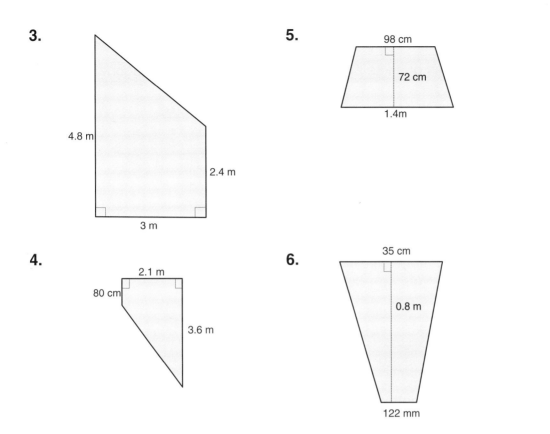

4.8 m
2.4 m
3 m

5.

98 cm
72 cm
1.4m

4.

2.1 m
80 cm
3.6 m

6.

35 cm
0.8 m
122 mm

7. This is the cross-section of a metal ingot.
What is the area of the cross-section?

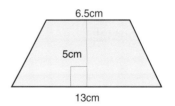

6.5cm
5cm
13cm

8. This is the cross-section of a squash court:

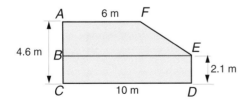

A   6 m   *F*
4.6 m *B*   *E*
            2.1 m
C   10 m   *D*

(a) What is the area of the rectangle *BCDE* ?
(b) Find the length *AB*.
(c) What is the area of *ABEF* ?
(d) What is the total cross-section area of the squash court?

Area of a kite, a rhombus and other quadrilaterals

One of the properties of a kite and of a rhombus is that their diagonals cross at right angles:

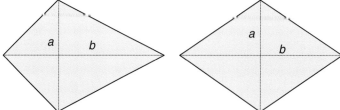

It may not be immediately obvious to see how this helps us to find the area, so let's put a rectangle round the shapes:

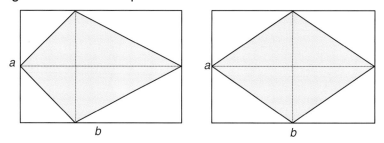

Now you can see that both the kite and the rhombus fill exactly half the rectangle.

The area of the rectangle is base × height, which happens to be the product of their diagonals!

Example:

A rhombus has diagonals of 8 cm and 12 cm. What is its area?

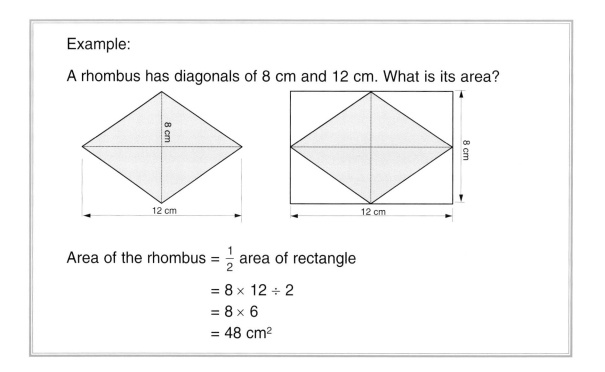

Area of the rhombus = $\frac{1}{2}$ area of rectangle

$$= 8 \times 12 \div 2$$
$$= 8 \times 6$$
$$= 48 \text{ cm}^2$$

Exercise 13.10

1. Find the areas of these:

(a)

(c)

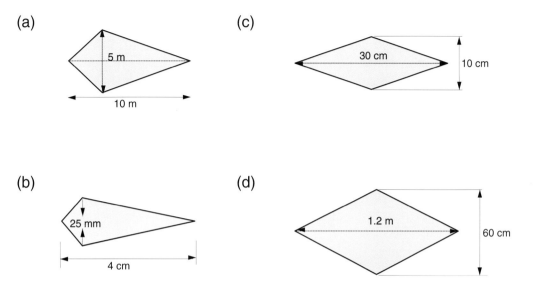

(b)

(d)

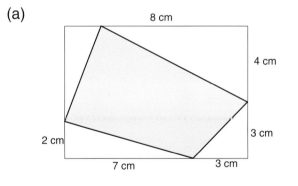

2. Find the shaded areas of these shapes:

(a)

(b)

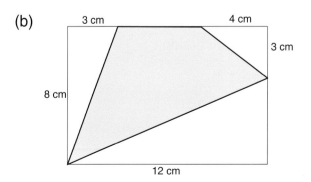

Exercise 13.11: Extension questions – Units of area

All the calculations we have done so far have used one unit of area per question, either mm², cm², m² or km².

There are times when we start out with one unit of area and then need to change to another. This is more complicated than it looks. Look at these two squares. We know that 1 m = 100 cm

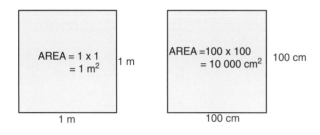

Therefore   **1 m² = 10 000 cm²**

This is very important. Just remember that there are **not** 100 cm² in 1 m². If you can remember this, it will stop you making many mistakes.

1. Draw squares like the two above to find how many:
   (a) square millimetres in a square centimetre
   (b) square millimetres in a square metre
   (c) square metres in a square kilometre
   (d) square metres in a square centimetre
   (e) square metres in a square millimetre
   (f) square kilometres in a square metre

These are not easy to remember. If you have a question where you need to write the answer in different units from those that you are given, it is much easier to change the units **first**. If you cannot do that, **always** draw a square and make sure that you have the correct conversion.

2. A square is 4 m by 4 m. Give its area in:
   (a) square centimetres
   (b) square kilometres

3. A triangle has base 5 m and height 3 m. Give its area in:
   (a) square millimetres
   (b) square centimetres

4. A rectangle has a base of 30 cm and a height of 4 m. Give the area of the rectangle in:
   (a) square centimetres
   (b) square metres

5. A rectangle has an area of 2 m² and a width of 20 cm. What is its length?

6. A triangle has an area of 1 m² and a height of 20 mm. What is its base?

7. A square has an area of 4 km². What is the length of a side in metres?

8. A triangle of base 40 cm has an area of 10 000 mm². What is its height?

   A hectare is a measure of larger areas:
   1 hectare = 10 000 m²
   100 hectares = 1 km²

9. (a) How many m² are there in 3.6 hectares?
   (b) How many hectares are there in 5.7 km²?
   (c) What is the area, in hectares, of a parallelogram with base 1.2 km and height 800 m?

10. A farmer has a 30 hectare field. It is in the shape of a trapezium with parallel sides of 500m and 700m.

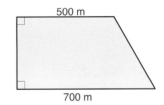

500 m

700 m

   (a) What is the perpendicular distance between the two parallel sides?
   (b) The farmer decides that he wants to divide his field up into two triangles. Calculate the area of the two new fields in hectares.
   (c) What is the ratio of the area of the larger field to the smaller field?
   (d) After doing his calculations, the farmer then decides to divide the original field up into a smaller trapezium and a triangle, both with the same area. Show how he can do this. Illustrate your answer with a clear diagram showing the dimensions of the fields.

11. Bill and Ben are having an argument. Bill has a field in the shape of a kite. The diagonals of the kite are 1.8 km and 0.6 km. Ben has a field in the shape of a trapezium. The parallel sides are 400 m and 500 m long, and the perpendicular distance between them is 1.2 km. Both Bill and Ben think his field is the larger. Who is right?

Exercise 13.12: Mixed questions

1. Write down the formula for:
   (a) the area of a parallelogram
   (b) the area of a triangle
   (c) the area of a trapezium

2. Find the area of these shapes:

   (a)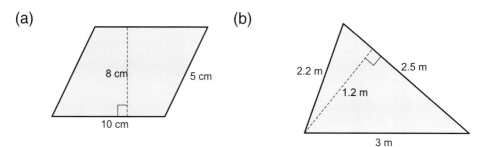

   (b)

3. Find the height of a triangle of area 72 cm² and base 12 cm.

4. I have cut a triangle of base 12 cm and height 7 cm out of a piece of paper 21 cm by 30 cm. What area of paper remains?

   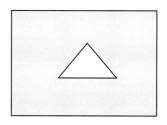

5. This is the cross-section of a stand at a sports stadium:

   CD, BE and *AF* are parallel and
   AB = *BC* = *DE*

   (a) Find the area of: (i) *BCDE*
   (ii) *ABEF*

   (b) Hence find the area of the cross section.

   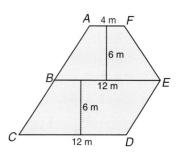

6. This is a company logo which is made up of a parallelogram on top of a trapezium. The parallelogram has height 22 mm and base 44 mm and the trapezium has the same height but the base length is twice as long as the length of the top. What is the surface area of the logo?

   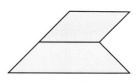

End of chapter 13 activity: The shape game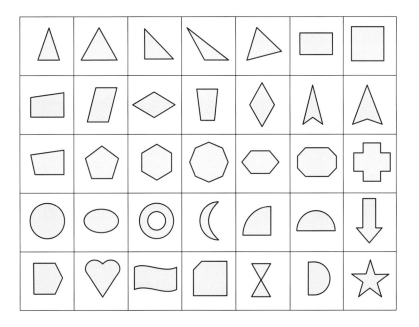

On the worksheet you will see the following table of shapes. They all have names and certain properties. Some have more than 4 sides, some have line symmetry, some have rotational symmetry, some have diagonals that cross at right angles and so on.

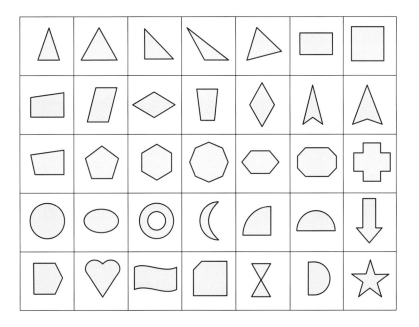

Here's how to play the game (you can play this as a class but is in best in pairs):

1. Choose a shape. Do not tell anyone what it is.

2. When your opponent has chosen his or her shape, toss a coin to see who starts.

3. Player no.1 asks player no.2 a question to which the answer can only be 'yes' or 'no'.

    For example, 'Does you shape have more than four sides?'

4. When player no.2 has answered, player no.1 should cross off all the shapes on his sheet that match the answer. For example, if the answer to the question above had been 'no', they would cross off everything except the triangles, quadrilaterals and curved shapes.

5. The players take it in turns to ask questions. The player who guesses the other player's shape first wins!

Chapter 14: Straight line graphs

In mathematics a graph is a drawing showing the relationship between certain quantities plotted on a grid with reference to a set of axes.

The axes are very important. When drawing, or looking at, a graph, you should always start with the axes. The axes should be labelled carefully to show what each one represents:

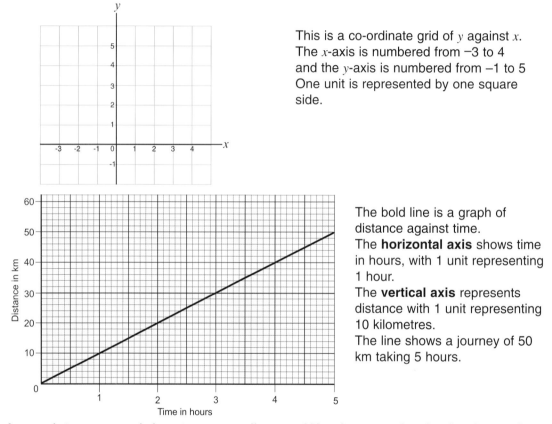

This is a co-ordinate grid of y against x. The x-axis is numbered from −3 to 4 and the y-axis is numbered from −1 to 5 One unit is represented by one square side.

The bold line is a graph of distance against time.
The **horizontal axis** shows time in hours, with 1 unit representing 1 hour.
The **vertical axis** represents distance with 1 unit representing 10 kilometres.
The line shows a journey of 50 km taking 5 hours.

Any point on a graph has two co-ordinates. We always write the **horizontal** co-ordinate first.

To remember this think of how you wake up: horizontal – then you stand up – vertical:

Horizontal first, then ...   vertical.

Graphs parallel to the axes

Let us look at a grid. Any point on the grid has a pair of co-ordinates:

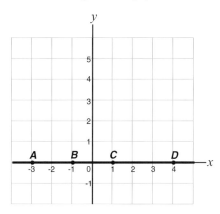
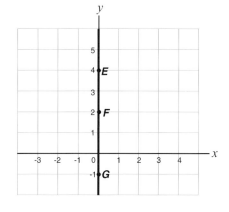

These points are on the *x*-axis:

A(−3, 0)   B(−1, 0)
C(1, 0)   D(4, 0)

All the points on the *x*-axis have a *y* co-ordinate of 0

Therefore the **x-axis** is the line **y = 0**

These points are on the *y*-axis:

E(0, 4)   F(0, 2)
G(0,−1)

All the points on the *y*-axis have an *x* co-ordinate of 0

and the **y-axis** is the line **x = 0**

Exercise 14.1

Copy this pair of axes into your exercise book:

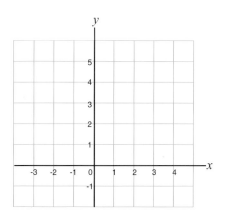

1. Plot these points:

    A (3, 1)   B (3, 0)   C (0, 3)
    D (2, 0)   E (0, 2)   F (2, −1)
    G (−1, 0)   H (−1, 4)   I (0, −1)

2. List the points that lie on the *x*-axis.

3. List the points that lie on the *y*-axis.

By looking at pairs of co-ordinates, we saw that all the points on the *x*-axis have 0 for the *y* co-ordinate, so the rule, or equation, for the **x-axis** is **y = 0**

Similarly all the points on the *y*-axis have 0 for the *x* co-ordinate, so the rule, or equation, for the **y-axis** is **x = 0**

In this next exercise, we are going to look at lines parallel to the x and y axes, and find the rule, or equation, for each of them.

Exercise 14.2

On each grid there is a straight line graph with some points on the line marked by letters.

Find the co-ordinates of the lettered points. From these, write down the equation of that line.

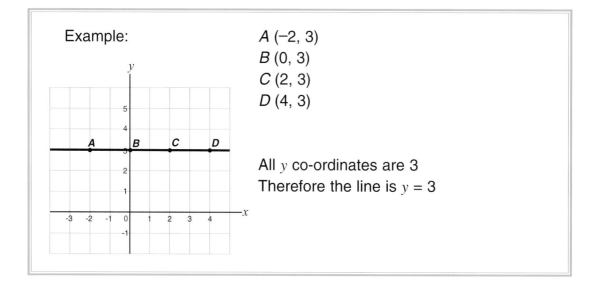

Example:

A (−2, 3)
B (0, 3)
C (2, 3)
D (4, 3)

All y co-ordinates are 3
Therefore the line is $y = 3$

1.

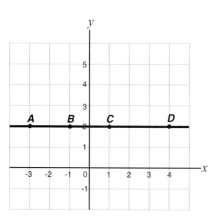

2.

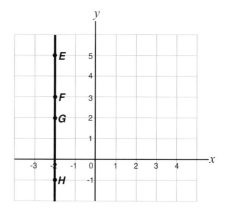

3.

5.

4.

6.

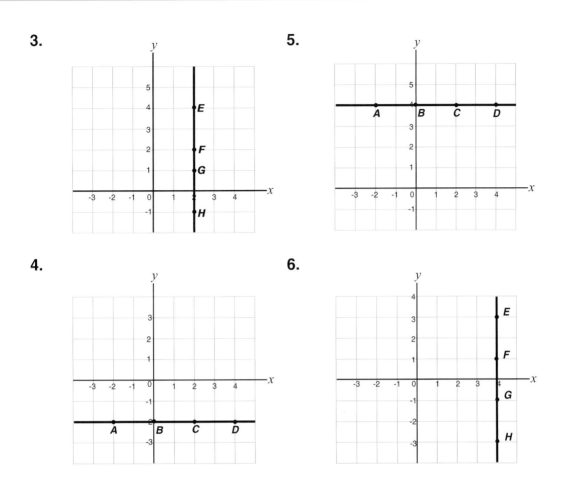

Here are two special lines, not parallel to an axis:

7.

8.

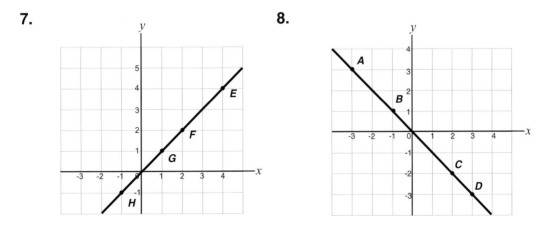

Exercise 14.3

Draw 6 grids with pairs of axes numbered from −4 to 4
Use one pair of axes for each of questions 1 to 6

1. Draw the lines given by the equations: $x = 3$, $y = -1$
    Write down the co-ordinates of the point where the two lines intersect.

2. Draw the lines given by the equations: $x = -2$, $y = 0$
    Write down the co-ordinates of the point where the two lines intersect.

3. Draw the lines given by the equations: $x = 4$, $y = 1$
    Write down the co-ordinates of the point where the two lines intersect.

4. Draw the lines given by the equations: $x = -2$, $y = x$
    Write down the co-ordinates of the point where the two lines intersect.

5. Draw the lines given by the equations: $x = 0$, $y = 3$
    Write down the co-ordinates of the point where the two lines intersect.

6. Draw the lines given by the equations: $x = 2$, $y = -x$
    Write down the co-ordinates of the point where the two lines intersect.

In the next exercise, you will draw several lines on one co-ordinate grid. The region enclosed by the lines is a shape.

Example:

On a grid with axes numbered from −4 to 4, draw the four lines given by the following equations:

$x = -2$, $y = 1$, $x = 2$, $y = -3$

Name the shape formed by the four lines and find its area.

The shape is a square.

Area $= 4 \times 4$
$= 16$ sq units

Exercise 14.4

1. On a co-ordinate grid with values of both x and y from −3 to 3, draw the four lines given by the following equations:

   $x = -2$, $y = -1$, $x = 1$, $y = 2$

   Find the area of the square formed by the four lines.

2. On a co-ordinate grid with values of both x and y from −4 to 4, draw the four lines given by the following equations:

   $x = 4$, $y = -2$, $x = -3$, $y = 3$

   Name the shape formed by the four lines and find its area.

3. On a co-ordinate grid with values of both x and y from −4 to 4, draw the four lines given by the following equations:

   $x = 3$, $y = -1$, $x = -2$, $y = 4$

   Name the shape formed by the four lines and find its area.

4. On a co-ordinate grid with values of both x and y from −3 to 3, draw the three lines given by the following equations:

   $x = -2$, $y = -1$, $y = x$

   Find the area of the triangle formed by the three lines.

5. On a co-ordinate grid with values of both x and y from −5 to 5, draw the three lines given by the following equations:

   $x = -1$, $y = 4$, $y = -2$

   Draw a fourth line so that the four lines form the outline of a rectangle of area 30 square units. Write down the equation of the fourth line.

6. On a co-ordinate grid with values of both x and y from −4 to 4, draw the three lines given by the following equations:

   $x = 3$, $y = -2$, $x = -3$

   Draw a fourth line so that the four lines form the outline of a square. Write down the equation of the fourth line and calculate the area of the square.

Straight lines not parallel to the axes

Almost all the lines we have drawn so far have been parallel to the x-axis or the y-axis.

The two that were not were:

$y = x$ and $y = {}^-x$

In both of these the lines ran through the origin (0,0).

Now let's look at this graph:

The sloping line is straight; it does not pass through the origin but through the point (0, 3).

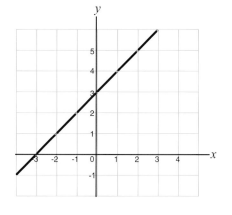

To find the equation for this line, start by looking at points that lie on the line:

(−3, 0), (−1, 2), (0, 3) and (2, 5)

In each case, the y co-ordinate is 3 more than the x co-ordinate. This allows us to work out the equation for the line.

The line therefore is $y = x + 3$

Any straight line can be described by an equation.

If we know the equation of a line, we can calculate points on the line like this:

If the line is $y = x + 3$

When $x = 0$, then: $y = 0 + 3$
$= 3$

When $x = 2$, then: $y = 2 + 3$
$= 5$

When $x = 4$, then: $y = 4 + 3$
$= 7$

If we plot the points (0, 3), (2, 5) and (4, 7), we can draw a line through them to represent: $y = x + 3$

Before we do this, it is a good idea to practise substitution.

Exercise 14.5

Example:

If $y = 2x$, find y when $x = 2$

When $x = 2$ $y = 2 \times 2$
                           $= 4$

1. If $y = 3x$, find y when x equals:
    (a) 2   (b) 4   (c) 1   (d) 0

2. If $y = x + 5$, find y when x equals:
    (a) 3   (b) 0   (c) 7   (d) 2

3. If $y = 7 - x$, find y when x equals:
    (a) 4   (b) 2   (c) 0   (d) 3

4. If $y = 2x + 3$, find y when x equals:
    (a) 1   (b) 3   (c) 7   (d) 0

5. If $y = \frac{x}{2}$, find y when x equals:
    (a) 4   (b) 2   (c) 0   (d) 1

Substituting negative numbers

There is no reason why the values of x cannot be negative. Just remember the rules for negative numbers:

$$(+2) \times (+2) = +4 \qquad (+2) \times (-2) = -4$$
$$(-2) \times (+2) = -4 \qquad (-2) \times (-2) = +4$$

Always use brackets round negative numbers, so that you do not confuse the signs:

$$+ (+2) = 2 \qquad + (-2) = -2 \qquad - (+2) = -2 \qquad - (-2) = +2 \text{ or } 2$$

Example:

If $y = x^2 + 3$ find y when $x = -2$
    $y = (-2)^2 + 3$
      $= (-2) \times (-2) + 3$
      $= 4 + 3$
      $= 7$

Exercise 14.6

1. If $y = -x$, find y when x equals:
    (a) −1   (b) −4   (c) 2   (d) 0

2. If $y = 3x - 2$, find y when x equals:
    (a) −2   (b) 0   (c) −3   (d) 1

3. If $y = 3 + x$, find y when x equals:
    (a) −4   (b) −1   (c) 0   (d) −3

4. If $y = 2 - x$, find y when x equals:
    (a) −1   (b) −3   (c) 0   (d) 1

5. If $y = 1 - 3x$, find y when x equals:
    (a) −1   (b) 0   (c) −3   (d) 2

To draw a graph from an equation, we need at least two points but we generally plot at least three to make sure that we have not made a mistake.

Step 1:   First write down the equation.
Step 2:   Next choose at least three values for x and put them into a table.
Step 3:   Then calculate the corresponding values of y.
Step 4:   Finally draw the graph. Plot the points with a dot or better a cross.
Step 5:   Join the dots or crosses to draw the graph of the line.

Example:

Draw a graph of the equation $y = x + 2$

x	−2	−1	0	1	2
y	0	1	2	3	4

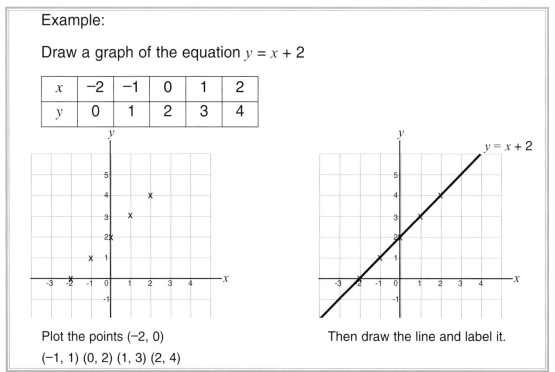

Plot the points (−2, 0)   Then draw the line and label it.
(−1, 1) (0, 2) (1, 3) (2, 4)

Exercise 14.7

The worksheet may be used for this exercise.

1. (a) For the equation copy and complete this table of values for x and y.

x	−2	−1	0	1	2
y					

(b) Draw the graph of $y = x - 2$

Once you have drawn a line, you may want to find other values of x and y that lie along that same line. The way you do this is to draw a **dotted line** from the value you are given to the line you have just plotted. When you reach the line, you then draw another dotted line back to the other axis. This then gives you the value you want to find. Here is an example to show you what we mean.

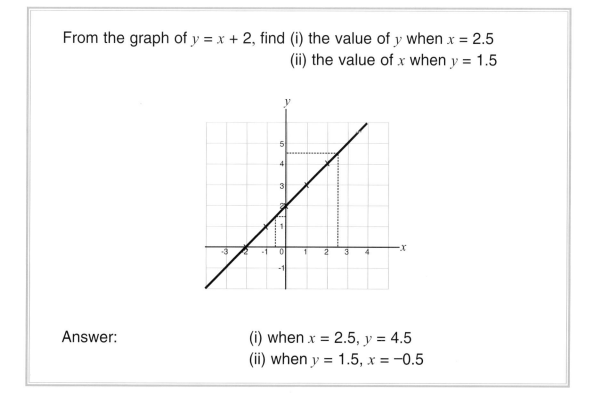

From the graph of $y = x + 2$, find (i) the value of y when $x = 2.5$
(ii) the value of x when $y = 1.5$

Answer: (i) when $x = 2.5$, $y = 4.5$
(ii) when $y = 1.5$, $x = -0.5$

2. (a) For the equation $y = 2x + 1$, copy and complete this table of values for x and y.

x	-2	-1	0	1	2
y					

(b) Draw the graph of $y = 2x + 1$

(c) From your graph find (i) the value of y when $x = 1.5$
(ii) the value of x when $y = 2$

3. (a) For the equation $y = 3 - x$, copy and complete this table of values for x and y.

x	-2	-1	0	1	2
y					

(b) Draw the graph of $y = 3 - x$

(c) From your graph find (i) the value of y when $x = -0.5$
(ii) the value of x when $y = 2.5$

4. (a) For the function $y = 1 + 3x$, copy and complete this table of values for x and y.

x	-2	-1	0	1	2
y					

(b) Draw the graph of $y = 1 + 3x$

(c) From your graph find (i) the value of y when $x = 2.5$
(ii) the value of x when $y = 5$

For more complicated functions you may find that an extra row of working helps you to calculate the value of y.

5.   (a) For the function $y = 2x - 3$, copy and complete this table of values for x and y.

x	−2	−1	0	1	2
$2x$	−4	−2	0	2	4
y	−7				

    (b) Draw the graph of $y = 2x - 3$

    (c) From your graph find (i) the value of y when $x = 1.5$

                                   (ii) the value of x when $y = -2$

6.   (a) For the function $y = 4 - 2x$, copy and complete this table of values for x and y.

x	−2	−1	0	1	2
$2x$	−4	−2	0	2	4
y	8				

    (b) Draw the graph of $y = 4 - 2x$

    (c) From your graph find (i) the value of y when $x = -1.5$

                                   (ii) the value of x when $y = 5$

7.   (a) For the function $y = 2 - \dfrac{x}{2}$,complete a table of values for x and y with values of x between −3 and 3

    (b) Draw the graph of $y = 2 - \dfrac{x}{2}$

    (c) From your graph find (i) the value of y when $x = 1.5$

                                   (ii) the value of x when $y = -0.75$

8.   (a) For the function $y = \dfrac{x}{2} - 3$, complete a table of values for x and y with values of x between −3 and 3.

    (b) Draw the graph of $y = \dfrac{x}{2} - 3$

    (c) From your graph find (i) the value of y when $x = 1.5$

                                   (ii) the value of x when $y = -1.5$

Exercise 14.8: Extension questions

Before you do this exercise, let's look at this graph (you have seen it before on page 276) and remind ourselves of some of the things it tells us, and how we can work out the equation for this line:

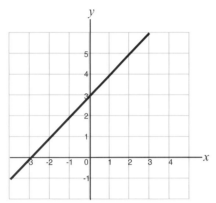

The sloping line is straight, but does not pass through the origin.

Points that lie on the line include:

(−3, 0), (−1, 2), (0, 3) and (2, 5)

In each case, the y co-ordinate is 3 more than the x co-ordinate.

The line is $y = x + 3$

1.   Look at this graph:

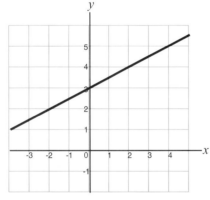

Write down the co-ordinates of the points that lie on the line.

From your list of points decide whether the line is:

(a) $y = 2x + 3$ (b) $y = \dfrac{x}{2} + 3$ (c) $y = x + 3$

Look at the graphs in the next four questions. In the same way as you did in Q1, write out the co-ordinates of several points and then write down the equation of the line.

2.

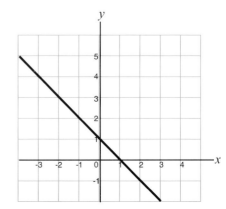

3.

4.   **5.**

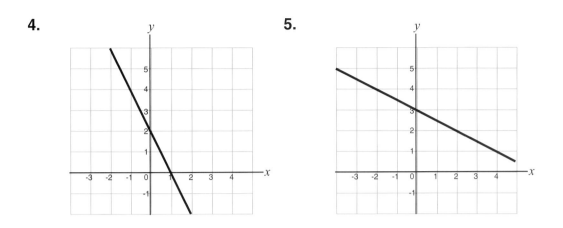

6. Look at your answers and the lines.
Can you see any connection between your equations and where the lines cut the y-axis?

7. Look at your answers and the lines.
Can you see any connection between your equations and where the lines slope up to the right or up to the left?

8. Look at your answers and the lines.
Can you see any connection between your equations and the steepness of the lines?

9. (a) Draw a co-ordinate grid with values of x and y from −5 to 5

    (b) Draw graphs of the following equations:
       (i) $y = 0$ (ii) $y = 2x - 1$ (iii) $x = -1$

    (c) Calculate the area of the triangle formed by the three lines.

10. (a) Draw a co-ordinate grid with values of x and y from −5 to 5

    (b) Draw graphs of the following equations:
       (i) $y = -3$ (ii) $y = 1 - x$

    (c) Draw a third line so that the three lines form an isosceles triangle.

    (d) Calculate the area of the triangle.

    (e) Write down the equation of the third line.

11. (a) Draw a co-ordinate grid with values of x and y from −5 to 5

(b) Draw graphs of the following equations:
 (i) $y = x$ (ii) $y = 2x - 4$

(c) Draw a third line so that the three lines form a triangle of area 9 square units.

(d) Write down the equation of the third line.

Exercise 14.9: Summary exercise

1. (a) If $y = x + 5$, find y when $x = 4$

(b) If $y = x - 3$, find y when $x = -2$

(c) If $y = 2x + 3$, find y when $x = 2$

(d) If $y = 2x + 1$, find y when $x = -1$

(e) If $y = 1 - x$, find y when $x = 4$

(f) If $y = 3 - x$, find y when $x = -3$

(g) If $y = \dfrac{x}{2} + 5$, find y when $x = 4$

2. The lines on this graph have all been labelled **incorrectly**. Copy the diagram and write the correct equation of each line.

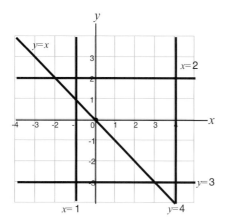

3. (a) Copy and complete this table of values for the equation $y = 2x - 4$

x	−2	−1	0	1	2
$2x$	−4	−2	0	2	4
y	8				

(b) Draw a graph of this equation on a grid with x axis numbered from −2 to 2 and y axis numbered from −8 to 2

(c) Where does this graph cross:
(i) the x axis?
(ii) the y axis?

(d) From your graph find:
(i) the value of y when $x = 1.5$
(ii) the value of x when $y = -0.5$

End of chapter 14 activity: Real life graphs

Many companies use graphs to try to sell their products. Here is an example of a bar graph from a brand of herbal bubble bath:

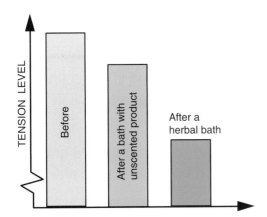

It appears from the graph that the herbal bath has a wonderful effect on tension levels.

But look carefully at the vertical axis. That little zig-zag means that the scale is not continuous. Also notice that there are no values given on the tension level axis, so we don't know how tension is measured.

The full graph could actually be:

like this: or this: or even this:

It could be that the herbal bath makes very little difference at all. One has to remember that the company is interested in selling lots of the product and wants us to feel as though their herbal bath is great at reducing stress levels, even if it does probably exaggerate the real effect and is a bit misleading.

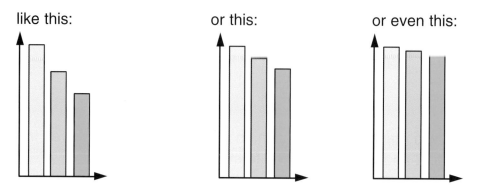

1.   Make a class collection of all the graphs and charts you can find that are used to promote or advertise products. You will need to look in newspapers and magazines, in product information and on packaging.

2.   Divide the graphs into two groups, accurate and informative graphs and misleading graphs. Write a short report on how the graphs are misleading.

3.   Look again at the first group. Are you sure they are accurate? See if any of them could be sneakily misleading after all.

4.   In a small group, decide on a product you would like to market. Draw up two graphs showing the wonderful properties or incredible popularity of your product. One graph should be accurate, the other misleading. How sneaky can you be?

Chapter 15: More about numbers

When you carry out calculations, particularly when using a calculator, you can get seamingly meaningless answers. Here's an example to show you what we mean:

VAT is $17\frac{1}{2}$ %. What is the VAT on a pair of shoes costing £29.50?

$$17\frac{1}{2} \text{ % of £29.50} \quad = 0.175 \times 29.5$$
$$= 5.1625$$

You cannot have 5.1625 pounds and so we must round off the price to the nearest penny, or to two decimal places. i.e. £5.16

In this chapter we will look at various ways of rounding numbers.

Decimal places: Zooming in on the number line

If you look at the centimetre scale of your ruler, you will see that it looks like this:

Each space between two digits is divided into ten, so each subdivision must be worth one tenth or 0.1 of a whole number.

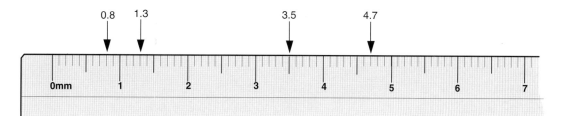

We say that the numbers with one digit after the decimal point are written to **one decimal place.**

You can see that each of these lies between two whole numbers, and we can round these to the nearest whole number, seeing which whole number they are nearest to. Digits **below 5 'round down'**. Digits **5 and above 'round up'**.

For example:

> 3.5 is in the middle. We say it is nearest to 4
> 0.8 is nearest to 1
> 1.3 is nearest to 1
> 4.7 is nearest to 5

If we **zoom** in on the number line, we can look at numbers to **two** decimal places.

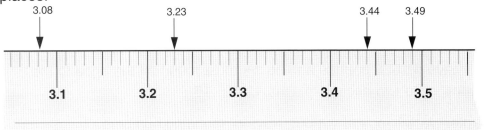

We can round these numbers to one decimal place, by following the same principle as above: 0-4 round down, 5-9 round up.

3.08 lies between 3.0 and 3.1   3.08 is 3.1 (to 1 decimal place)
3.23 lies between 3.2 and 3.3   3.23 is 3.2 (to 1 d.p.)
3.44 lies between 3.4 and 3.5   3.44 is 3.4 (to 1 d.p.)
3.49 lies between 3.4 and 3.5   3.49 is 3.5 (to 1.d.p.)

Now **zoom** in again to see numbers to three decimal places.

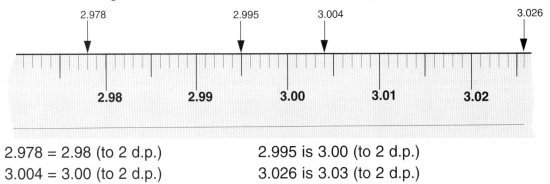

2.978 = 2.98 (to 2 d.p.)   2.995 is 3.00 (to 2 d.p.)
3.004 = 3.00 (to 2 d.p.)   3.026 is 3.03 (to 2 d.p.)

If you consider a number with even more decimal places, e.g. 3.034 589, we can still say that this number lies between 3.03 and 3.04 and is nearer to 3.03

> 3.034 589 is 3.03 (to 2 d.p.)

The digit to consider is the digit **immediately after** the **required place** of decimals:

If it is 5 or more, you should round up, 4 or less stays the same.

Thus, to write 3.034 589 to:

1 d.p., look at the 2nd decimal place: 3.0**3**4 589 3.034 589 is 3.0 (to 1 d.p.)
2 d.p., look at the 3rd decimal place: 3.03**4** 589 3.034 589 is 3.03 (to 2 d.p.)
3 d.p., look at the 4th decimal place: 3.034 **5**89 3.034 589 is 3.035 (to 3 d.p.)
4 d.p., look at the 5th decimal place: 3.034 5**8**9 3.034 589 is 3.034 6 (to 4 d.p.)
5 d.p., look at the 6th decimal place: 3.034 58**9** 3.034 589 is 3.034 59 (to 5 d.p.)

Exercise 15.1

Write these numbers to: (a) 1 d.p.   (b) 2 d.p.   (c) 3 d.p.

Example:

18.3074

(a) 18.3074 = 18.3   (to 1 d.p.)
(b) 18.3074 = 18.31   (to 2 d.p.)
(c) 18.3074 = 18.307   (to 3 d.p.)

---

1.   105.6149

2.   2.7137

3.   0.3752

4.   6.0574

5.   14.905 43

6.   25.00765

7.   0.043 536

8.   0.0207

9.   4.5555

10. 0.9999

11. 10.0909

12. 199.9999

Significant figures

Consider this problem:

I buy a plank of wood 2 m long and I cut it into 7 equal lengths. How long is each length?

$$\begin{aligned} \text{Length} &= 2 \div 7 \\ &= 0.285\ 714\ 285 \text{ m} \\ &= 28.571\ 43 \text{ cm} \end{aligned}$$

Now I could cut my plank to the nearest mm, which would be 28.6 cm, but the other numbers are irrelevant.

Three figures, whether they be 0.286 m or 28.6 cm or 286 mm, are all I need to know. Notice that whatever the units: mm, cm or m, we have the same 3 figures. We call this 'rounding to three **significant figures**'.

What exactly is a significant figure? A significant figure is a number which tells us the number of units, tens, hundreds etc. in the number being considered.

Zeros are important. For a number like 0.0024 they are **not** significant; they tell us the value of the other numbers. For numbers like 2056 or 0.205 the 0s following the first significant figure are also significant.

So in 203 455

2 is the 1st significant figure – it tells us that we have 2 hundred thousands.
0 is the second significant figure – it tells us there are no ten thousands.
3 is the third significant figure – it tells us we that have 3 thousands.

Now look at 0.000 452

4 is the first significant figure: it tells us that we have 0.0004 or 4 ten thousandths.
5 is the second significant figure and 2 is the third.

None of the zeros before 4 is significant as they are only there to put the 4 in the correct place.

Exercise 15.2

1. Write down the value of the 1st significant figure in each of these numbers:

    (a) 542   (b) 0.034   (c) 34.052   (d) 0.003 45

2. Write down the value of the 2nd significant figure in each of these numbers:

    (a) 3456   (b) 0.0324 78   (c) 34.052   (d) 0.009 78

3. Write down the value of the 3rd significant figure in each of these numbers:

    (a) 2354   (b) 3.004 5   (c) 590 034   (d) 0.098 876

4. Write down the value of the 4th significant figure in each of these numbers:

    (a) 23 876   (b) 0.065 725   (c) 340 405   (d) 0.000 567 87

Rounding

When we round to a number of significant figures, we use the same rule as rounding to the nearest ten, or to the nearest 2 decimal places.

Look at the number 235 674 below. First of all imagine a line drawn after the required significant figure. If the number to the right of your imaginary line is 5 or more, round the number to the left of your imaginary line up; if it is 4 or less, it stays the same:

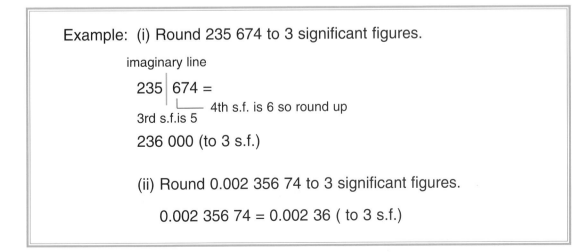

Example: (i) Round 235 674 to 3 significant figures.

imaginary line

235 | 674 =

4th s.f. is 6 so round up

3rd s.f.is 5

236 000 (to 3 s.f.)

(ii) Round 0.002 356 74 to 3 significant figures.

0.002 356 74 = 0.002 36 (to 3 s.f.)

Exercise 15.3

1. Round these numbers to one significant figure:
    (a) 245   (b) 304 567   (c) 0.0465   (d) 0.309

2. Round these numbers to two significant figures:
    (a) 3065   (b) 946   (c) 0.0755   (d) 0.309

3. Round these numbers to three significant figures:
    (a) 25 099   (b) 3494   (c) 0.005 893   (d) 0.460 27

4. Round these numbers to four significant figures:
    (a) 34 599   (b) 120 519   (c) 0.035 465   (d) 0.339 452

5. Round these numbers to 3 significant figures:
    (a) 1.99999   (b) 24.999   (c) 0.99999   (d) 99.999

6. Round these numbers to 3 significant figures:
    (a) 0.050906   (b) 305 099   (c) 0.100490 5 (d) 55.0709

It is important not to get significant figures and decimal places confused. Make sure you understand this difference before you move on.

> **24.5** is written to **1 decimal place** but to **3 significant figures**.
> **0.005** is written to **3 decimal places** but to **1 significant figure**.

Exercise 15.4

1. Consider these numbers:
    (i) 516   (ii) 3.9   (iii) 34.785   (iv) 6.16

    (a) How many decimal places is each number written to?
    (b) How many significant figures is each number written to?

2. Consider these numbers:
    (i) 0.567   (ii) 0.38   (iii) 0.001 789   (iv) 0.000 156

    (a) How many decimal places is each number written to?
    (b) How many significant figures is each number written to?

3. Consider these numbers:
    (i) 51 006   (ii) 3.0906   (iii) 34.005   (iv) 6.100 64

    (a) How many decimal places is each number written to?
    (b) How many significant figures is each number written to?

4. Consider these numbers:

(i) 51 000   (ii) 0.072 0   (iii) 34.000   (iv) 7.000 040

(a) How many decimal places is each number written to?

(b) How many significant figures is each number written to?

5. In the last question you had numbers with 0s as their last digit.

(a) Give an example of a number that could be rounded to 2.40 to 3 significant figures.

(b) Give an example of a number that could be rounded to 2.070 to 3 decimal places.

Large and small numbers

Most problems we have to work out have quite ordinary numbers but as we explore the world of science, geography and astronomy we often come across very large numbers and very small numbers.

Consider these facts about the Earth:

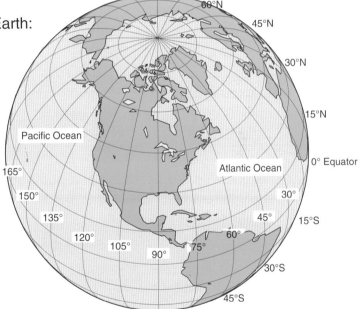

The Earth is the fifth largest of the planets and is on average about 149 700 000 km from the Sun.

The total mass of the Earth is about 6 694 000 000 000 000 000 000 tonnes (i.e. 6 694 million million million).

The population of China was approximately 1 115 000 000 in 1990

The relative density of hydrogen is about 0.000 089 9

The distance between atoms in copper is about 0.000 000 000 34 m.

Now, if you look at your calculator, you will see that the display can only show 8 or 10 digits. This makes it very difficult to do any calculations with these very large and very small numbers. We have to find a way of writing them in **shorthand** so that we can use a calculator.

Writing these numbers in shorthand not only makes it easier to calculate with them but also to compare their relative sizes. It is also quicker to write shorthand.

Decimals as powers of ten

Remember how earlier on in this book we looked at the column headings of large numbers, Units, Tens, Hundreds, Thousands, Ten thousands etc. as being written as powers of ten:

Ten thousand	$= 10\,000$	$= 10 \times 10 \times 10 \times 10$	$= 10^4$
One thousand	$= 1000$	$= 10 \times 10 \times 10$	$= 10^3$
One hundred	$= 100$	$= 10 \times 10$	$= 10^2$
Ten	$= 10$	$= 10$	$= 10^1$

But what happens as we get smaller? Look at the sequence of the index numbers, 4, 3, 2, 1 the next must be 0

> This gives us the definition of a number to the power 0
> $$x^0 = 1$$
> $$\text{Unit} = 1 = 10^0$$

Next we have a tenth (0.1)   1 tenth $= \dfrac{1}{10}$

Let's look at how can we write $\dfrac{1}{10}$ as a power of ten. Remember the sequence of index numbers:

4, 3, 2, 1, 0, ... it follows that the next number must be −1, then −2 and so on.

> This gives us the definition of a negative index number:
> $$x^{-1} = \dfrac{1}{x}, \quad x^{-2} = \dfrac{1}{x^2}, \quad x^{-3} = \dfrac{1}{x^3} \text{ etc.}$$

This means we can continue the column headings as:

One tenth $= 0.1 \quad = \dfrac{1}{10} \quad = 10^{-1}$

One hundredth $= 0.01 \quad = \dfrac{1}{100} \quad = \dfrac{1}{10^2} \quad = 10^{-2}$

One thousandth $= 0.001 \quad = \dfrac{1}{1000} \quad = \dfrac{1}{10^3} \quad = 10^{-3}$ and so on.

As a little check, you can see that the number of 0s in 1000 is 3 and that reminds us that the index number is 3

(Do remember to write decimals as 0.35, not just .35)

Exercise 15.5

Write these numbers as powers of ten:

Example: (i) $10\,000 = 10^{4}$

(ii) $0.000\,001 = 10^{-6}$

1.	100 000	7.	10 000
2.	100	8.	0.001
3.	0.01	9.	1 000 000 000
4.	0.000 1	10.	0.000 01
5.	100 000 000	11.	0.1
6.	0. 000 000 001	12.	1

Exercise 15.6

Write these numbers as a single figure multiplied by an index number:

> Example: (i) $4\,000 = 4 \times 1000$
> $= 4 \times 10^{3}$
>
> (ii) $0.007 = 7 \times 0.001$
> $= 7 \times 10^{-3}$

1. 200 000

2. 0.000 002

3. 0.3

4. 0.005

5. 0.000 000 006

6. 400 000 000

7. 0.000 009

8. 0.000 02

9. 200

10. 0.000 000 000 000 8

11. 5 000

12. 30 000

Exercise 15.7

Write these numbers out in full. Remember to put the space in the correct position after each group of three numbers:

> Example: (i) $3 \times 10^{4} = 3 \times 10\,000$
> $= 30\,000$
>
> (ii) $7 \times 10^{-5} = 7 \times 0.000\,01$
> $= 0.000\,07$

1. 7×10^{2}

2. 8×10^{6}

3. 9×10^{-1}

4. 5×10^{2}

5. 9×10^{5}

6. 3×10^{1}

7. 2×10^{-3}

8. 7×10^{7}

9. 8×10^{-5}

10. 4×10^{-3}

11. 6×10^{6}

12. 2×10^{-2}

Standard index form

The way of writing numbers as a number multiplied by a power of ten is called the 'standard index form'. The definition of standard index form is:

A number between one and ten multiplied by a power of ten.

The numbers we have just looked at have all been just single numbers but there is no reason why we cannot have decimals. Often we have to have decimals:

$3.4 \times 10^3 = 3.4 \times 1000$ Note the 3 is multiplied by 1000, so the answer will be
$ = 3400$ three thousand and something, not thirty-four thousand.

Exercise 15.8

Write these numbers out in full:

1. 4.5×10^2

2. 2.3×10^3

3. 1.82×10^4

4. 7.34×10^5

5. 9.02×10^{-1}

6. 3.71×10^{-2}

7. 4.1×10^{-3}

8. 6.72×10^{-4}

9. 5.45×10^3

10. 3.65×10^{-2}

Exercise 15.9

Write these numbers in standard index form:

> Example: (i) $230\,000 = 2.3 \times 100\,000$
> $ = 2.3 \times 10^5$
>
> (ii) $0.000\,305 = 3.05 \times 0.0001$
> $ = 3.05 \times 10^{-4}$

1. 420

2. 12 000

3. 234 000 000

4. 102 000

5. 3000

6. 55

7. 600 000 000 000

8. 19 909

9. 340 000

10. 5 060 000

11. 0.003

12. 0.004 51

13. 0.000 056

14. 0.000 000 705

15. 0.12

16. 0.009 712

17. 0.105 67

18. 305

19. 67 900 000

20. 0.000 045 56

Exercise 15.10

Give your answers to these in standard index form:

> Example:
>
> Write 400 litres in millilitres.
>
> $$400 \text{ litres} = 400 \times 1000 \text{ millilitres}$$
> $$= 400\ 000$$
> $$= 4 \times 10^5 \text{ ml}$$

1. Write 4 km in millimetres.

2. Write 6 kg in grams.

3. How many seconds are there in a day?

4. Write 5 millimetres in km.

5. What is 5 g in tonnes?

6. Write 4.24 millimetres in km.

7. 'Mega' is the prefix for one million. A megabuck is one million dollars. Write 150 megabucks as dollars in standard index form.

8. 'Micro' is the prefix for one millionth. One microsecond is one millionth of a second. Write 90 microseconds in seconds in standard index form.

9. Dinosaurs roamed the Earth 150 million years ago. Write the number of years in standard index form.

10. Pico is a million millionth. Write 15 picoseconds as seconds in standard index form.

11. The Big Bang is supposed to have taken place 10^{10} years ago. How many years is that?

12. The total mass of the Earth is 6 694 000 000 000 000 000 000 tonnes (i.e. 6 694 million million million). Write this mass in standard index form.

13. The relative density of Hydrogen is 0.000 089 9
    Write this in standard index form.

14. The distance between copper atoms is about 3.4×10^{-10} m. Write this distance out in full.

Standard index form and the scientific calculator

Try this calculation on a scientific calculator.

  450 000 × 250 000

The display showing the answer may look something like this:

   1.125^{11} or 1.125×10^{11}

This is the calculator's own shorthand for 1.125×10^{11} or 112 500 000 000

Now do the calculation 0.000 004 ÷ 500 000
The answer on the display might be something similar to:

   8.00^{-12} or 8×10^{-12}

This is the calculator saying 8×10^{-12} or 0.000 000 000 008

When you write your answers, you must write down the calculation correctly.

You **must not** write the calculator shorthand, as 8^{-12} is in fact $\dfrac{1}{8^{12}}$ and must not be confused with 8×10^{-12}

More estimating

Sometimes you have to deal with calculations where it is not worth giving an exact answer because the values change a little all the time, for example questions on population sizes.

> Example:
>
> If the population of London is 6 767 500 and the population of Belfast is 301 600, how much larger is the population of London than Belfast?
>
> London is approximately 6 800 000 and Belfast is approximately 300 000 and so London is 6 800 000 ÷ 300 000 = 22.7 or 23 times larger than Belfast.

Exercise 15.11

1. The population of Coventry is roughly four times as big as the population of the Isle of Jersey. If the population of Jersey is 80 212, estimate the population of Coventry.

2. The population of the Isle of Wight is about one sixth of the population of Glasgow. If the population of Glasgow is 733 784, estimate the population of the Isle of Wight.

3. Estimate the number of seconds in one year.

4. If there are 1760 yards in a mile, roughly how many yards are there in 496 miles?

5. There are 23 boys in my form. To eat comfortably they each need a 65 cm width at the dining table. Estimate the minimum perimeter of dining table that will seat the whole class. Give some suitable dimensions, in metres, for the length and width of the table.

6. After a recent survey we found that the average weekly pocket money in my class of 24 was £1.78 (to the nearest penny). Estimate the total amount of pocket money the class receives altogether.

7. Our school photocopier uses 45 packets of 500 sheets of paper in one term. There are 11 weeks in the term. There are 5 days a week and 9 working hours in a day. Estimate the number of sheets used in one hour.

8. The school photographer is coming to take each pupil's photograph. There are 443 children in the school. It takes her on average 3 minutes to take each child's photograph. Estimate the number of hours that the photographer needs to spend at the school.

9. My teacher is writing our school reports. She says that she has to write reports for 9 classes. There are on average 19 pupils in each class. She says it takes her about 12 minutes to write each report. Estimate the number of hours my teacher spends writing our reports.

10. I have just finished a really good book. There were 298 pages in the book and about 12 words a line on 30 lines. I read the book in a total of 8 hours and 40 minutes. Estimate my reading speed in number of words per minute.

Exercise 15.12: Extension questions

In this next set of questions you need to make some decisions before you calculate the answers. It is quite acceptable for your answers to be estimates because the exact answer could depend on so many variables.

Example:

How many apples have you eaten in your lifetime?

I assume I am 12 years and 3 months old and that I have eaten about 3 apples a week since I was 2 years old.

Number of apples I have eaten in my lifetime $\approx 10.25 \times 52 \times 3$
$$\approx 1600 \text{ apples}$$

---

1. Estimate the number of times you have blinked in your lifetime.

2. How many hours of television have you watched in your lifetime?

3. How many kilograms of chips have you eaten?

4. How long have you spent doing homework?

5. How many books have you read?

6. If you were to answer every single question in this book, how long would it take you?

7. How many tennis balls could you fit into your classroom?

8. How many footballs could you fit into your school hall?

9. How many litres of water have you drunk in total?

10. If you had saved all the money you have ever been given, how much would you now have in total?

11. If you were to make a pile of all the books you have ever read, how high would it be?

12. If you were to put all the teachers you have ever had on the weighing scales, what would their total mass be?

Exercise 15.13: Summary exercise

1. Round 19.4085 to:
    (a) 1 decimal place   (b) 2 decimal places   (c) 3 decimal places

2. Round 7.04996 correct to:
    (a) 1 decimal place   (b) 2 decimal places   (c) 3 decimal places

3. Write 304.983 correct to:
    (a) 1 significant figure   (c) 2 significant figures
    (b) 3 significant figures   (d) 4 significant figures

4. Write 0.004 098 23 correct to:
    (a) 1 significant figure   (c) 2 significant figures
    (b) 3 significant figures   (d) 4 significant figures

5. (a) Write ten million as a power of ten.
    (b) Write one millionth as a power of ten.
    (c) How would you describe the number 10^9?

6. Write these numbers in full:
    (a) 1.7×10^3 (c) 6.3×10^{-6} (e) 8.1×10^5
    (b) 6.025×10^6 (d) 9.51×10^{-5} (f) 5.804×10^{-3}

7. Write these numbers in standard index form:
   (a) 56 000 000   (c) 0.000 24   (e) 4 050 000 000
   (b) 0.004   (d) 31 205 000   (f) 0.000 501 23

8. What is 3.5×10^{-6} km in millimetres?

9. The first prize for a 'best pet' competition is the weight of your pet in £1 coins. My pet elephant won the competition and he weighs 5 tonnes.
   (a) How many grams is that? Give your answer in standard index form.
   (b) A £1 coin weighs about 10 g. How much money did my elephant and I win in the competition?

10. Estimate the number of hours that you have watched television in the last year. State clearly any assumptions that you have made.

End of chapter 15 activity: Calculator games

Space invaders

You can play this with either a scientific or a non-scientific calculator.

In these two games the numbers on the calculator display are the invaders and you have to defeat them by 'firing' numbers at them. Each game has slightly different rules about which numbers you can 'fire'.

Game 1 (Basic but helps to get the idea for Game 2)

Enter these numbers on your calculator:

$$1\,2\,3\,4\,.\,5\,6\,7\,8$$

You can only 'fire' numbers by subtracting them. The numbers that you fire can contain only **one** digit that is not zero, they can contain as many 0s as you like and a decimal point if you wish.

Make a table:

Fire	Display
	1 2 3 4 . 5 6 7 8

Decide what you are going to fire first, say 0.06

Enter $\boxed{-}$ $\boxed{0}$ $\boxed{.}$ $\boxed{0}$ $\boxed{6}$ and press the equals sign. The figures on your display will become 1234.5078

Write these figures in your table:

Fire	Display
	1 2 3 4 . 5 6 7 8
−0.06	1 2 3 4 . 5 0 7 8

Keep going until you have eliminated all the aliens and your calculator reads 0

Game 2

The rule this time is that you can only 'fire' single digits – i.e. a number in the units column. You still 'fire' by subtracting.

To move a number into the units column, you must multiply or divide all the numbers on the display; you can × 10, × 100 or × 1000, or ÷ 10, ÷ 100 or ÷ 1000

Let us look at the start of the game:

Fire	Display
	1 2 3 4 . 5 6 7 8
−4	**1 2 3 0 . 5 6 7 8**
÷ 10	**1 2 3 . 0 5 6 7 8**
−3	**1 2 0 . 0 5 6 7 8**
x?	

Now, you continue. Remember you cannot multiply or divide by a power of ten greater than a thousand, and you must make one move only between fires. Put in some different starting displays of *aliens* and try those too.

Game 3

This is a two-player version of Game 2

Player 1 **fires** the first shot, then **passes** the calculator to Player 2
Player 2 **moves**, then **fires** a shot, then **passes** the calculator to player 1
Player 1 **moves**, then **fires** etc.

The aim of the game is to get the other player into a position where he cannot fire: e.g. 0. 0005678 and he is stuck.

Game 4

Game 4 is a whole class version of Games 2 and 3

Everyone starts with the same display.
Each player **fires**, then **passes**.
Next each player **moves**, then **passes.**
Next each player moves, then **fires**, then **passes** etc.

If you cannot fire on your go, then you are out. Continue until only one person is left.

Chapter 16: Circles

There are some special names for parts of the circle.

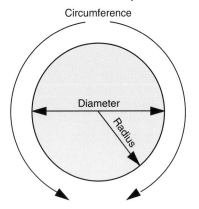

Circumference

Diameter

Radius

The **circumference** is the distance round the outside.
The **radius** is the distance from the centre to the edge.
The **diameter** is the distance across the middle.

From this information you can see that you can make an equation to calculate the diameter of a circle:

Diameter = 2 × radius

If you draw a circle on your page, you will find that you can measure the diameter and the radius with your ruler, but it is hard to measure the circumference.

The easiest way to measure a circumference is by wrapping a piece of string round your circle, marking off the length of the circumference and then measuring the string against a ruler.

Exercise 16.1

1. Draw 3 circles of different sizes in your exercise book.

2. Measure their diameters and their circumferences.

3. Put the results in a table like this:

Diameter (d)	Circumference (c)	$c \div d$

4. Now divide each circumference by the diameter. What do you notice?

Ask your friends if they get the same result. Amazing! If you all measured accurately, you should all have an answer of about 3, or even 3.1, to the calculation **circumference ÷ diameter,** regardless of the sizes of your circles.

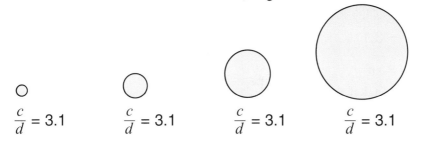

$$\frac{c}{d} = 3.1 \qquad \frac{c}{d} = 3.1 \qquad \frac{c}{d} = 3.1 \qquad \frac{c}{d} = 3.1$$

But is it really so amazing? As the diameter gets bigger, then the circumference must also get bigger. We should not be surprised that there is a link between them. We can say that the diameter and the circumference are in proportion:

the ratio   circumference : diameter
is   3.1 : 1

But, as we said before, ratios should not include decimals, so we usually write:

Circumference = 3.1 × diameter

$$c = 3.1 \times d$$

Now, the ratio is not really 3.1. In fact the ratio has been calculated very precisely and is a number that has an infinite number of decimal places:

3.141 592 653 589 793 238 462 643 383 279...

This number is known by the **Greek letter π (pi).**

Using this our formula, for the circumference now becomes:

$$c = \pi d \quad or \quad c = 2\pi r$$

If you push the π button on your calculator, you will see that it gives 3.1415926 or 3.141592654 (or it may give 3.1415927 which tells you that the last figure has been rounded up). It depends on the type of calculator you are using. You can use this when you calculate with π.

In practice we very rarely ever need to know a dimension to so many decimal places and so we often use an approximation, either 3.1 or 3.14 or the fraction $\frac{22}{7}$ or $3\frac{1}{7}$. Remember that all these values are approximations.

Exercise 16.2

> **Example:** Taking $\pi = 3.1$, find the circumference of a circle of diameter 4 cm.
>
> $$\pi = 3.1 \qquad d = 4 \text{ cm}$$
>
> $$c = \pi d$$
> $$= 3.1 \times 4$$
> $$= 12.4 \text{ cm}$$

1. Without using a calculator, find the circumferences of these circles, taking $\pi = 3.1$

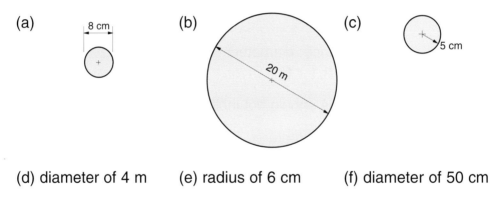

(a) 8 cm

(b) 20 m

(c) 5 cm

(d) diameter of 4 m   (e) radius of 6 cm   (f) diameter of 50 cm

> **Example:** Taking $\pi = \frac{22}{7}$, find the circumference of a circle with a diameter of 14 cm.
>
> $$\pi = \frac{22}{7} \qquad d = 14 \text{ cm}$$
>
> $$c = \pi d$$
>
> $$= \frac{22}{\cancel{7}_1} \times \cancel{14}^2$$
>
> $$= 22 \times 2$$
> $$= 44 \text{ cm}$$

2. Without using a calculator, find the circumferences of these circles, taking $\pi = \dfrac{22}{7}$

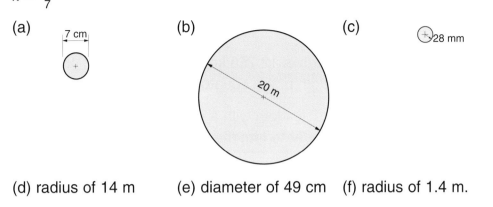

(a) 7 cm

(b) 20 m

(c) 28 mm

(d) radius of 14 m   (e) diameter of 49 cm   (f) radius of 1.4 m.

Example: Using the π button on your calculator, find the circumference of a circle with a diameter of 14 cm. Give your answer to 1 decimal place.

$d = 14$ cm

$c = \pi d$

$ = \pi \times 14$

$ = 43.982\ 297\ldots$

$ = 44.0$ cm   (to 1 d.p.)

N.B. Write out most of the digits on the calculator followed by 3 dots before you round the result.

---

3. Find the circumferences of these circles, using the π button on your calculator. Give your answers correct to 3 significant figures. Remember that you must write down all your working even though you are using a calculator this time:

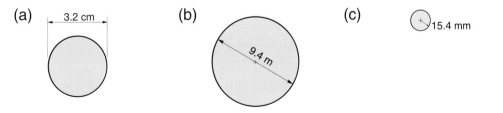

(a) 3.2 cm

(b) 9.4 m

(c) 15.4 mm

(d) diameter of 0.45 m   (e) diameter of 1.4 km   (f) radius of 75 cm

Exercise 16.3

Use the π button on your calculator to answer these questions. Give your answers to 3 significant figures.

1.   If the diameter of the Earth is 12 756 km, use the π button on your calculator to find the length of the equator.

2.   I am making a circular table cloth with a diameter of 2.8 m. What length of ribbon must I buy in order to trim the edge of my tablecloth?

3.   I have made a model tank out of a cotton reel, a match stick, a drawing pin and a rubber band. If the cotton reel has a radius of 3 cm, find how far my tank will go in one full turn of the cotton reel.

4.   My bicycle has wheels of diameter 84 cm. How far will my bicycle go in one turn of the wheels?

5.   I have a round hat of radius 18 cm. What length of ribbon do I need to go all the way round it?

6.   A tin can has a diameter of 8 cm. What length of label fits exactly round the can?

Area of a circle

If it was hard to measure the circumference of a circle, it is even harder to measure the area! You will start off the next exercise by drawing circles on squared paper and counting the squares.

Exercise 16.4

1.   Draw three circles of different radii on graph paper.

2.   You can work out the area of most of your circles by drawing a square and four rectangles, and calculating their area, then counting the remaining squares:

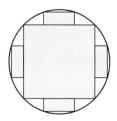

3. Put the radius and area results from q.2 in a table like this:

Radius (r)	Area (A)	$A \div r^2$

4. Now divide each area by the radius squared ($A \div r \div r$) and put the results in the third column of the table above. What do you notice?

Note **area** is in **square units** and is **not** measured in **cm, m** or **km** but in **cm²**, **m²** or **km²**. This means that we divide the area by the radius squared or simply written as $\dfrac{A}{r^2}$

Look at the figures you calculated when dividing A by r^2. What have you found? If you have been accurate, you should find our old friend 3.1, otherwise known as π.

We can now create a formula for calculating the area of a circle:

$$\frac{A}{r^2} = \pi \qquad \text{or} \qquad A = \pi r^2$$

Exercise 16.5

Example: Find the area of a circle of diameter 14 cm, taking $\pi = \dfrac{22}{7}$

$d = 14$ cm and therefore the radius $r = 7$ cm

$$A = \pi r^2$$

$$= \frac{22}{7_1} \times \cancel{7}^1 \times 7$$

$$= 22 \times 1 \times 7$$

$$= 154 \text{ cm}^2$$

1. Using $\pi = \frac{22}{7}$, find the areas of these circles:

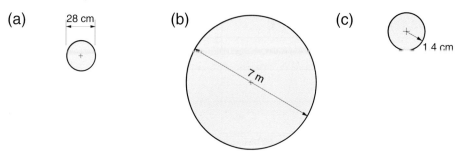

(a) 28 cm   (b) 7 m   (c) 1 4 cm

2. Using $\pi = 3.1$, find the areas of these circles:

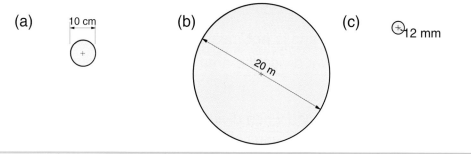

(a) 10 cm   (b) 20 m   (c) 12 mm

Example: Using the π button on your calculator, find the area of a circle of diameter 14 cm. Give your answer to 1 decimal place.

d = 14 cm and therefore the radius r = 7 cm

$A = \pi\, r^2$

   $= \pi \times 7 \times 7$

   $= 153.938\ldots$

   $= 154.0$ cm²   (to 1 d.p.)

N.B. Write out most of the digits on the calculator followed by 3 dots before you round the results.

---

3. Use the π button on your calculator and find the areas of these circles; give your answers to 3 significant figures:

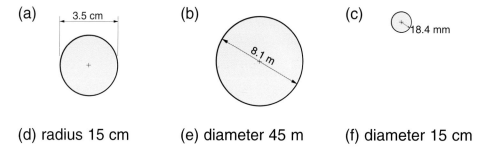

(a) 3.5 cm   (b) 8.1 m   (c) 18.4 mm

(d) radius 15 cm   (e) diameter 45 m   (f) diameter 15 cm

Exercise 16.6

Use the π button on your calculator to answer these questions; give your answers to 3 significant figures:

1.   I cut a slice of orange. The slice has a diameter of 8 cm. Find the area of my slice.

2.   A table mat has a diameter of 12 cm. Find its area and its circumference.

3.   I have a glass with a base diameter of 7 cm. Find the area of the base.

4.   (a) My mother has just cut a wooden lid to fit my baby sister's round sand pit. The lid has a radius of 1.5 m. Calculate the area of the lid.

   (b) The lid needs a length of wooden trim round the circumference. What length of wooden trim does my mother need?

5.   How many circles of diameter 5 cm can be cut from a strip of paper 5 cm wide and 1 m long? (Be careful!)

6.   I have a cucumber. I cut a slice out of the middle of the cucumber and find that it has a diameter of 3.2 cm. I then cut a slice off the end of the cucumber and find that has a diameter of 1.2 cm. Find the difference between the areas of the two slices.

Semi-circles and quadrants

So far, we have calculated the circumferences and areas of whole circles using the formulae. We can also use these to find perimeters and areas of fractions of a circle.

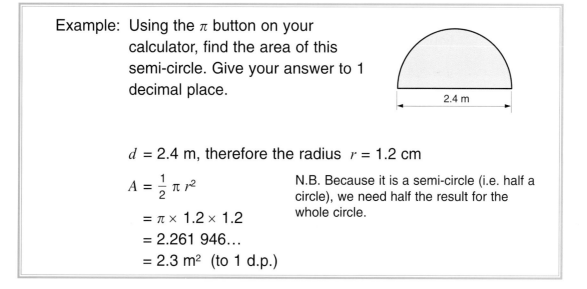

Example: Using the π button on your calculator, find the area of this semi-circle. Give your answer to 1 decimal place.

2.4 m

d = 2.4 m, therefore the radius r = 1.2 cm

$A = \dfrac{1}{2}\,\pi\,r^2$

N.B. Because it is a semi-circle (i.e. half a circle), we need half the result for the whole circle.

$= \pi \times 1.2 \times 1.2$

$= 2.261\ 946...$

$= 2.3$ m² (to 1 d.p.)

Exercise 16.7

Use the π button of your calculator for this exercise and give all answers to 1 decimal place.

1. Find the areas of these shapes:

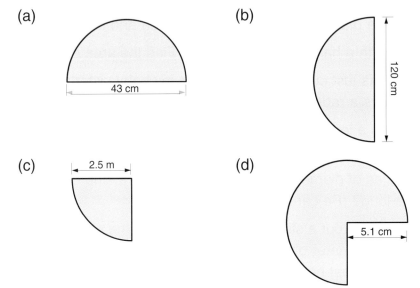

(a) 43 cm

(b) 120 cm

(c) 2.5 m

(d) 5.1 cm

Perimeters

Look at the above shapes and think about the perimeters.

For each one you will need to find the **curved length** and then add on the **straight bits**.

Example: Using the π button on your calculator, find the perimeter of this semi-circle. Give your answer to 3 significant figures.

d = 2.4 m

2.4 m

Perimeter = curved length + straight length

$= \frac{1}{2} \pi d + d$

$= \frac{1}{2} \pi \times 2.4 + 2.4$

N.B. Because it is a semi-circle (i.e. half a circle), we need half the diameter of a whole circle.

$= 3.76991... + 2.4$

$= 6.1699...$

$= 6.17$ m (to 1 d.p.)

Exercise 16.8

Use the π button of your calculator for this exercise and give all answers to 1 decimal place.

1. Find the perimeters of these shapes:

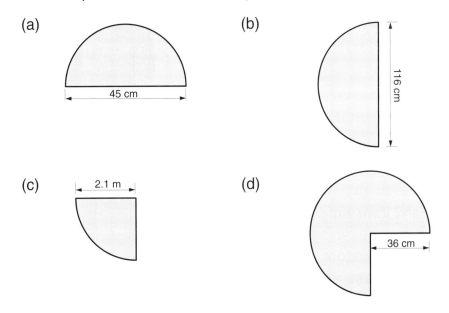

(a)

45 cm

(b)

116 cm

(c)

2.1 m

(d)

36 cm

2. A pond is in the shape of a semicircle with radius of 1.8 m.
   (a) What is the surface area of the pond?
   (b) What is the distance round the edge of the pond?

Exercise 16.9: Extension questions – The history of π

Early and quite primitive civilisations recognised the fact that there was a fixed ratio between **circumference** and **diameter** of a circle and between **area** and the **square of the radius**. However, different civilisations attached different values to this ratio.

The symbol π was first used in 1706 by William Jones. We now know that the value of π is a number with an infinite number of non-repeating decimal places (as is $\sqrt{2}$). We call these numbers irrational numbers. However, early mathematicians lived in an age of reason, and to them this concept seemed unreasonable. The early estimations for the value of π therefore were based on either rational numbers or as the result of a series. In the next set of questions you will discover some of the ways some early mathematicians tackled this problem.

Using your calculator, work out these values of π. Write any non-exact answers to six decimal places. (Bear in mind that to 15 decimal places we now know π to be 3.141 592 653 589 793 ...)

1. Pre 2000 BC, the temple builders of Iraq used 3 as the value of π. What did the builders in the Old Testament use? (Kings 1, chapter 7)

2. In the Rhind Papyrus c1500 BC (now in Moscow) the Egyptian scribe Ahmes wrote:

$$A = \left[\frac{8d}{9}\right]^2 \text{ and if we write } d \text{ as } 2r, \text{ this becomes } A = \left[\frac{16r}{9}\right]^2$$

and the ratio is therefore $16^2 : 9^2 = 256 : 81$
What does this make π?

3. The Ancient Greeks c. 240 BC: Archimedes worked on polygons with increasing numbers of sides and calculated the ratio as between $3\frac{10}{71}$ and $3\frac{1}{7}$

    Ptolemy calculated the ratio as $3 + \frac{8}{60} + \frac{30}{3600}$
    What does this make π?

4. The Ancient Chinese c. 200-500 AD were fascinated by ratio and came to some very accurate estimates:

    Tsu Ch'ung Chi (430-501 AD) came to the closest approximation to π in the ancient world. He did this by applying a continuous fraction series:

    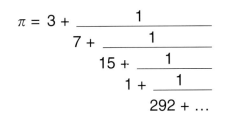

    $$\pi = 3 + \cfrac{1}{7 + \cfrac{1}{15 + \cfrac{1}{1 + \cfrac{1}{292 + \ldots}}}}$$

    To do this on your calculator, enter 292, then press the 'reciprocal button' which is marked $\frac{1}{x}$

    The display on your calculator will give you the answer to $\frac{1}{292}$
    Then add 1 and then press the reciprocal button again to give the answer to
    $\frac{1}{1 + \frac{1}{292}}$ Then add 15 etc.

    Where do you think the series 7, 15, 1, 292 comes from? Tsu Ch'ing-Chih 's calculations are lost, but he was able to carry them on further and found the value of π to be between 3.141 592 6 and 3.141 592 7

5. What do these estimates make π?

    In India c5-800 AD   (a) Baudhayana used $\frac{49}{16}$

    (b) Arya-Bhata used $\frac{62832}{20000}$

    (c) Brahmagupta used $\sqrt{10}$

Remember that the Asians had their numeral system while the Greeks were still battling with symbols. But once the Arab numerals had come to the western world and men started thinking in terms of numerical patterns, the estimates for π became more accurate. Work out these estimates for π :

6. Fibonacci in 1228 gave the ratio as $\dfrac{1440}{458\frac{1}{2}}$

7. In the sixteenth century Cusa thought the ratio was $\frac{3}{4}(\sqrt{3} + \sqrt{6})$

8. In 1673 Leibniz discovered that the following series gave a value of π:

$$\pi = 4 \left(1 - \frac{1}{3} + \frac{1}{5} - \frac{1}{7} + \frac{1}{9} - \frac{1}{11} \ldots\right)$$

How far do you have to continue this series to get an accurate estimate for π?

9. In 1680 John Wallis produced a very neat formula – (this involved much guesswork but sound mathematical intuition – a typical mathematics scholar!):

$$\frac{\pi}{2} = \frac{2 \times 2 \times 4 \times 4 \times 6 \times 6\ldots}{1 \times 3 \times 3 \times 5 \times 5 \times 7\ldots}$$

10. It is nice to know that the early mathematicians have still left us something to discover. As recently as 1914 Ramanujan suggested this approximation:

$$\pi = \sqrt{\sqrt{\frac{2143}{22}}}$$ Can you do better?

Exercise 16.10: Summary exercise

1. Take $\pi = \frac{22}{7}$ and find the circumference of a circle of diameter 63 cm.

2. Take $\pi = \frac{22}{7}$ and find the area of a circle of radius 7 cm.

3. Using the π button on your calculator, calculate:
    (a) The circumference of a circle of radius 5 cm. Give your answer correct to 2 decimal places.
    (b) The area of a circle of diameter 17 cm. Give your answer correct to 3 significant figures.

4. Use the π button on your calculator and give non-exact answers to 1 decimal place for this question:

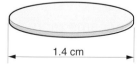

1.4 cm

(a) This disc is a token for a game machine. What is the area of the token?
(b) The tokens are cut from a sheet measuring 1 m by 1 m. How many tokens can be cut from one sheet?

5. Use the π button on your calculator and find the perimeter of this mirror. Give your answers to 2 decimal places.

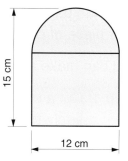

15 cm

12 cm

6. Bales Ales have just brought out a novelty beer mat. The mat has a radius of 7 cm and has a hole cut out of it so that you can put the neck of your bottle through the hole. The hole has a diameter of 3 cm. Take $\pi = 3.1$ and find the remaining area of the beer mat.

BALES

Ales

End of chapter 16 activity: Drawing spirals

(Graph paper will be useful for this activity.)

The spiral of a snail's shell is just one example of a geometrical shape occurring in nature. Nature has realised that a thin shell is much stronger when its curved, and the progressive curves of a spiral give additional strength as well as additional protection. Architects, in conjunction with structural engineers, have used this theory to produce the stunning curves of the Sydney Opera House and the gentle spiral of the Guggenheim Art Gallery.

A spiral may look simple but how exactly do you draw one?

The Fibonacci series we discovered earlier, 1, 1, 2, 3, 5, 8, 13 etc., is formed by adding the two previous numbers together to get the next number. If we illustrate this with each number in the series being the side of a square, we get a spiral of squares:

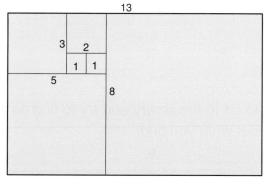
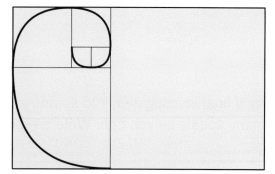

If you then draw a quarter circle in each square, you can produce a spiral.

Copy the pattern of squares shown above and extend the pattern as far as your piece of paper will allow. Then draw the spiral.

You can make a device for drawing a spiral like this:

Step 1: Cut a circle with a radius of 3 cm from a piece of thick card and glue it firmly to the centre of a piece of paper.

Step 2: Cut another circle, but this time with a radius of 3.5 cm. Cut a small slit in the edge of this circle. Glue this circle firmly on top and in the centre of the first slightly smaller circle.

Step 3: Then get a piece of button thread 70 cm long and tie a knot in one end. Slip the thread through the slit you cut and pull it until the knot stops it pulling through any further. It should now be securely attached. At the other end of the thread tie a small loop, large enough to get a pencil through. Then wind the thread round the circle (under the rim of the larger circle) until only the loop is showing.

Step 4: Put a pencil in the loop. Then, keeping the thread taught, put the tip of the pencil on the paper and move it so that you start to unwind the thread. As you do this you will see that you are drawing a spiral.

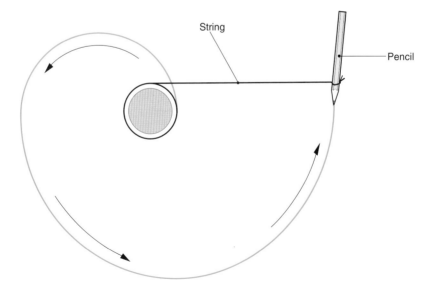

As a final investigation into spirals you could go to the library and try to find as many spirals as you can. Write a report about what you find.

Chapter 17: Transformations

Reflections

Lines of symmetry occur in many mathematical shapes and in many patterns. Sometimes we draw a pattern that is symmetrical about a line and at other times we have a pattern where we have to find the line of symmetry. If our pattern is drawn on a co-ordinate grid, then it makes it simpler to describe the exact position of the line of symmetry, of the object being reflected and its image.

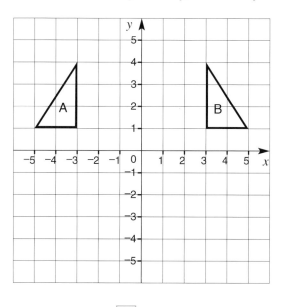

In this example triangle B is the image of triangle A after a reflection in the y-axis (the line $x = 0$).

Exercise 17.1

A worksheet is available for use in this exercise. If you are not using the worksheet, you will need to draw several grids like the one above.

1. Copy the above triangles A and B on to the first grid on the worksheet. Draw the reflections of both A and B in the x-axis.

2. On the second grid on the worksheet draw the square P with vertices at (3, 3) (3, 5) (5, 5) and (5, 3). Draw the line $y = 2$
    Draw the square Q which is a reflection of P in $y = 2$

3. On the third grid on the worksheet draw the triangle X with vertices at (3, −1) (3, −4) and (5, −1). Draw the line $x = 1$ and then draw the triangle Y which is the image of X after a reflection in $x = 1$

4. On the fourth grid on the worksheet draw the triangle R with vertices at (−1, 3) (−4, 1) and (−4, 3). Draw the line $y = -1$
Draw the triangle S which is the image of R after a reflection in $y = -1$

5. On the fifth grid on the worksheet draw the square A with vertices at (−1, 1) (−2, −1) (−4, 0) and (−3, 2). Draw the line $x = 1$
Draw the square B which is the image of A after a reflection in $x = 1$

6. On the sixth grid on the worksheet draw the trapezium P with vertices at (2, 4) (1, 1) and (5, 1) and (4, 4). Draw the line $x = 2$
Draw the trapezium Q which is the image of P after a reflection in $x = 2$

7.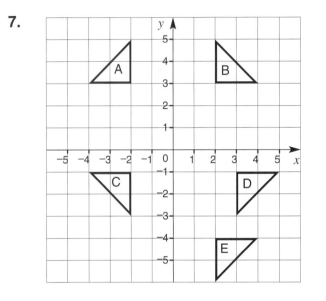

Describe the reflection which maps:
(a) A to B
(b) A to C
(c) C to D
(d) B to E

8.

Describe the reflection which maps:
(a) A to B
(b) A to C
(c) B to C
(d) E to A
(e) D to B

Rotation

An image may be also be obtained from an object that is rotated. To draw a rotation on a co-ordinate grid, we need **three** pieces of information:

1: the **centre of rotation 2**: the **angle of rotation 3**: the **direction of rotation**.

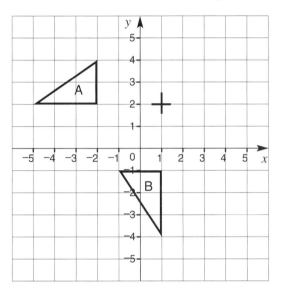

B is the image of A after a **rotation of 90° anticlockwise** about the point **(1, 2)**

A is the image of B after a **rotation of 90° clockwise** about the point **(1, 2)**.

It is very useful to use tracing paper when drawing rotations and when checking the centre of rotation. First trace over the object, and then put the point of your pencil on the centre of rotation. Once you have done this, you can rotate the tracing paper accordingly and you will then easily be able to see the position of the image.

Exercise 17.2

A worksheet is available for use in this exercise, otherwise you will need to draw several grids like the one above to answer the following questions. You will also need some tracing paper.

1. Draw the triangle A with vertices at (2, 1) (5, 1) and (2, 3).
   (a) Draw the triangle B, a rotation of A of 90° clockwise about the origin.
   (b) Draw the triangle C, a rotation of A of 180° about the origin.
   (c) Draw the triangle D, a rotation of A of 270° clockwise about the origin.

2. Draw the triangle P with vertices at (2, 2) (3, 4) and (1, 4).
   (a) Draw the triangle Q, a rotation of P of 90° clockwise about the point (1, 0).
   (b) Draw the triangle R, a rotation of P of 180° about the point (1, 0).
   (c) Draw the triangle S, a rotation of P of 270° clockwise about the point (1, 0).

3. Draw the triangle W with vertices at (1, 2) (1, 5) and (0, 5).
   (a) Draw the triangle X, a rotation of W of 90° clockwise about the point (1, 2).
   (b) Draw the triangle Y, a rotation of W of 180° about the point (1, 2).
   (c) Draw the triangle Z, a rotation of W of 270° clockwise about the point (1, 2).

4. Draw the rhombus A with vertices at (2, 0) (1, 2) (2, 4) and (3, 2). Draw the image B, a rotation of A of 90° anticlockwise about the point (2, −1). Draw the image C, a rotation of B of 90° anticlockwise about the point (2, −1).

5. Draw the trapezium P with vertices at (0, 0) (2, 1) (2, −3) and (0, −2). Draw the image Q, a rotation of P of 180° about the point (−1, 1).

6. Draw the kite Y with vertices at (−3, 5) (−1, 4) (−3, −1) and (−5, 4). Draw the image Z, a rotation of Y of 90° clockwise about the point (0, 1).

7.

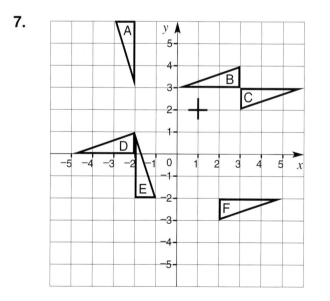

Describe the rotation that maps:
(a) B to C
(b) D to E
(c) A to E
(d) B to A
(e) B to F

8.

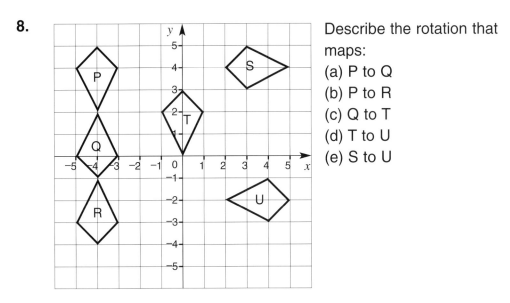

Describe the rotation that maps:
(a) P to Q
(b) P to R
(c) Q to T
(d) T to U
(e) S to U

9. If an object A is rotated 90° clockwise about a point to an image B, and B is rotated 90° clockwise about the same point to an image C, what single transformation will map A to C?

10. In the diagram for q.8 what **reflection** will map P to Q?

Translation and vectors

In reflections and rotations the image is in a different place from the object, and is a different way round. Sometimes we just want an image to be in a new place, but the **same** way round. To do this the object **slides** across the page. This slide is called a **translation**:

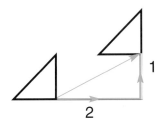

A translation is described in the same order as a pair of co-ordinates, i.e. the x-direction first and then the y-direction. We usually write a translation as a **vector**. A vector is an arrow used to describe a movement.

The translation in the above diagram would be written: $\begin{pmatrix} 2 \\ 1 \end{pmatrix}$

This is 2 units right and 1 unit up.

Example:

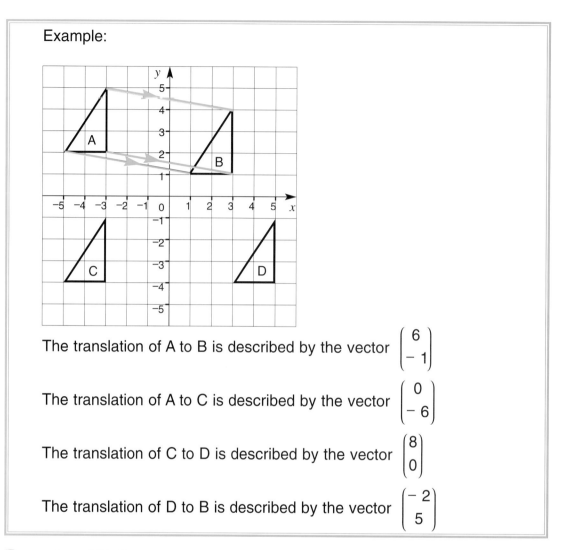

The translation of A to B is described by the vector $\begin{pmatrix} 6 \\ -1 \end{pmatrix}$

The translation of A to C is described by the vector $\begin{pmatrix} 0 \\ -6 \end{pmatrix}$

The translation of C to D is described by the vector $\begin{pmatrix} 8 \\ 0 \end{pmatrix}$

The translation of D to B is described by the vector $\begin{pmatrix} -2 \\ 5 \end{pmatrix}$

Exercise 17.3

1.

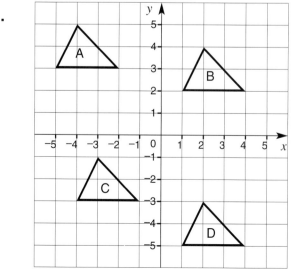

Describe the translation that maps:
(a) A to B
(b) C to B
(c) C to D
(d) B to D
(e) D to A

2

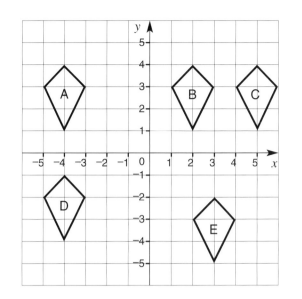

Describe the translation that maps:

(a) A to B

(b) B to C

(c) D to B

(d) A to D

(e) D to E

(f) E to A

3. On a co-ordinate grid with x and y axes numbered from −5 to 5, draw a triangle A with vertices at (5, 5) (5, 3) and (2, 4).

(a) Draw the triangle B, the image of A after a translation by the vector $\begin{pmatrix} -4 \\ -3 \end{pmatrix}$

(b) Draw the triangle C, the image of B after a translation by the vector $\begin{pmatrix} -2 \\ 1 \end{pmatrix}$

(c) Draw the triangle D, the image of C after a translation by the vector $\begin{pmatrix} 5 \\ 4 \end{pmatrix}$

(d) Describe the translation that will map triangle D to triangle A.

4. On a co-ordinate grid with x and y axes numbered from −5 to 5, draw a kite K with vertices at (−4, −4) (−3, −5) (−2, −4) and (−3, −2).

(a) Draw the kite L, the image of K after a translation by the vector $\begin{pmatrix} 4 \\ 3 \end{pmatrix}$

(b) Draw the kite M, the image of L after a translation by the vector $\begin{pmatrix} -3 \\ 2 \end{pmatrix}$

(c) Draw the kite N, the image of M after a translation by the vector $\begin{pmatrix} 5 \\ -4 \end{pmatrix}$

(d) Describe the translation that will map kite M to kite L.

Mixed transformations

A transformation is a general term for an application that transforms the original object into its image. A transformation can be a rotation, a reflection, a translation or an enlargement.
Sometimes it can be could be more than one of these.

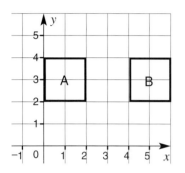

B is the image of A after any one of these:

a reflection in the line $x = 3$

a rotation of 180° about the point (3, 3)

a rotation of 90° clockwise about the point (3, 1)

a rotation of 270° anticlockwise about the point (3, 5)

a translation given by the vector $\begin{pmatrix} 4 \\ 0 \end{pmatrix}$.

Remember:

Reflection in a line
Translation by a vector
Enlargement by a scale factor with a centre
Rotation through an angle in a direction about a point

We covered enlargement in Chapter 10, so you might like to do a quick bit of revision on that subject before you do this next exercise.

Exercise 17.4

1.

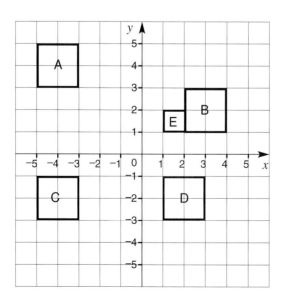

(a) Describe the reflection that maps A to C

(b) Describe the rotation that maps C to D

(c) Describe the translation that maps D to B

(d) Describe the enlargement that maps E to B

2.

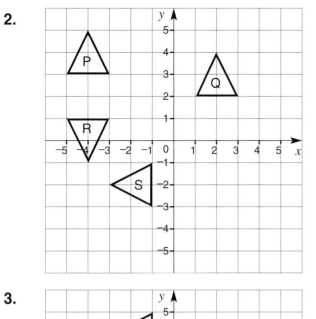

Describe the transformation that maps:

(a) ΔP to ΔR

(b) ΔR to ΔS

(c) ΔP to ΔQ

(d) ΔR to ΔQ

3.

Describe the transformation that maps:

(a) ΔA to ΔB

(b) ΔB to ΔC

(c) ΔB to ΔD

(d) ΔC to ΔE

(e) ΔD to ΔE

(f) ΔB to ΔE

4.

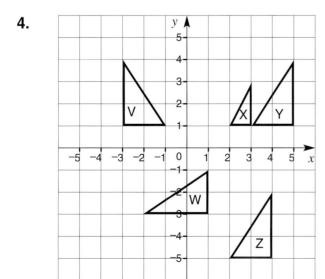

Describe the transformation that maps:

(a) ΔV to ΔY

(b) ΔX to ΔY

(c) ΔV to ΔW

(d) ΔY to ΔZ

You can use the worksheet for Exercise 17.4 for the next six questions:

5.   Draw a triangle A with vertices at (3, 5) (3, 3) and (5, 3).
     (a) Draw the image B, the reflection of A in the y axis.
     (b) Draw the image C, the rotation of A through 90° clockwise about the
         origin.
     (c) Draw the image D, the translation of A given by the vector $\begin{pmatrix} -6 \\ -3 \end{pmatrix}$
     (d) Describe a single transformation that will map B to C.

6.   Draw a triangle W with vertices at (1, 2) (3, 2) and (3, 3).
     (a) Draw the image X, the rotation of W of 90° anticlockwise about the
         point (1, 2).
     (b) Draw the image Y, the enlargement of W by scale factor 2, centre of
         enlargement (1, 2).
     (c) Draw the image Z, the reflection of W in the line $x = -1$

7.   Draw the rhombus P with vertices given by (2, 4) (4, 3) (6, 4) and (4, 5).
     (a) Draw the image Q, the reflection of P in the line $x = 1$
     (b) Draw the image R, the reflection of P in the line $y = 2$
     (c) Draw the image S, the image of P after a translation by the vector $\begin{pmatrix} -6 \\ -4 \end{pmatrix}$
     (d) Describe the rotation that maps Q to R.
     (e) Describe the translation which maps S to Q.

8.   Draw the trapezium A, with vertices at (−5, 3) (−4, 4) (−3, 4) and (−2, 3).
     (a) Draw the image B, the reflection of A in the line $y = 1$
     (b) Draw the image C, the rotation of B of 180° about the point (0, 2).
     (c) Draw the image D, the translation of C by the vector $\begin{pmatrix} -4 \\ -2 \end{pmatrix}$
     (d) Describe the reflection that maps D to A.
     (e) Describe the rotation that maps B to D.

9.   The kite K has vertices at (−3, 0) (−2, 1) (−3, 4) and (−4, 1). Draw K.
     (a) Draw the image L, the reflection of K in the line $y = 1$
     (b) Draw the image M, the rotation of K of 180° about the point (−2, 1).
     (c) Describe a transformation that could map L to M.
     (d) Draw the image N, the rotation of K through 90° clockwise about the
         point (−3,−2).
     (e) Draw the image P, the reflection of L in the y axis.
     (f) Describe the transformation that maps N to P.

10. Draw the triangle W with vertices at (−3, 1) (−2, 0) and (−2, 2).

    (a) Draw the image X, the reflection of W in the line $x = 1$

    (b) Draw the image Y, the translation of W by the vector $\begin{pmatrix} 2 \\ 0 \end{pmatrix}$

    (c) Draw the image Z, the rotation of Y through 90° anticlockwise about the point (0, 2).

Exercise 17.5: Extension questions

1. Some interesting transformations can be seen by reflecting objects in the lines $y = x$ and $y = -x$. Copy this diagram and reflect the triangles A and B in $y = x$ and $y = -x$.

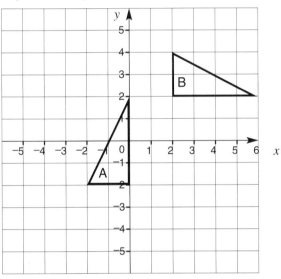

Copy and complete this table giving the co-ordinates of the six vertices of the two triangles:

Triangle	Co-ordinates	Image after reflection in $y = x$	Image after reflection in $y = -x$
A	(0, −2)		
	(0, 2)		
	(−2, −2)		
B	(2, 4)		
	(2, 2)		
	(6, 2)		

What do you notice about the co-ordinates after the reflections?

2. Sometimes we need two transformations to map an object to the image:

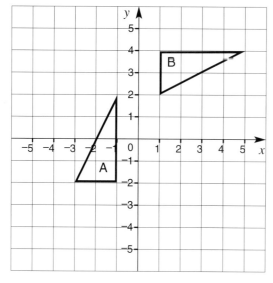

(a) Explain why you cannot map A to B as a single transformation.
(b) If the first transformation of A is a reflection in the x-axis, what is the second?
(c) If the first transformation is a reflection, and the second a translation, can you write down the exact transformations?
(d) Can you find another pair of transformations?

3. Sometimes there is more than one transformation from object to image:

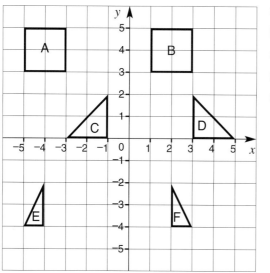

Give all the possible single transformations that will map:
(a) A to B
(b) C to D
(c) E to F

Which pair has the most possibilities and which the least? Can you explain your answer?

4.

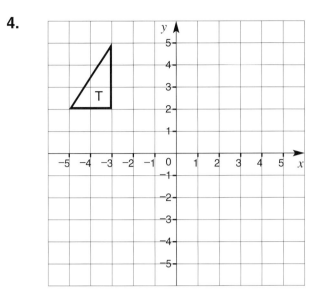

Copy this diagram. Rotate triangle T through 90° clockwise about (−3, −1) to give an image R.

A certain reflection of R will give the same image as a certain reflection of T. Draw this image and clearly mark the two lines of symmetry.

5.

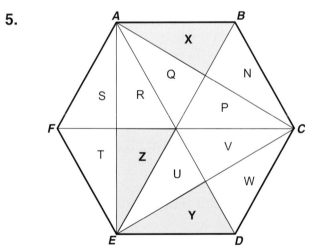

The hexagon *ABCDEF* is divided into 12 congruent triangles.

(a) Describe the **single** transformation that maps triangle X on to triangle Y.

(b) Describe the **single** transformation that maps triangle Y on to triangle Z.

(c) Describe **as many other pairs** of consecutive transformations that map triangle X on to triangle Z.

(d) How many of the other triangles, N, P, Q, R, S, T, U, V and W, can be filled by a single transformation of triangle X? Describe each transformation carefully.

Exercise 17.6: Summary exercise

1.

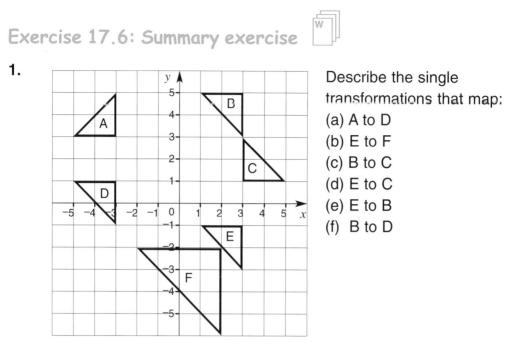

Describe the single transformations that map:

(a) A to D
(b) E to F
(c) B to C
(d) E to C
(e) E to B
(f) B to D

2. A triangle A is drawn on the worksheet.
(a) Draw the reflection of the triangle in the x-axis and label this image B.
(b) Draw the rotation of A by 180° about the origin, and label this image C.
(c) The translation of A given by the vector $\begin{pmatrix} 3 \\ -2 \end{pmatrix}$ and label this image D.

3. A triangle P is drawn on the worksheet.
(a) Draw the image Q, the reflection of P in the line $x = 2$
(b) Draw the image R, the rotation of P by 90° clockwise about the point (2, 1).
(c) Draw the image S, the translation of P given by the vector $\begin{pmatrix} 4 \\ -3 \end{pmatrix}$

4. A square W is drawn on the worksheet.
(a) Draw the enlargement of W by scale factor 3 and centre of enlargement the origin. Label this image X.
(b) Draw the translation of X by the vector $\begin{pmatrix} -3 \\ -4 \end{pmatrix}$. Label this image Y.
(c) Describe the enlargement that maps W to Y.

5. Draw the kite K with vertices at (−2,−1) (−1,−3) (−2, −5) and (−5,−3).
(a) Draw the reflection of K in the line $y = -1$ and label the image L.
(b) Draw the reflection of L in the line $x = -1$ and label the image M.
(c) Describe the transformation that maps K to M.

6. Draw the triangle Z with vertices at (4, −1) (3, 2) and (1, 0).

(a) Draw the image Y, the reflection of Z in the line $y = 1$

(b) Draw the image X, the rotation of Y 180° about the point (0, 2).

(c) Draw the image W, the translation of X by the vector $\begin{pmatrix} 0 \\ -2 \end{pmatrix}$

(d) Describe the transformation that maps W to Z.

End of chapter 17 activity: The four colour theorem

The four colour problem is famous and was unsolved for many years. Has it been solved? What do you think?

An outline of the problem

Ever since the time mapmakers began making the sort of maps which show distinct regions (such as countries or states), it has been understood that, if you plan well enough, you will never need to use more than four colours to colour them.

The basic rule for colouring a map is that no two regions that share a boundary can be the same colour.

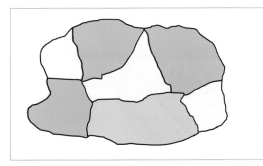

This map is coloured correctly.
No two adjacent regions are coloured the same.
It is fine for regions meeting at a point to be the same colour.

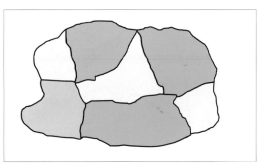

This map is not coloured correctly.
Two adjacent regions are coloured the same.

So how many different colours must you have if you want to colour a map where countries that share a boundary are not coloured in the same colour? In the mid-1800s this problem became known among a small group of mathematicians as a popular unsolved problem. Even at that time, it was common knowledge among mapmakers that 4 colours seemed to be sufficient. This wasn't actually proved, however, until 1976.

Even though we now know that only 4 colours are needed to colour any map, some maps can be coloured with three colours or even two. Finding a method to determine exactly the number of colours needed for any one particular map continues to daunt mathematicians today. Some mathematicians believe that a fast method to find out the minimum number of colours needed for a map is impossible (that is, they think a solution simply does not exist and hence can never be found).

Look at the maps on the worksheets for this exercise. Can you colour these with only four colours? Which ones need fewer colours? Can you put together any theories about why some need fewer colours than others?

Chapter 18: Volume

Cubes and cuboids

You can find the volume of a cuboid by multiplying the length by the width and then multiplying by the height. If you think of volume as a series of layers, you should be able to see why this is the way you calculate volume:

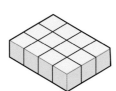 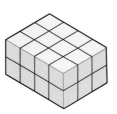 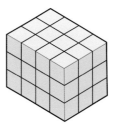

1 layer	2 layers	3 layers
12 cubic cm	24 cubic cm	36 cubic cm

The formula for the volume of a cuboid is:

Volume of cuboid = $l \times b \times h$ l is the length, b is the breadth (width) and h is the height

Written correctly in algebra terms, the formula becomes:
Volume of cuboid = lbh

When all the sides are the same length, then we have a cube.

The formula for the volume of a cube is:
Volume of cube = l^3

Make sure when you are writing down the formula for the area of shape that you specify what shape it is, for example *volume of a cube*. This is because formulae for volumes of different shapes are different. It is important that we use the correct one.

Exercise 18.1

Example: Find the volume of a cuboid of length 4 m, breadth 3.2 m and height 90 cm

$l = 4$ m $b = 3.2$ m $h = 0.9$ m

Before you do any calculations, remember to make sure that any measurements are expressed in the same units. In this example they are all now given in metres.

Volume of cuboid $= lbh$
$$= 4 \times 3.2 \times 0.9$$
$$= 11.52 \text{ m}^3$$

---

1. Find the volumes of these cuboids:
   (a) 3 cm by 5 cm by 7 cm
   (b) 5 m by 10 m by 12 m
   (c) 1.6 m by 1.2 m by 0.8 m

2. Find the volumes of these cubes:
   (a) of side 5 cm
   (b) of side 50 cm
   (c) of side 0.5 cm

3. Find the volumes of these cuboids:
   (a) length 1.2 m, breadth 90 cm and height 12 cm
   (b) length 4.8 cm, breadth 8 mm and height 1.4 cm
   (c) length 3.2 m, breadth 75 cm and height 0.9 m

For the next few questions remember that 1000 cm³ is equivalent to 1 litre

4. A water tank is 1 m long, 1.5 m wide and 80 cm deep. How many litres of water does it contain when it is full?

5. A fish tank is 30 cm wide, 20 cm deep and 20 cm tall. How many litres of water does it contain when it is three quarters full?

6. Calculate which has the greater volume:
   (a) a 125 litre water tank
   (b) a water tank in the shape of a cube of side 50 cm
   (c) a cuboid water tank with sides of 25 cm, 50 cm and 1 m

Now remember that 1000 ml = 1l and that 1 ml = 1 cm³

7.   (a) How many millilitres are there in 5 litres?
     (b) How many millilitres are there in 500 cubic centimetres?
     (c) How many cubic centimetres are there in 50 millilitres?

8.   What is the volume of a plastic cuboid of sides 4 cm, 7 cm and 8 cm.
     Give your answer in millilitres.

9.   Which volume is larger, a cube of side 8 cm, half a litre, or a cuboid with
     sides 5 cm, 9 cm and 11 cm?

10. (a) I have 24 centimetre cubes. Using all 24, how many different cuboids
         can I make?
     (b) I have 36 centimetre cubes. Using all 36, how many different cuboids
         can I make?
     (c) I have 35 centimetre cubes. Using all 35, how many different cuboids
         can I make?
     (d) I have 37 centimetre cubes. Using all 37, how many different cuboids
         can I make?

Finding the height or depth

By carefully substituting the correct values into the formula and then treating
the result as an equation, we can find the missing lengths.

Example: Find the height of a cuboid of length 4 cm, breadth 3 cm and
volume 60 cm³

Volume of cuboid = 60 cm³, l = 4 cm, b = 3 cm
Volume of cuboid = lbh

$$60 = 4 \times 3 \times h$$
$$60 = 12\,h \qquad (\div 12)$$
$$h = 5 \text{ cm}$$

Exercise 18.2

1. This cuboid has a base of area 12 cm² and a volume of 60 cm³. What is the height of the cuboid?

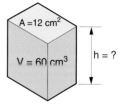

2. Find the heights of these cuboids:
    (a) base area of 9 cm², volume of 63 cm³
    (b) base area of 20 cm², volume of 150 cm³
    (c) base area of 40 cm²' volume of 24 000 cm³

3. If a cube has a volume of 125 cm³, what is the length of one side ?

4. Here is a cuboid with a width of 5 cm and a length of 12 cm. The volume of the cuboid is 7.2 litres. What is the height of the cuboid?

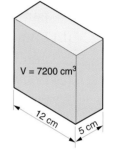

5. Give the heights of these cuboids:
    (a) volume 1 litre, length 10 cm and width 10 cm
    (b) volume 5 litres, length 25 cm and width 8 cm
    (c) volume 300 litres, length 2.5 m, width 1.2 m

6. A cuboid of base 25 cm² is filled from a jug containing 500 ml of water. What is the depth of the water in the cuboid?

7. A cuboid of length 40 cm and width 20 cm is filled from a jug containing 2 litres of water. What is the depth of the water in the cuboid?

Solving volume questions

When you are looking at questions relating to the cost per ml, or the mass per cubic metre, look carefully at the word 'per'. When we worked with percentages, we translated the word percent into 'divide by 100'. In mathematics, the word per can be thought of as meaning 'divide'.

So, to find the **cost per ml**, **divide** the **total cost** by the **total volume**.

Example:

Which is better value, 125 ml of orangeade for 45p, or 175 ml of lemonade for 65p?

Cost of orangeade = $\frac{45}{125}$ Cost of lemonade = $\frac{65}{175}$

= 0.36 p per ml   = 0.3714... p per ml

The orangeade is better value.

Exercise 18.3

1. Which is better value, 225 ml of banana milkshake for 75p, or 175 ml of banana and raspberry smoothie for 60p?

2. I can buy one shampoo that costs £1.20 for 750 ml, and another shampoo for £1.50 a litre. Which one is better value?

3. A box of muesli 5 cm by 15 cm by 30 cm costs £1.80
    Is this better value than 1 litre bag of the same muesli costing £1?

4. I have a water tank that holds 400 litres. In order that it fits through my loft door, it must have a maximum height of 1 m and a maximum width of 50 cm. What must the minimum length of the tank be?

5. A cereal packet has a base of 10 cm by 24 cm and a height of 30 cm. It contains 750 g of Wheeties. What is the mass per cubic cm of Wheeties?

6. A hollow cube of side 5 cm is filled with water which is then poured into a cuboid 25 cm by 10 cm by 15 cm. How many cubefuls does it take to fill the cuboid?

7. (a) How many cubes of side 2 cm will fit into a larger cube of side 8 cm?
    (b) How many cubes of side 2 cm will fit into a larger cube of side 7 cm?

8. A brick of sides 5 cm, 10 cm and 15 cm is dropped into a rectangular bowl of water. If the rectangular bowl has sides of length 30 cm and 40 cm, by how much does the water level go up?

Prisms

You may have used a glass prism like this one in science, to separate light into its spectrum of seven different colours:

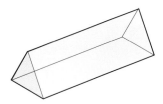

This glass prism's correct name is a **triangular prism**.

A prism is a shape that has a **constant cross-section**. This means that the shape can be sliced into slices of the same area:

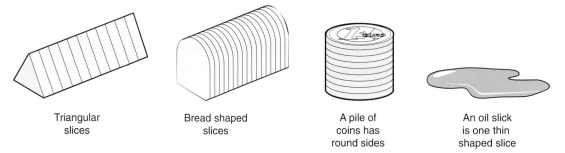

| Triangular slices | Bread shaped slices | A pile of coins has round sides | An oil slick is one thin shaped slice |

These are all prisms. Note that the slices of each prism are parallel to its ends.

To work out the volume of the prism, we need to know the area of one slice, the thickness of each slice and the number of slices. Imagine one loaf of bread cut into thick slices and a second loaf cut into thin slices. The slices of both loaves could have the same area but the volume of each loaf would depend on the thickness of the slices and the number of slices.

Exercise 18.4

1. This prism has 7 slices – each slice is in the shape of a triangle:

    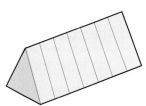

    (a) If the triangle has a base of 6 cm and a height of 5 cm, what is the area of the triangle?
    (b) If the slices are all 1 cm thick, what is the volume of one slice?
    (c) What is the volume of the seven slices?
    (d) If three extra slices, of the same thickness, were added to this prism, what would the volume be?
    (e) If the original 7-sliced prism had the same cross-section but a length of 5.2 cm, what would the volume be?

2. Here are four identical slices of bread, each with an area of 80 cm² :

    (a) If the slices are all 1 cm thick what is the volume of one slice?
    (b) If the slices are all 0.5 cm thick, what is the volume of one slice?
    (c) If the four slices are each 1 cm thick, what is the volume of the pile?
    (d) If there were 16 slices each 0.8 cm thick, then what would be the volume of the pile?

3. Here is a pile of six coins. The flat surface of each coin has an area of 2.25 cm²:

    (a) Each coin is 0.4 cm thick. What is the volume of one coin?
    (b) What is the volume of the pile of coins?
    (c) If the pile were 20 coins high, what would be the volume of the pile?

4. You will need to turn square metres into square centimetres for this question.

    This oil slick has a surface area of 400 m².
    (a) If it has a thickness of 1 cm, what is its volume?

    In fact an oil slick is very thin and has a thickness of about 0.2 mm.
    (b) What is the volume of oil?
    (c) What is this volume in litres?

From the above questions you should be able to see the general rule:

Volume of a prism = area of cross-section x length (or height or depth)

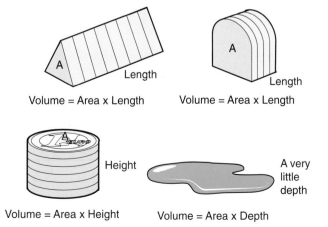

Volume = Area x Length   Volume = Area x Length

Volume = Area x Height   Volume = Area x Depth

Volume of a prism

Example: Find the volume of a prism of length 12 cm and a triangular cross-section of base 6 cm and height 5 cm.

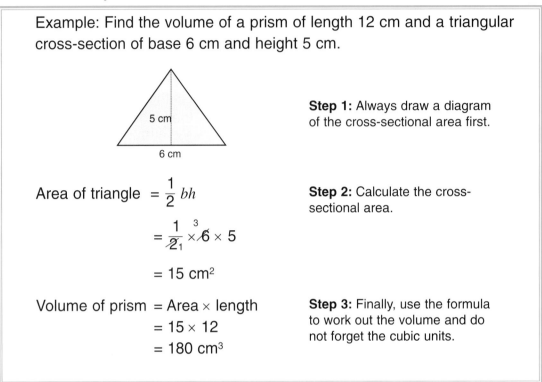

Step 1: Always draw a diagram of the cross-sectional area first.

Area of triangle $= \dfrac{1}{2} bh$

Step 2: Calculate the cross-sectional area.

$$= \frac{1}{2_1} \times \overset{3}{6} \times 5$$

$$= 15 \text{ cm}^2$$

Volume of prism $=$ Area $\times$ length

$$= 15 \times 12$$

$$= 180 \text{ cm}^3$$

Step 3: Finally, use the formula to work out the volume and do not forget the cubic units.

Exercise 18.5

1. Find the volume of a triangular prism where the triangular cross-section has a base of 8 cm and a height of 6 cm. The prism is 20 cm long.

2. This prism has a cross-section in the shape of a parallelogram. What is the volume of the solid?

3. Here is the cross-section of a solid block from my baby brother's block sorting set:

   The block is 4 cm thick. What is the volume of the block?

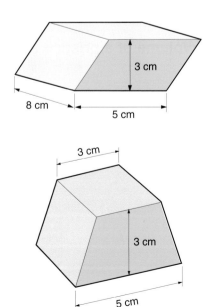

4. This is the cross-section of a barn which is 10 m long. What is the volume of the barn?

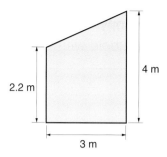

5. A triangular prism has a volume of 120 cubic centimetres and a length of 15 cm. What is the area of the cross-section?

6. A triangular prism has a volume of 200 cm³, and a base of area 10 cm². What is the height of the prism?

Exercise 18.6: Extension questions – Maximum volume

A cuboid can be made from a net. The net of a hollow cuboid looks like this:

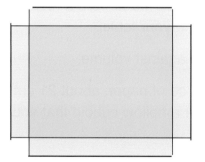

It is a rectangle with a square cut from each corner.

What size of square will give the maximum volume of the cuboid? Let each square have side x. The rectangle is 10 cm by 8 cm:

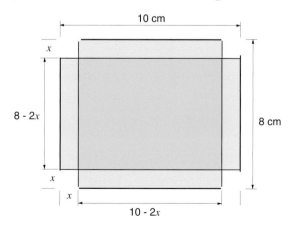

You can see that the sides of the cuboid are therefore $(8 – 2x)$ and $(10 – 2x)$

1. Copy and complete this table to find the value of x that would give a cuboid with the greatest volume possible:

x	$8 - 2x$	$10 - 2x$	Volume
1	6	8	48
1.5			
2			
2.5			
3			
3.5			

2. Repeat q.1 but this time for the net of a box made from a square 20 cm by 20 cm. You will need more rows in your table.

3. Repeat q.1 but this time for the net of a box made from a rectangle 15 cm by 20 cm. You will need more rows in your table.

4. From the table in q.3 draw a graph of x against volume.

5. A4 is the name for a standard-sized piece of paper, about 21 cm by 29 cm. What is the maximum volume of a hollow cuboid that you can make from a piece of A4 paper?

The questions so far have been about volume, but you could also look at the surface area. Let's consider our first box:

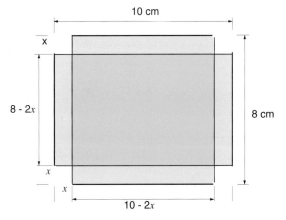

The areas of the five rectangles (can you identify these?) that make up the box are:

$$x(8 - 2x), \quad x(8 - 2x), \quad x(10 - 2x), \quad x(10 - 2x) \text{ and } (8 - 2x)(10 - 2x)$$

However, it is much easier to look at the whole shape and calculate the surface area. We do this by calculating the area of the whole rectangle (10 cm by 8 cm) and then subtracting the areas of the four squares we cut out ($4 \times x^2$). We can see that the surface area is in fact:

$10 \times 8 - 4 \times x^2$ which is $80 - 4x^2$

6.   Copy and complete the table below and draw a graph to show the change in the surface area:

x	x^2	$4x^2$	$80 - 4x^2$
1	1	4	76
1.5			
2			
2.5			
3			
3.5			

If you can use Excel or another spreadsheet program, then you can do some further investigation into volumes and surface areas.

Exercise 18.7: Summary exercise

1.   What is the volume of a cube of side 6 cm?

2.   If a cube has a volume of 64 cm³, what is the length of one side?

3.   (a) A cuboid has a length of 80 cm, a width of 50 cm and a height of 90 cm. What is its volume in cm³?
       (b) What is the volume in litres?

4.   This cuboid has a width of 50 cm, a length of 2.5 m and a height of 4 m.

Give its volume in
(a) cm³
(b) m³

5. A cuboid has a base area of 15 cm and a volume of 60 cm. What is the height of the cuboid?

6. Here is the cross-section of a metal ingot. The length of the ingot is 50 cm. Give its volume in:
   (a) cm³
   (b) litres

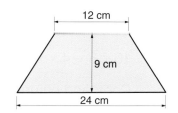

7. A water tank is in the shape of a hexagonal prism. It has a volume of 40 litres and a base of area 250 cm. What is the height of the tank?

8. What is better value, 1.2 litres of OZO washing powder at £2.25 per litre or 2 litres of DAX at £3.10 per litre?

9. An empty water tank measuring 2 m by 1.2 m by 80 cm is filled by a 4-litre bucket. How many bucketfuls does it take to fill the water tank?

10. A square hole 2 cm wide is cut through a cube of side 5 cm. What is the volume of the solid, once the hole has been made?

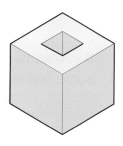

End of chapter 18 activity: Euler's theorem

More Polyhedra

(If you have access to Polydrons, they are very useful for this investigation.) A polyhedron is a solid shape with faces that are planes.

There are five Platonic solids whose faces are all the same regular polygon:

Tetrahedron: 4 equilateral triangles   Cube: 6 squares   Octahedron: 8 equilateral triangles   Dodecahedron: 12 regular pentagons   Icosahedron: 20 equilateral triangles

There are many other solids whose faces may be different shapes:

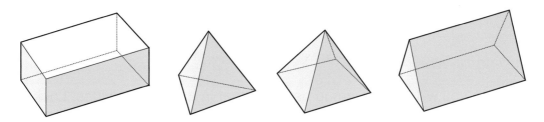

Solids have plane **faces** and have straight **edges** which join together at points or **vertices**. A cube thus has 6 faces, 12 edges and 8 vertices.

We would expect there to be some relationship between these three values. Can you find what it is?

1. Count the faces, edges and vertices of the cuboid, tetrahedron, pyramid and triangular prism above.

2. Make a table like this and fill it in:

Solid	Faces	Edges	Vertices
cube	6	12	8

3. Now look at the remaining 3 Platonic solids and add them to the table.

4. Add the prisms that you made at the end of Chapter 8.

5. Now make some more solids and add them to the table.

5. With all this information can you now find the relationship between F (faces), E (edges) and V (vertices)?

This relationship was proved by the mathematician **Leonhard Euler** (1707-1783). He opened up many new areas of mathematics and was the originator of the Konigsburg Bridge problem which may be familiar to your parents and even your grandparents. Ask your teacher for the puzzle.

Chapter 19: More data

Grouping data

Sometimes you will need to group data together in a range of values. Look at the first two questions about rainfall. It would not be sensible to have a frequency for each value to the nearest mm. In this type of example the individual pieces of data are collected together and put into sensibly-sized groups.

Exercise 19.1

1. The following figures show the daily record of rainfall in centimetres during April:

2.2	0	3.4	0.2	0	2.8	1.6	2.5	3.5	2.4
3	6.7	1.7	2.9	0	1.5	2.6	3.1	1.7	0.6
2.7	0.6	3.2	1.1	5.6	3.4	2.3	0	2.4	1.3

    (a) Copy and complete this frequency table:

Rainfall in cm	Tally	Frequency
0 – 0.9		
1.0 – 1.9		
2.0 – 2.9		
3.0 – 3.9		
4.0 – 4.9		
5.0 – 5.9		
6.0 – 6.9		
Total		30

    (b) Draw a frequency diagram to show the daily rainfall during April.

2. This data shows the daily rainfall in centimetres over the month of June. Draw a frequency table, and then a frequency diagram to display this information. Use the same groups of data as you did in q.1:

1.6	0	3.1	0	0.2	2.8	1.6	2.5	3.2	2.5
1.4	0	0.6	2.6	1.4	1.9	2.3	0	0	0.4
2.3	0	0.3	1.2	0.8	3.1	2.3	0	1.7	1.3

3. Using the information in q.1 and q.2, find the range and the mean rainfall for each of the months of April and June. What do all your results tell you about the two months?

4. Each member of my year was asked to hold his or her breath for as long as possible. Here is a frequency table showing the results:

Time in seconds	Tally	Frequency
25.5 – 34.4	$\cancel{||||}$	5
34.5 – 44.4	$\cancel{||||}$ II	7
44.5 – 54.4	$\cancel{||||}$ $\cancel{||||}$ I	11
54.5 – 64.4	$\cancel{||||}$ III	8
64.5 – 74.4	$\cancel{||||}$ I	6
74.5 – 84.4	III	3

(a) How many pupils are there in the class?
(b) Draw a frequency diagram to illustrate this information.
(c) What is the modal group?
(d) If I took one of the class at random, what is the probability that he held his breath for between 44.5 and 54.4 seconds?
(e) Do this experiment with your class and draw a frequency diagram to show your results.
(f) Compare your results with the results above. What are the differences?

5.   32 boys took a maths exam. Here are their results as percentages:

56	64	78	58	90	72	55	90
62	63	75	68	83	94	52	81
86	67	87	73	78	82	66	74
63	76	81	70	67	78	71	79

(a) What is the mean percentage? What is the median mark?

Because most of the marks are different, finding the mode for this set of data is not sensible, nor is it sensible to draw a bar chart from these results. Instead, we need to group the marks together to get a better picture of the distribution.

(b) Work out the groups that you need and draw a frequency table.
(c) What is the modal group?
(d) Draw a frequency diagram of this distribution.
(e) Another set of 16 papers was then marked, and the results were as follows:

| 55 | 62 | 58 | 71 | 52 | 80 | 64 | 50 |
| 71 | 60 | 72 | 74 | 62 | 66 | 58 | 61 |

Draw another frequency table to show all 48 marks, and then draw another frequency diagram.

(f) What are the differences in the frequency diagrams?
(g) What are the new mean, median and modal group?

Pie charts

Here is the breakdown of the votes from the 2001 election:

% of poll:	Labour:	40%
	Conservatives:	36%
	Lib. Dems:	20%
	Others:	4%
	Total:	100%

This can be shown on a pie chart. Remember from Chapter 5 how we worked out how many degrees should represent each measure. In this example we can say that because 100% is a full circle, i.e.360°, then 1% will be represented by $\frac{360}{100}$

Thus the angles at the centre of the circle are:

$$\text{Labour} = \frac{360}{100} \times 40 = 144°$$

$$\text{Conservatives} = \frac{360}{100} \times 36 = 129.6 \approx 130°$$

$$\text{Lib. Dems} = \frac{360}{100} \times 20 = 72°$$

$$\text{Other} = \frac{360}{100} \times 4 = 14.4 \approx 14°$$

Before you draw the pie chart, you should just check that the angles you have calculated add up to 360°

In this case we have: 144° + 130° + 72° + 14° = 360°
(The check is important because some of the degrees have been rounded to the nearest whole degree, and sometimes the addition comes to 361° or 359° and further adjustments have to be made.)

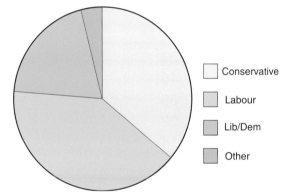

You may need to use a calculator to work out the angles, but write down the calculations that you do. The easiest thing to do is to make a table to show your calculations.

Exercise 19.2

1. A market research company asked the pupils at my school about their favourite television programmes. These are their results as percentages of the total number of pupils at the school:

Enemies	43%
Cuffy the hamster slayer	35%
The Bob	9%
The News	5%
Other	8%

(a) Copy and complete this table:

Programme	Percentage	Calculation	Angle
Enemies	43%	0.43×360	155°
Cuffy	35%		
The Bob	9%		
The News	5%		
Other	8%		
Total	100%		360°

(b) Show this information on a pie chart.

2. 220 children were asked how they preferred to spend their free time. These were their first choices:

Watching Television	53
Playing Computer Games	46
Sport (Football / Rugger)	35
Sport (Tennis / Badminton)	22
Riding	14
Reading	12
Art / Modelling / Pottery	8
Music (listening / playing)	6
Other	24

(a) Make a table like the one in q.1 and calculate the angles.

(b) Draw a pie chart to illustrate these results.

(c) What percentage of children chose tennis or badminton as their first choice?

(d) What percentage of children chose watching television or computer games as their first choice?

(e) If a child were chosen at random, what is the probability that riding would be his or her first choice?

3. We asked 190 children about which school lunch they liked the least. These were the results:

Curried eggs	53
Mushy peas	45
Spring greens	36
Fish cakes	21
Cheese pie	15
Spinach pie	12
Other	8

(a) Make a table like the one in q.1 and calculate the angles.
(b) Draw a pie chart to illustrate these results.
(c) What percentage of children chose curried eggs as their worst lunch?
(d) What percentage of children chose a green vegetable as their worst lunch?
(e) If a child were chosen at random, what is the probability that cheese pie would be his worst choice?

4. The top 6 classes in the school all raised money for charity. This is how much they collected:

6X	Cake stand	£53
6Y	Washing cars	£25
7X	Sponsored silence	£44
7Y	Bring and buy	£61
8X	Sponsored walk	£72
8Y	Face painting	£12

(a) Make a table like the one in q.1 and calculate the angles.
(b) Draw a pie chart to illustrate these results.
(c) Now show the results in a bar chart.
(d) Which do you think illustrates the results better? Explain your answer.

Scatter graphs

When we looked at big hands and big feet in Book 1, we compared one value with another. This is quite a useful way of looking at the relationship between two sets of values. Some relationships you would expect, for example as people get taller they weigh more. There is a range of weights that you would expect for a person of a certain height. If someone is outside that range, then they are either underweight or overweight.

You come across scatter graphs in science. Look at the results of these two experiments. The first experiment compares the amount of fertiliser used to feed six identical plants against the height of those plants after four weeks:

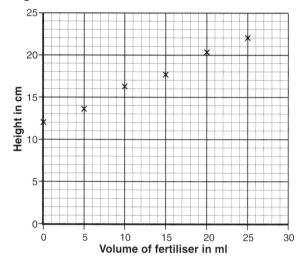

This scatter graph tells us that as the millilitres of fertiliser used increases, so the height of the plant in cm increases. This graph demonstrates a **positive correlation.**

This second experiment compares the amount of insecticide applied to six identical plants against the height of those plants after four weeks:

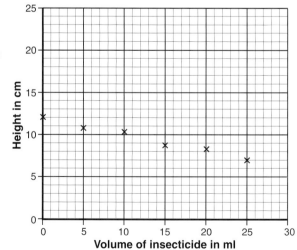

In this case, as the amount of insecticide increases, the height decreases. We say that this graph demonstrates a **negative correlation.**

Exercise 19.3

1. Here is a table of values showing the shoe sizes and heights of ten pupils. Draw a scatter graph to show the relationship between the two. What type of correlation does this show?

Height in mm	1.42	1.55	1.63	1.35	1.59	1.60	1.51	1.38	1.72	1.50
Shoe size	36	38	40	33	39	41	36	35	43	35

2. Here is a table showing the percentage marks scored in maths and English exams by 14 pupils. Draw a scatter graph to show the relationship between the two. Write about your graph.

Mathematics	56	63	72	68	80	76	45	90	81	73	62	65	76	84
English	61	67	74	65	85	67	56	83	78	80	70	58	80	75

When all the points have been plotted it is sometimes possible to draw a line of best fit. A line of best fit should have the same number of points plotted above it as below it and should be as close to them as possible. Let's look again at the two scatter graphs from the previous page.

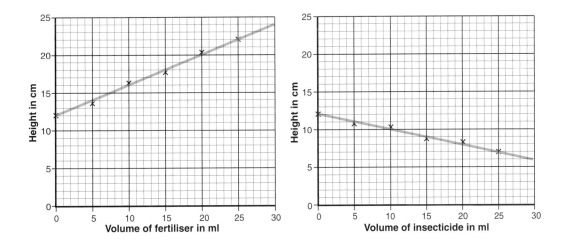

3. Draw the lines of best fit on your graphs in q.1 and q.2.

4. We sat two maths papers. Here is a table of the results of maths paper 1 against maths paper 2:

Paper 1	81	65	71	90	55	63	74	75	77	52	62	68
Paper 2	45	34	42	48	26	40	19	43	43	27	30	36

(a) Draw a scatter graph to compare the two results.
(b) Fred was not feeling well when he took paper 2. Circle the cross that you think might show Fred's marks.
(c) Draw a line of best fit.
(d) Mary was away for paper 2 but scored 85 on paper 1. Use the line of best fit to predict what Mary might have scored on paper 2.

Exercise 19.4: Extension questions

When finding the answers to the following questions, you may need to use the formula:

Total = mean average × number of items

Algebra and statistics

1. The average age of a class of 20 is x months. Write an expression in x for the sum of their ages.

2. The average age of a class of x children is 10 years 5 months. Write an expression in x for their total age in months.

3. There are x children in the class and the sum of their ages is 1980 months.
    (a) Write an expression in x for their average age in months.
    (b) What is their average age in years, in terms of x?

4. I have £x, India has £2 more and Archie has £5 less. If the mean amount of money is £12, what is x?

5.   Here is a table of the ages of a group of children:

Age:	9	10	11	12
Number of children:	4	6	x	2

(a) If the mean age of the children is 10 exactly, what is x?

(b) If the median age is 10, what is the maximum number of children and hence the maximum value of x?

(c) If the modal group is 10, what is the maximum value of x and hence the maximum number of children?

6.   Here is a table of the ages of another group of children:

Age:	4	5	6	7
Number of children:	$2x$	$x - 1$	x	$x + 3$

(a) If the mean average age is 6, what is the value of x?

(b) How many 5 year olds are there?

7.   Here is a bar chart showing the number of patients visited by Dr Bones last week:

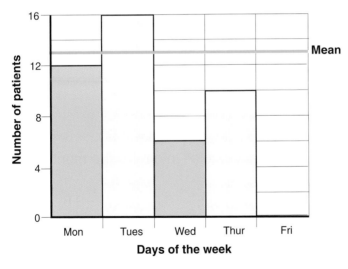

Dr Bones cannot remember how many patients he visited last Friday, but the bar chart shows the mean number of patients he visited over the five days. Calculate the number of patients he visited on the Friday.

8. There are x children in the school. A quarter of them walk to school, two thirds come by car and the rest by bus.
    (a) Write an expression in x for the number of children who come to school by bus.
    (b) If the number that come to school by bus is 19, form an equation in x and solve it to find the number of children in the school.

9. There are x employees in the SunLite Factory, and they are rarely ill. In fact, the mean number of days that they have taken off this last year is 1.75.
    (a) How many man-days have been lost over the year?
    (b) Three times as many employees have been ill as have not been ill at all. Write an expression in x for the number of employees who have been ill?
    (c) No one has had more than five days off and the number of people who have had two days off is the same as the number who have had four days off. Half of this number have had 5 days off, and twice as many (as the number that had 2 days off) have had 1 day off. No one was off exactly 3 days. What fraction of the people who had any days off had 5 days off?
    (d) Write expressions in x for the number of people who had 0, 1, 2, 3, 4 and 5 days off. Make sure that the total adds up to x.
    (e) If 24 more people were never ill than the number who took 5 days off, write an equation in x and solve it to find the total number of employees.

Exercise 19.5: Summary exercise

1. The following figures show the daily rainfall in cm for the month of September.

5.1	1.9	5.3	0	0.4	2.5	5.5	6.3	0	3.8
3.1	0.7	2.6	3.9	0	1.2	0	0	0	0.6
3.2	2.7	0.3	0	0	0	2	0.6	1.9	3.3

    (a) Collect these results in a frequency table. You will need to group the data in suitable classes.
    (b) Illustrate the information on a frequency diagram.
    (c) Find the range and the mean rainfall.

2. We asked 175 children how many books they had read this term. These were the results:

More than 10	17
8 or 9	25
6 or 7	20
4 or 5	58
2 or 3	43
fewer than 2	12

    (a) Make a table to calculate the angles.
    (b) Draw a pie chart to illustrate these results.
    (c) What percentage of children had read more than 10 books?

3. Here is a table showing the heights and masses of people in my class:

Height in cm	155	160	158	143	135	150	163	157	152	146	139	151
Mass in kg	44	52	45	37	28	40	55	43	43	40	30	42

    (a) Draw a scatter graph to compare the two sets of results.
    (b) Draw a line of best fit.
    (c) One child was away on the day of the survey, but he is 154 cm tall. Use your graph to estimate how much he weighs.

End of chapter 19 activity: A Fibonacci number trick

Here is a little trick you can perform on your friends. It will appear to show them that you are a mathematical genius.

Before you can do the actual trick, you must learn a clever bit of wizardry – how to multiply a number by 11 quickly.

Take the number 24 for example.

You can tell by estimating that the $11 \times 24 \approx 10 \times 20 \approx 200$

And you know that the last digit will be $1 \times 4 = 4$

So $11 \times 24 = 2\_4$

You need a quick way to find the middle digit.

If you think of 11 as 10 + 1, then you have 11 × 24= 10 × 24 + 1 × 24

$$= 240 + 24$$
$$= 264$$

You see the middle digit is the two numbers added together!

Suppose you have a three-digit number, for example 348

Think of 11 as 10 + 1; then you have 11 × 348= 10 × 348 + 1 × 348

$$= 3480 + 348$$

It is easiest to see in a frame:

Th	H	T	U
3	4	8	0
+	3	4	8
3	8	2	8
	1		

So 11 × 348 = 3828

For any three-digit number calculation where we are multiplying by 11 follow these steps:

The multiplication is 348 × 11
Give each digit in the three digit number a letter. In this case we have the number 348, so 3 is *a*, 4 is *b* and 8 is *c*.

To calculate the answer, you begin with the number on the right.

Step 1: The number to go in the units column is *c*, i.e. 8

Step 2: The number to go in the tens column is the last digit of the calculation *b* + *c*. So *b* + *c* is 4 + 8 = 12, and the last digit is 2.
This 2 goes in the tens column.

Step 3: The number to go in the hundreds column is the last digit of *a* + *b*. Add 1 to this answer if you had any carry numbers from the answer in step 2. So *a* + *b* is 3 + 4 = 7 and add another 1 to make 8 because there was a carry number from the answer 12 in step 2.

Step 4: Finally the number that goes in the thousands column is *a*, and add an extra 1 if you had a digit to carry from step 3. In this case *a* is 3 and there wasn't a carry number.

The final number, and the answer to your calculation, is 3828

Try doing this a few times for the following numbers, check the answers with a calculator and then go on to the trick:

11×27 Units (7); Tens (2 + 7 = 9); Hundreds (2)
So $11 \times 27 = 297$

11×275 Units (5), Tens (5 + 7 = 12 which is 2 carry 1);
Hundreds (7 + 2 = 9 plus 1 to give 10 which is 0 carry 1);
Thousands (2 plus 1 to give 3)
So $11 \times 275 = 3025$

Try these:

11×86 11×863
11×97 11×976

Now you should be ready for the trick:

Stage 1: Ask your friend to choose any two numbers that he or she likes, but suggest that they should not be too big because he or shey will have to do some calculations with them.

(For example 16 and 23)

Stage 2: Get your friend to write them down one over the other and then add them up.

$$
\begin{array}{r}
16 \\
+\ 23 \\
\hline
39
\end{array}
$$

Stage 3: Now get your friend to add the 2nd number he or she chose to the answer in stage 2

$$
\begin{array}{r}
16 \\
+\ 23 \\
\hline
+\ 39 \\
\hline
62
\end{array}
$$

Stage 4: Now he has to add that answer to the previous answer. Keep adding the answer just calculated to the number before it and put the new sum underneath. He should stop when he has 10 numbers written down (this should include the two numbers first chosen).

16

23
___
39

62

101

163

264

427

691

1118

Stage 5: Ask him to tell you the 7th number in the column of 10 (in this case 264) but do not look at any of the others. Tell your friend to add up all the ten numbers. Before he can work it out you can tell him that the answer is 2904 by using the method you perfected above.

How do you do it?

The sum of all ten numbers is just eleven times the fourth number from the bottom. Go on, try it a few times and convince yourself.

Why does it work?

You can see how it works using algebra.

Start with A and B as the two numbers that your friend chooses.

What does he write next? Just A + B in algebraic form. Keep going with each stage, then add up your ten algebraic terms and you should see how it works!

Chapter 20: Algebra 3 – More equations

In all the equations we have looked at so far we have only had one x term. Let's now look at something slightly different. Suppose I am told:

🎁 🎁 + 24p = 🎁 🎁 🎁 + 2p

"2 presents and 24 pence is the same value as 3 presents and 2 pence"

I should be able to write an equation to find the price of one present. If we say the price of a present is x, then we can write the following equation:

$$2x + 24 = 3x + 2$$

We can **solve** this equation in the same way we solved simpler equations. The way we do that is to **simplify** the equation until we end up with a **value of x equaling a number.**

To simplify the equation above, we can first take $2x$ away from both sides to give $24 = x + 2$. We then continue as before. It is always helpful to explain what we are doing to both sides of the equation as we are going along.

Example:

$$2x + 24 = 3x + 2$$
$$(- 2x)$$
$$24 = x + 2$$
$$(- 2)$$
$$22 = x$$
$$x = 22$$

Remember to take the equation step by step:

Step 1. Take the smaller x term from both sides.

Step 2. Now take away the remaining number term from both sides.

Step 3. Finally divide by the coefficient of x. (The **coefficient** of x is the number that multiplies x.)

Keep the equals signs underneath each other and always show what you are doing to both sides of the equation, in brackets down the right-hand side.

Exercise 20.1

Solve these equations:

1. $2x + 4 - x + 8$

2. $2x + 14 = 3x + 8$

3. $4x + 12 = 5x + 5$

4. $6x + 10 = 7x + 6$

5. $7x + 9 = 8x + 4$

6. $3x + 2 = x + 8$

7. $4x + 2 = x + 11$

8. $2x + 14 = 5x + 8$

9. $2x + 12 = 6x + 8$

10. $7x + 4 = 5x + 8$

In the above examples we only had to subtract numbers. In the next exercise you may have to add them:

Example:

$$4x + 12 = 7x - 3$$
$$\qquad\qquad (-4x)$$
$$12 = 3x - 3$$
$$\qquad\qquad (+3)$$
$$15 = 3x$$
$$\qquad\qquad (\div 3)$$
$$5 = x$$

or $\qquad x = 5$

Exercise 20.2

Solve these equations:

1. $2x - 4 = x + 1$

2. $4x - 7 = 3x + 3$

3. $5x - 3 = 4x + 2$

4. $3x + 3 = 2x + 7$

5. $4x + 1 = 5x - 6$

6. $7x + 9 = 9x - 5$

7. $8x - 5 = 5x + 1$

8. $2x + 1 = 4x - 9$

9. $2x - 3 = 15 + 4x$

10. $7x - 7 = x + 11$

Sometimes, when one term has been removed, a negative number is left.

It is very important that this is written down clearly.

Example:

$$5x - 12 = 3 + 8x$$
$$\quad\quad\quad\quad\quad (- 5x)$$
$$-12 = 3 + 3x$$
$$\quad\quad\quad\quad\quad (- 3)$$
$$-15 = 3x$$
$$\quad\quad\quad\quad\quad (\div 3)$$
$$-5 = x$$

or $\quad x = -5$

Exercise 20.3

Solve these equations:

1. $3x + 1 = 2x - 4$ **6.** $6x + 2 = 4x - 4$

2. $3x - 1 = 4x - 5$ **7.** $2 + 4x = 7x - 7$

3. $5x + 7 = 4x - 4$ **8.** $5x + 7 = x - 1$

4. $4x - 1 = 5x - 7$ **9.** $7x + 1 = 2x - 4$

5. $7 + 6x = 5x - 3$ **10.** $3x - 1 = 7 + 5x$

Remember, that although all the answers so far have been whole numbers, there is no reason why the answer should not be a fraction, or even a negative fraction:

Example:

$$3 + 6x = 3x - 1$$
$$\quad\quad\quad\quad\quad (- 3x)$$
$$3 + 3x = -1$$
$$\quad\quad\quad\quad\quad (- 3)$$
$$3x = -4$$
$$\quad\quad\quad\quad\quad (\div 3)$$
$$x = -\frac{4}{3} = -1\frac{1}{3}$$

11. $4x - 1 = x + 1$

12. $5x - 6 = 3x + 1$

13. $x - 1 = 2 + 3x$

14. $3 + 6x = x + 7$

15. $3x - 7 = 4 + 8x$

16. $3 + 2x = 4x - 2$

17. $7x - 1 = x + 4$

18. $3 + 2x = 8x + 9$

19. $3x - 10 = 7x + 4$

20. $5 + 6x = 3x - 2$

In solving the above equations, there was a pattern. As long as you followed this pattern, you should have arrived at the solution.

However, there are two special cases where things may seem a little strange:

1. The vanishing term:

$$3x + 2 = x \qquad\qquad (-x) \quad 2x + 2 = ?$$
$$\text{help no } x! \text{ So write } 0$$
$$2x + 2 = 0 \qquad\qquad (-2)$$
$$2x = -2 \qquad\qquad (\div 2)$$
$$x = -1$$

2. The negative term:

$$2x + 2 = 4 + 3x \qquad (-3x)$$
$$-x + 2 = 4 \qquad\qquad (-2)$$
$$-x = 2 \qquad\qquad (\div -1)$$
$$x = -2$$

To avoid the negative x term (and it is easy to make mistakes with negative numbers) it is a good idea to find the smallest x term first and eliminate that. This is particularly important when the x term is negative because it is not easy to spot the smaller term immediately.

Exercise 20.4

Solve these equations:

Example: $x + 3 = 4 - 2x$

The x terms are x and $-2x$.
$-2x$ is the smaller, so we go $- (-2x)$ or $+ 2x$

$$x + 3 = 4 - 2x$$
$(+ 2x)$
$$3x + 3 = 4$$
$(- 3)$
$$3x = 1$$
$(\div 3)$
$$x = \frac{1}{3}$$

---

1. $3x + 4 = 2x$

2. $4x = 7x - 5$

3. $8 + 3x = 2x$

4. $6x + 4 = 3x$

5. $7 - 3x = 4x$

6. $4 - 2x = x$

7. $4x = 5 - 7x$

8. $3x = 7 - 2x$

9. $8x - 2 = 2x$

10. $5x = 3 - 7x$

You must simplify the next ten questions before you solve them:

Example:

$$3x - x + 3 = x + 4 - 2x$$
(simplify)
$$2x + 3 = 4 - x$$
$(+ x)$
$$3x + 3 = 4$$
$(- 3)$
$$3x = 1$$
$(\div 3)$
$$x = \frac{1}{3}$$

---

11. $7x - 4 + 4x = 8$

12. $3x = 3 - 2x + 6$

13. $2 = 6 - 8x \quad x$

14. $3 - 2x + x = 8 + 3x - 4$

15. $4x - 1 + 3x = 3x - 6 - x$

16. $12x = 3x + 1 - 7x$

17. $11 - 2x = 3 + 2x - 9$

18. $5(2 + 2x) = 7 - 3x$

19. $7 - x = 4x - 3(x - 3)$

20. $3(5 - 4x) = 2(1 + 5x)$

You have now solved equations in various different forms. See how quickly you can do the next 20 questions – time yourself.

Exercise 20.5

1. $4 + x = 6$

2. $2 = 5 - x$

3. $9x = 15$

4. $\dfrac{x}{4} = 5$

5. $2x + 1 = 7$

6. $9 - 3x = 3$

7. $3(x + 1) = 2$

8. $7 = 2(x - 3)$

9. $\dfrac{1}{8}(x + 4) = 2$

10. $7 = \dfrac{x - 5}{3}$

11. $3(x - 2) = 1$

12. $3x + 3 = 2x + 7$

13. $5x - 5 = 6x + 9$

14. $3x - 1 = 4 + x$

15. $7x + 4 = 5 + 2x$

16. $5x + 3 = 2x$

17. $8 - x + 4x = 5$

18. $4 - 3x - 7 = 5x + 12 - 2x$

19. $5(1 - 3x) = 7(2 - x)$

20. $7 - 4x = 3(3 + 2x)$

Using algebra to solve problems

Now that you are good at solving equations, you can use these principles to solve real problems. When you do this, you need to decide what you are representing by the letters you choose. It could be a **quantity**, for example **cost**, **weight**, **age** or just an unknown **number**.

Example:

I am given the same amount of pocket money each week. One week I bought 4 tennis balls and had 27p left over. The following week I bought 2 tennis balls and had £1.45 left over. How much do the tennis balls cost and how much pocket money do I get each week?

Let the tennis balls cost x pence.

One week I had: $4x + 27$ Next week I had: $2x + 145$

$$4x + 27 = 2x + 145$$
$$(-2x)$$
$$2x + 27 = 145$$
$$(-27)$$
$$2x = 118$$
$$(\div 2)$$
$$x = 59$$

Tennis balls cost 59 pence each and I get £2.63 pocket money.

Exercise 20.6

1. I have just enough money to buy four packets of Jellos or to buy two packets of Jellos and 15 sticks of liquorice at 2p a stick.
    (a) If a packet of Jellos costs x, what is the cost of 4 packets in terms of x?
    (b) What is the cost of 2 packets of Jellos and the 15 sticks of liquorice, in terms of x?
    (c) Form an equation in x and solve it.
    (d) How much does a packet of Jellos cost and how much money did I have to start with?

2. Buns cost 12p. The cost of 4 cakes and 6 buns is the same as the cost of 3 buns and 5 cakes.
    (a) If cakes cost x pence, write an expression in x for the cost of 4 cakes and 6 buns.
    (b) Write an expression in x for the cost of 3 buns and 5 cakes.
    (c) Write an equation in x and solve it.
    (d) What is the cost of 5 cakes?

3. Here are two angles on a straight line:

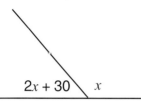

$2x + 30$ x

Form an equation in x and solve it to find the two angles.

4. (a) What is the angle sum of this triangle ?

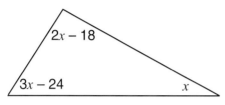

$2x - 18$

$3x - 24$ x

(b) Form an equation in x and solve it to find the three angles in the triangle.

5. I have three pieces of string. The second piece is 5 cm shorter than the first piece and the third piece is 10 cm longer than the first piece.
(a) If the first piece is x cm long, write an expression in x for the length of the second piece.
(b) Write an expression in x for the length of the third piece.
(c) The first and second piece together are the same length as the third piece. Write an equation in x and solve it.
(d) What is the total length of all three pieces of string?

6. My grandfather gave me some money. He gave my elder brother ten pounds more than he gave me and he gave my younger sister two pounds less than he gave me.
(a) If my grandfather gave me £ x, how much, in terms of x, did he give my brother and my sister?
(b) How much did my grandfather give us altogether?
(c) If the total amount that my grandfather gave us was four times the amount that I received, how much, in terms of x, did my grandfather give us?
(d) Form an equation in x and solve it to find out how much we each received.

7. Louis baked x cakes and India baked three times as many. Archie baked 15 cakes more than Louis.
    (a) How many cakes did India bake?
    (b) How many cakes did Archie bake?
    (c) If Archie baked the same number of cakes as Louis and India together, form an equation in x and solve it to find out how many cakes each child baked.

8. On Mother's day my son gave me one red rose for each year of his age, and my daughter gave me two white roses for each year of her age. My son is 4 years older than my daughter and I received 28 roses altogether.
    (a) If my son is x years old, how many roses did he give me?
    (b) How old is my daughter in terms of x?
    (c) How many roses did my daughter give me, in terms of x?
    (d) Form an equation in x and solve it to find the ages of my two children.

In each of these questions form an equation in x and solve it:

9.

$2x - 5$

$3x + 1$

The perimeter of the above rectangle is 52 cm. Form an equation in x and solve it to find the length and width or the rectangle.

10.
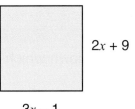

$2x + 9$

$3x - 1$

For our maths homework I worked out that the length of the side of a square must be $2x + 9$
My friend worked out that it was $3x - 1$
As it happened, we were both correct!

Form an equation in x and solve it, then find the area of the square.

11. I have to write 1000 lines. I have written most of them and now I have to write one third of the amount that I have already written plus 20 lines. How many lines have I already written?

12. Kola Cola costs 6p more per can than Perli Cola. I can buy 4 tins of Perli Cola for the same as I can buy 3 cans of Kola Cola. What is the cost of each brand of cola?

Exercise 20.7: Extension questions

New operations

In the exercises on algebra and arithmetic we did not need to define the symbols. They all had a known meaning.

It can be quite fun to set up your own special code. You may wish to define some new symbols that have a meaning which only you know about.

The new symbols should represent a new sequence of +, −, x or ÷, or other operations:

Example: If # means 'is 4 more than' then:

12 # 8   4 # 0 2^3 # 2^2 etc

If x # 7 then $x = 11$ 11 is '4 more than' 7

If 20 # x^2 then $x^2 = 16$

and $x = 4$ or -4

---

1. (a) If # means 'is 4 more than' write down which of these statements is true:

(i) 10 # 6   (ii) 3 # 7   (iii) 4^3 # 4^2

(b) Find a value of x that makes each of these statements true:

(i) 7 # x (ii) x # 15   (iii) $2x$ # x

(iv) 5 # $\frac{1}{x}$ (v) $\frac{20}{x}$ # 0   (vi) $\frac{24}{x}$ # $\frac{x}{2}$

You may find that it helps to turn the operation into an equation in order to find x.

> Example:
>
> $$6 \,\#\, \frac{1}{x}$$
>
> $$6 = 4 + \frac{1}{x}$$
>
> $$2 = \frac{1}{x}$$
>
> $$x = \frac{1}{2}$$

2. If $‡$ means 'is 3 less than' then

   $1 ‡ 4$ 1 is 3 less than 4

   $-1 ‡ 2$ −1 is 3 less than 2

   (a) Write down which of these statements is true:

       (i) $5 ‡ 2$ (ii) $-5 ‡ -2$ (iii) $2 \times 3 ‡ 3^2$

   (b) Find a value of x that makes each of these statements true:

       (i) $39 ‡ x$ (ii) $x ‡ -5$ (iii) $4x ‡ x$ (iv) $x ‡ 2\,x$ (v) $\dfrac{1}{2x} ‡ \dfrac{x}{2}$

3. If the symbol Δ between two numbers means 'is one more than half of', then $5 \,\Delta\, 8$ (5 is one more than 4 which is half of 8).

   (a) Write down which of these statements is true:

       (i) $4 \,\Delta\, 6$ (ii) $3 \,\Delta\, 1$ (iii) $\dfrac{1}{2} \,\Delta\, -1$

   (b) Find a value of x that makes each of these statements true:

       (i) $x \,\Delta\, 1$ (ii) $6 \,\Delta\, x$ (iii) $\dfrac{3}{2} \,\Delta\, x$ (iv) $x \,\Delta\, \dfrac{1}{2}$ (v) $\dfrac{1}{x} \,\Delta\, -4$ (vi) $x \,\Delta\, 3x$

4. If the symbol $\lozenge$ means 'the remainder when the second number is divided by 9', then $3 \,\lozenge\, 21$ $21 \div 9 = 2$ remainder 3

   (a) Write down which of these statements is true:

       (i) $1 \,\lozenge\, 19$ (ii) $5 \,\lozenge\, 13$ (iii) $3 \,\lozenge\, 3$

   (b) If $x \,\lozenge\, y$, are there any values of x and y such that x is greater than y?

   (c) Write a value of x, that lies between 20 and 30, which make each of these statements true:

       (i) $0 \,\lozenge\, x$ (ii) $8 \,\lozenge\, x$ (iii) $5 \,\lozenge\, x$

   (d) Find as many values of x that you can to make the statement $x \,\lozenge\, 4x$ true.

Exercise 20.8: Summary exercise

1. Solve these equations:

    (a) $3x + 8 = 2x + 5$
    (b) $x + 8 = 2x - 3$
    (c) $5 - 2x = 2x + 1$

    (d) $4 - 3x = 5 + x$
    (e) $5(x + 1) = 2(x + 5)$
    (f) $9 - x + 8 = 2x - 3 + 7x$

2. Jamie, Henry, Charlie and Oliver are on the school ski trip. Jamie has twice as many euros to spend as Charlie. Henry has 10 euros more to spend than Charlie. Oliver has 7 euros. Together Jamie, Charlie and Oliver have the same amount of euros as Henry.
    (a) If Charlie has x euros, how many has   (i) Jamie
                                                  (ii) Henry.
    (b) Form an equation in x and solve it to find how many euros Charlie has.
    (c) How much money do the four of them have altogether?

3. For the same amount of money I can either buy 5 sticks of liquorice and 8 penny sweets or 4 sticks of liquorice and 12 penny sweets.
    (a) If the cost of a stick of liquorice is x pence, what is the cost, in terms of x, of 5 sticks of liquorice and 8 penny sweets?
    (b) What is the cost, in terms of x, of 4 sticks of liquorice and 12 penny sweets?
    (c) Write an equation in x and solve it to find the cost of a stick of liquorice.

4. I have won the school mathematics prize and have a book token to spend. When I go to the book shop, I find that they have some special offer books at half price. I can either buy 5 books at the normal price and have £1.50 change or I can buy 11 special offer books and have 55p change.
    (a) If the special offer price is x pence, what will the normal price be?
    (b) Write an equation in x and solve it to find the normal price of books.
    (c) What was the value of my book token?

End of chapter 20 activity: A music genius test

These numbers occur in lines of well-known songs or are the titles of pieces of music. How many of them can you fill in over the next twenty-four hours? (Some are traditional, some are classical and some are pop songs. Not all are recent, so you are allowed to ask suitable people for help!)

> Example: 2 L_ _ _ _ _ B _ _ _ H _ _ 2 L_ _ _ _ _ T_ _ _
> Answer: 2 little boys had 2 little toys (Rolf Harris)

There are bonus marks for the artist or composer!

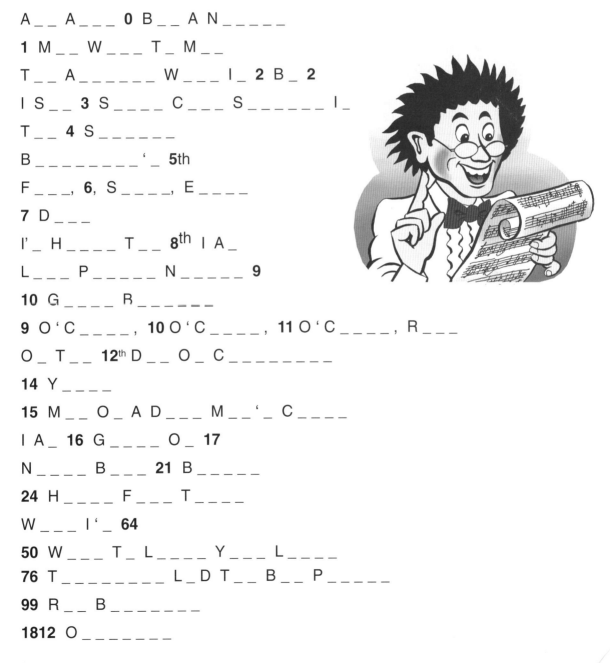

A _ _ A _ _ _ **0** B _ _ A N _ _ _ _ _

1 M _ _ W _ _ _ T _ M _ _

T _ _ A _ _ _ _ _ _ W _ _ _ I _ **2** B _ **2**

I S _ _ **3** S _ _ _ _ C _ _ _ S _ _ _ _ _ _ I _

T _ _ **4** S _ _ _ _ _ _

B _ _ _ _ _ _ _ _ ' _ **5th**

F _ _ _, **6**, S _ _ _ _, E _ _ _ _

7 D _ _ _

I' _ H _ _ _ _ T _ _ **8th** I A _

L _ _ _ P _ _ _ _ _ N _ _ _ _ _ **9**

10 G _ _ _ _ B _ _ _ _ _ _

9 O ' C _ _ _ _, **10** O ' C _ _ _ _, **11** O ' C _ _ _ _, R _ _ _

O _ T _ _ **12th** D _ _ O _ C _ _ _ _ _ _ _ _

14 Y _ _ _ _

15 M _ _ O _ A D _ _ _ M _ _ ' _ C _ _ _ _

I A _ **16** G _ _ _ _ O _ **17**

N _ _ _ _ B _ _ _ **21** B _ _ _ _ _

24 H _ _ _ _ F _ _ _ T _ _ _ _

W _ _ _ I ' _ **64**

50 W _ _ _ T _ L _ _ _ _ Y _ _ _ L _ _ _ _

76 T _ _ _ _ _ _ _ _ L _ D T _ _ B _ _ P _ _ _ _ _

99 R _ _ B _ _ _ _ _ _ _

1812 O _ _ _ _ _ _ _

Chapter 21: Sequences

Look at these sequences of numbers:

2, 4, 6, 8, 10, 12, 14, …

1, 3, 5, 7, 9, 11, 13, 15, …

3, 6, 9, 12, 15, 18, 21, …

The first sequence is **even numbers**, the second is **odd numbers** and the third is the three times table, or **multiples of three**.

These are familiar sequences. If you were asked to find the 100th even number, odd number or multiple of three, you could do that quite easily:

100th even number is 200   2 × 100
100th odd number is 199   1 less than the 100th even number
100th multiple of three is 300   3 × 100

Other sequences are not so easy to recognise, or to calculate their 100th terms.

Exercise 21.1

1. (a) Write out the next three terms of each of these sequences:
       (i) 5, 10, 15, 20, 25, …, …, …,
       (ii) 6, 11, 16, 21, 26, …, …, …,

   (b) Write down the 100th term of each of the above sequences, showing your calculations clearly.

2. (a) Write out the next three terms of each of these sequences:
       (i) 4, 8, 12, 16, 20, …, …, …,
       (ii) 3, 7, 11, 15, 19, …, …, …,

   (b) Write down the 100th term of each of the above sequences, showing your calculations clearly.

3. (a) Write out the next three terms of each of these sequences:
       (i) 6, 12, 18, 24, 30, …, …, …,
       (ii) 9, 15, 21, 27, 33, …, …, …,

   (b) Write down the 100th term of each of the above sequences, showing your calculations clearly.

Did you notice that the sequences in the last three questions went in pairs? If you did, you may also have seen a connection between the first and second in each pair. Now try these. They are like the second sequence in each pair:

4.   (a) Write out the next three terms of each of these sequences:
        (i) 2, 5, 8, 11, 14, ..., ..., ...,
        (ii) 5, 12, 19, 26, 33, ..., ..., ...,
        (iii) 4, 9, 14, 19, 24, ..., ..., ...,

      (b) Write down the 100th term in each sequence above, showing your calculations clearly.

For other sequences it is harder to find the pattern. See if you can recognise these:

5.   (a) Write out the next three terms of each of these sequences:
        (i) 1, 4, 9, 16, 25, ..., ..., ...,
        (ii) 1, 3, 6, 10, 15, ..., ..., ...,
        (iii) 1, 1, 2, 3, 5, 8, 13, ..., ..., ...,

      (b) Write down the **10th term** in each sequence above, showing your calculations clearly.

Many sequences are generated by geometrical patterns. Drawing patterns can help us to work out the rule behind a particular sequence.

Exercise 21.2

1.   Look at this sequence of patterns:

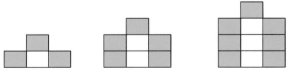

      (a) Draw the next two patterns.
      (b) Copy and complete this table:

White rectangles	1	2	3	4	5	100
Green rectangles						

      (c) Write down the calculation you used to find the green rectangles in the 100th pattern.

2. Look at this sequence of patterns:

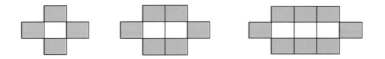

(a) Draw the next two patterns.
(b) Copy and complete this table:

White rectangles	1	2	3	4	5	10	20
Green rectangles							

(c) Write down the calculation you used to find the green rectangles in the 20th pattern.

3. Look at this sequence of patterns:

(a) Draw the next two patterns.
(b) Copy and complete this table:

White rectangles	1	2	3	4	5	10	20	100
Green rectangles								

(c) Write down the calculation you used to find the green rectangles in the 100th pattern.
(d) What is the name of the sequence of numbers you have generated in the green rectangles column?

4. Look at this sequence of patterns, drawn on square spotty paper:

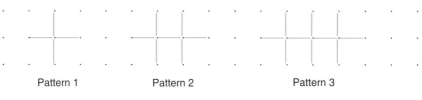

Pattern 1   Pattern 2   Pattern 3

(a) Draw the next two patterns.

(b) Copy and complete this table:

Pattern number	1	2	3	4	5	10	20	100
Number of lines								

(c) Write down the calculation you used to find the lines in the 100th pattern.

5. Look at this sequence of patterns, drawn on triangular spotted paper:

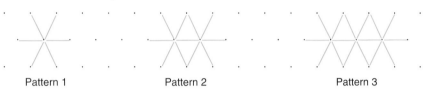

Pattern 1   Pattern 2   Pattern 3

(a) Draw the next two patterns.
(b) Draw a table like the one in q.4 and fill it in.
(c) Write down the calculation you used to find the lines in the 100th pattern.

6. Look at these patterns:

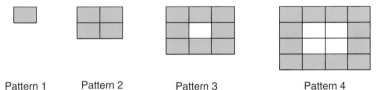

Pattern 1   Pattern 2   Pattern 3   Pattern 4

(a) Draw the next two patterns in the series.
(b) Copy and complete this table:

Pattern number	Green rectangles	White rectangles	Total rectangles
1	1	0	1
2	4	0	4
3			9
4			
5			
6			
10			

(c) Add an extra row for the 100th pattern number and explain how you calculate each of your answers.

7. Look at these patterns:

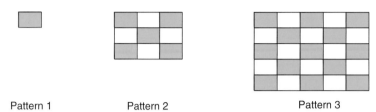

Pattern 1   Pattern 2   Pattern 3

   (a) Draw the next two patterns in the series.

   (b) Copy and complete a table like the one in q.6.

   (c) Add an extra row for the 100th pattern number and explain how you
       calculate each of your answers.

8.   (a) Make up a pattern of your own on squared paper.

   (b) Draw up a table like the ones you saw earlier.

   (c) Calculate the numbers in your 100th pattern, showing your calculations
       clearly.

In this exercise the patterns helped us to understand the relationship between
the pattern number and the rule.

Equations to sequences

Consider an equation, say $y = 2x + 1$

There is a value of y for each value of x.

If we consider the values of $x = 1, 2, 3, 4, 5, \ldots$, then the values of y are 3, 5,
7, 9, 11 etc.

We can write this in a different way, and say that the y numbers are a
sequence and the values of x tell us which number in the sequence we are
looking at.

Instead of x and y, sequences often use the letter n, where n stands for the
pattern or term number in the sequence:

       for the first term $n = 1$,
       for the second term $n = 2$,
       for the third term $n = 3$,

and thus the kth term is when $n = k$.

If we say that the rule for the term in the **sequence** is represented by **S**, then in the previous example:

If $n = 1$ $S_1 = 3$
   $n = 2$ $S_2 = 5$
   $n = 3$ $S_3 = 7$
   $n = 4$ $S_4 = 9$

and so the rule for the nth term of the sequence is $S_n = 2n + 1$

It is also helpful to think about sequences using the "What's in the box?" technique we saw in Book 1. The boxes contain machines. Each machine changes the number that goes in so that a new number comes out.
Here is a $\times 2$ machine:

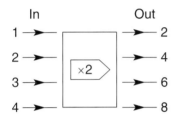

We can say that this function machine represents the function $T_n = 2n$ and so we can write:

$T_1 = 2$ $T_2 = 4$ $T_3 = 6$ $T_4 = 8$

Exercise 21.3

1. If the nth term of a sequence S is given by the formula: $S_n = n + 4$ find the:
   (a) 1st term   (b) 2nd term   (c) 3rd term   (d) 4th term

2. If the nth term of a sequence T is given by the formula: $T_n = n - 1$ find T_n when:
   (a) $n = 1$ (b) $n = 2$ (c) $n = 3$ (d) $n = 4$

3. If the nth term of a sequence W is given by the formula: $W_n = 3n + 2$ find W_n when:
   (a) $n = 1$ (b) $n = 2$ (c) $n = 7$ (d) $n = 10$

4. If the nth term of a sequence S is given by the formula: $S_n = 3 + 2n$ write down:
    (a) S_1 (b) S_3 (c) S_5 (d) S_8

5. If the nth term of a sequence T is given by the formula: $T_n = 5 + n$ write down:
    (a) T_1 (b) T_2 (c) T_6 (d) T_9

6. If the nth term of a sequence V is given by the formula: $V_n = 5n + 1$ write down:
    (a) V_1 (b) V_5 (c) V_{20} (d) V_{100}

Finding the rule

Relationship diagrams are a very useful way to help find the rules behind patterns of numbers. These are like the tables we used when we drew the patterns, or the 'In' and 'Out' lists on the function machines:

Example:

Can you find the next three terms in the series and hence the rule for T_n if:

$T_1 = 4$ $T_2 = 7$ $T_3 = 10$ $T_4 = 13$

$n \rightarrow T_n$
1 → 4
2 → 7
3 → 10
4 → 13
5 → 16
6 → 19
7 → 22

From the T_n column you can see that the numbers go up in threes. The three times table goes up in threes, and these numbers are just one more. So we can deduce from this that the rule must be:

$$T_n = 3n + 1$$

Exercise 21.4

1. Find the next three terms in the series and hence the rule for T_n if:

    $T_1 = 2$ $\qquad$ $T_2 = 5$ $\qquad$ $T_3 = 8$ $\qquad$ $T_4 = 11$

    (Draw a relationship diagram to help!)

2. Find the next three terms in the series and hence the rule for S_n if:

    $S_1 = 6$ $\qquad$ $S_2 = 11$ $\qquad$ $S_3 = 16$ $\qquad$ $S_4 = 21$

3. Find the next three terms in the series and hence the rule for V_n if:

    $V_1 = 2$ $\qquad$ $V_2 = 6$ $\qquad$ $V_3 = 10$ $\qquad$ $V_4 = 14$

4. Find the next three terms in the series and hence the rule for U_n if:

    $U_1 = 5$ $\qquad$ $U_2 = 12$ $\qquad$ $U_3 = 19$ $\qquad$ $U_4 = 26$

5. Find the next three terms in the series and hence the rule for S_n if:

    $S_1 = 3$ $\qquad$ $S_2 = 9$ $\qquad$ $S_3 = 15$ $\qquad$ $S_4 = 21$

6. Find the rules for the nth terms of the sequences of the green rectangles in q.1 to 5 of Exercise 21.2

A different rule

The rules we have looked at so far in this chapter have been for sequences where the difference between two consecutive terms went up equally:

For example:

The sequence 1, 5, 9, 13, ... has a constant difference of 4 and so is based on the 4 times table or $4n$.

Other sequences can be based on different patterns. You should recognise this pattern of square numbers:

1, 4, 9, 16, 25, ...

The differences have their own pattern:

$$1 \xrightarrow{+3} 4 \xrightarrow{+5} 9 \xrightarrow{+7} 16 \xrightarrow{+9} 25$$

Can you see the pattern in those differences? If you can, then you should recognise that the nth term is based on square numbers (n^2).

Exercise 21.5

1. Find the next three terms in the series and hence the rule for S_n if:

    $S_1 = 1$ $S_2 = 4$ $S_3 = 9$ $S_4 = 16$

2. Find the next three terms in the series and hence the rule for T_n if:

    $T_1 = 2$ $T_2 = 5$ $T_3 = 10$ $T_4 = 17$

3. Find the next three terms in the series and hence the rule for U_n if:

    $U_1 = 0$ $U_2 = 3$ $U_3 = 8$ $U_4 = 15$

4. Find the next three terms in the series and hence the rule for V_n if:

    $V_1 = 4$ $V_2 = 7$ $V_3 = 12$ $V_4 = 19$

5. Find the rules for the nth terms of the sequences in q.6 and q.7 of Exercise 21.2

Exercise 21.6: Extension questions – A pair of old friends

There were a couple of sequences in the first exercise that did not fit either the **constant difference pattern** or the **square number** pattern. Let us look at them again.

Sequence 1:

1, 3, 6, 10, 15, ..., ..., ...,

Let us examine the differences:

$$1 \xrightarrow{+2} 3 \xrightarrow{+3} 6 \xrightarrow{+4} 10 \xrightarrow{+5} 15$$

These differences go up by one each time. You may remember where we have seen this before; this diagram should give you a clue:

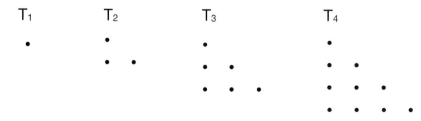

Whichever way you arrange the dots, they make the same number sequence:

$T_1 = 1 = 1$
$T_2 = 1 + 2 = 3$
$T_3 = 1 + 2 + 3 = 6$

Do you recognise them now? They are of course the triangle numbers.

How can we find a rule for the nth triangle number? Again, a picture may make more sense:

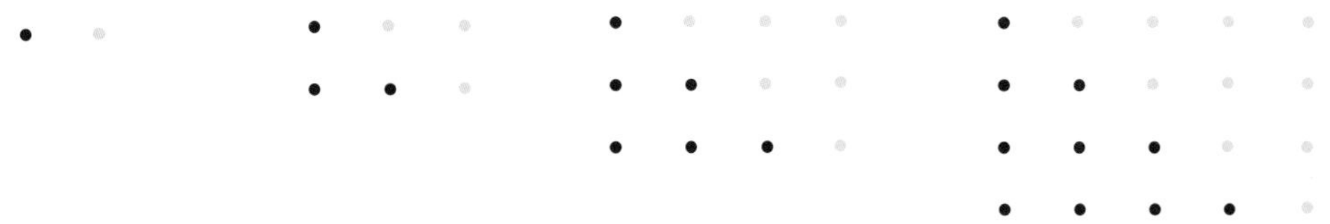

$2 \times T_1$	$2 \times T_2$	$2 \times T_3$	$2 \times T_4$
$= 1 \times 2$	$= 2 \times 3$	$= 3 \times 4$	$= 4 \times 5$
$= 2$	$= 6$	$= 12$	$= 20$

From the above it follows that:

$$2 \times T_n = n \times (n + 1)$$
$$= n(n + 1)$$

And therefore the formula for the nth triangle number must be:

$$T_n = \frac{1}{2} n(n + 1)$$

1. Write down the next three terms and then the rule for the nth term of these sequences:

    (a) 0, 2, 5, 9, 14, ...
    (b) 0, 1, 3, 6, 10, 15, ...
    (c) 2, 6, 12, 20, 30, ...

2. Try dividing up a circle into a number of regions:

(a) Copy the above diagrams and then draw the next three in the sequence. Every line must cross every other line.

(b) Copy and complete the following table:

No. of lines	1	2	3	4	5	6
No. of regions						

(c) From your table write a formula for R_n, the number of regions when you have n lines.

(d) Draw a circle divided up by 8 lines and check that your formula works when $n = 8$

Sequence 2:

1, 1, 2, 3, 5, 8, 13, ..., ..., ...,

Let us examine the differences:

$$1 \xrightarrow{+0} 1 \xrightarrow{+1} 2 \xrightarrow{+1} 3 \xrightarrow{+2} 5 \xrightarrow{+3} 8 \xrightarrow{+5} 13$$

The sequence of differences is the same as the original sequence. We looked at this pattern in Book 1, and is known as the Fibonacci Sequence. You may well come across other sequences that are formed in the same way.

3. Write down the next three terms of these sequences:
(a) 2, 5, 7, 12, 19, ..., ..., ...,
(b) 1, 3, 4, 7, 11, 18, ..., ..., ...,
(c) 0, 2, 2, 4, 6, 10, ..., ..., ...,

4. Fill in the missing numbers in these sequences:
(a) 2, ..., 5, 8, 12, ..., 23, ...,
(b) 1, 5, ..., 11, ..., 28, ...,
(c) ..., 7, 17, ..., 49, 71, ...,
(d) 50, 32, 18, ..., 4, ..., 4, ...,

Exercise 21.7: Summary exercise

1. (a) Write out the next three terms of each of these sequences:
    (i) 8, 16, 24, 32, 40, ..., ..., ...,
    (ii) 5, 13, 21, 29, 37, ..., ..., ...,

    (b) Write down the 100th term in each sequence above, showing your calculations clearly.

2. (a) Write out the next three terms of each of these sequences:
    (i) 9, 19, 29, 39, 49, ..., ..., ...,
    (ii) 7, 12, 17, 22, 27, ..., ..., ...,

    (b) Write down the 100th term in each sequence above, showing your calculations clearly.

3. Look at this series of patterns:

    (a) Draw the next three patterns in the series.
    (b) Copy and complete this table:

No. of green dots	1	2	3	4	5	6
No. of black dots						

    (c) How many black dots will there be if there are 10 white dots?
    (d) How many green dots will there be if there are 100 black dots?

4. If the nth term of a sequence S is given by the formula $S_n = 20 - 3n$, find:
    (a) S_1 (b) S_3 (c) S_6 (d) S_{12}

5. Find the next three terms in the series and hence the rule for T_n if:
    $T_1 = 1$ $T_2 = 5$ $T_3 = 9$ $T_4 = 13$
    (Draw a relationship diagram to help!)

6. Find the next three terms in the series and hence the rule for V_n if:
    $V_1 = 3$ $V_2 = 6$ $V_3 = 11$ $V_4 = 18$

End of chapter 21 activity: Dot patterns

Pentagonal and hexagonal numbers

We have looked at the patterns of triangles and squares, produced by dots, and have seen that they give us the triangle numbers and square numbers.

Copy and complete this table for the number of dots in each pattern number:

Number	1st	2nd	3rd	4th	5th	nth
Triangular	1	3	6			
Square	1	4				

The two next shapes in this sequence are pentagons and hexagons. Let us look at the patterns that these produce:

Pentagonal

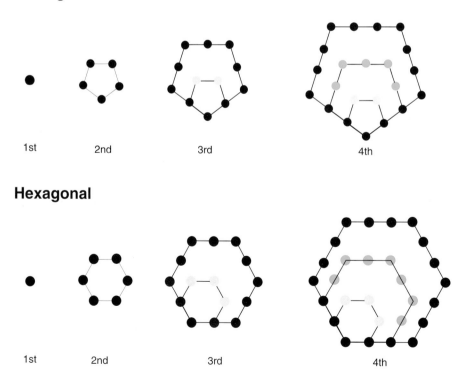

1st 2nd 3rd 4th

Hexagonal

1st 2nd 3rd 4th

Now add these to the table above and record these numbers:

Number	1st	2nd	3rd	4th	5th	nth
Triangular	1	3	6			
Square	1	4	9			
Pentagonal	1	5	12			
Hexagonal	1	6				

Can you work out the rule for the nth number?

Without drawing patterns can you extend the table for heptagonal and octagonal numbers?

Well done! You've made it!

Appendix 1

ISEB Mathematics syllabus revised Summer 2006 for examination in Spring 2008

The following table lists the changes to the syllabus and highlights where they are covered in *So you really want to learn Maths* books 1 and 2.

Attainment target 2: Number and algebra

Syllabus change	11+	13+	*So you really want to learn Maths*
Pupils use their understanding of place value to multiply whole numbers by 10 or 100.	Yes	Yes	Book 1: Chapter 4, p52-57 Additional exercise MP1.A available from www.galorepark.co.uk Book 2: Chapter 1
They begin to use formulae expressed in words.	Yes	Yes	Book 1: Chapter 15, p235-9 Additional exercise MP1.B available from www.galorepark.co.uk
They use four operations with decimals to two places. At 11+ multiplication and decimals will be by an integer less that 10. They should be able to round to the nearest integer.	Yes	Yes	Book 1: Chapter 8, p121-132 Book 2: Chapter 6 Book 1: Chapter 14, p218 Book 1: Chapter 8, p137-139 Additional exercise MP1.C available from www.galorepark.co.uk
At 13+ this should include rounding to 1 or 2 decimal places.		Yes	Book 1: Chapter 8, p137-139 Book 2: Chapter 6

Attainment target 2: Number and algebra (cont.)

Syllabus change	11+	13+	*So you really want to learn Maths*
They calculate fractional or percentage parts of quantities and measurements, using a calculator where appropriate.	Yes	Yes	Book 1: Chapter 7, p108-109 Book 1: Chapter 8, p140-1 Book 1: Chapter 13, p209-16 Book 1: Chapter 17, p271-81 Additional Exercise MP1.D available from www.galorepark.co.uk Book 2: Chapters 3 & 6
They understand and use an appropriate non calculator method for solving problems that involve multiplying and dividing any three digit number by any two digit number. (Multiplication only at 11+)	Yes	Yes	Book 1: Chapter 4, p59-67 Book 2: Chapter 1

Attainment target 3: Shape, space and measures

Syllabus change	11+	13+	*So you really want to learn Maths*
Pupils make 3D mathematical models by linking given faces or edges, they draw common 2D shapes in different orientations on grids. Candidates should be able to use a ruler, compasses, a protractor and set square. They should be able to construct triangles accurately to the nearest degree.	Yes	Yes	Book 1: Chapter 3, p36-50 Book 1: Chapter 16, p254-64 Book 2: Chapter 12

Attainment target 3: Shape, space and measures (cont.)

Syllabus change	11+	13+	*So you really want to learn Maths*
They find perimeters of simple shapes and find areas.	Yes	Yes	Book 1: Chapter 15, p235-252
When constructing models and when drawing or studying shapes, pupils measure and draw angles to the nearest degree, and use language associated with angle. Candidates should be able to draw nets accurately, using given data. At 13+ reasons may be required to justify explanations of properties of shapes.	Yes	Yes	Book 1: Chapter 16, p254-64 Book 2: Chapter 8
They know the rough metric equivalents of imperial units in common use. Units will be restricted to those in the NNS strategy for Year 7 (i.e. feet, miles, pounds, pints, gallons).			Book 1: Chapter 7, p120 Additional exercises MP1.E available from www.galorepark.co.uk
They understand and use the formula for the area of a rectangle. At 13+ this might include examples with algebra.	Yes	Yes	Book 1: Chapter 15, p235-252 Additional exercises MP2.A available from www.galorepark.co.uk Book 2: Chapter 7, p139-141 Book 2: Chapter 20, p371-3

In addition:

The topics listed below are required for 13+ examinations and are covered fully in *So you really want to learn Maths* Book 1:

- Negative numbers, addition and subtraction
- Angle sum of a triangle and sum of angles at a point
- Identify all the symmetries of 2D shapes
- Recognise and use common 2D representations of 3D objects
- Know and use the properties of quadrilaterals

Index